THE ILLUSTRATED DICTIONARY OF

ECOLOGY AND PLANT LIFE

Copyright © 1993 Merlion Publishing Ltd
First published 1993 by
Merlion Publishing Ltd
2 Bellinger Close
Greenways Business Park
Chippenham
Wiltshire SN15 1BN
UK

Series editor: Merilyn Holme
Assistant editor: Maureen Bailey

Design: Steven Hulbert
Illustrations: Peter Bull; David Graham; Sheila Galbraith and
Jeremy Gower (B.L. Kearley Ltd); Maltings Partnership; Maggie
Brand, Simon Chew and Miranda Gray (Maggie Mundy Illustrators'
Agency); Oxford Illustrators
Cover illustration: Jeremy Gower (B.L. Kearley Ltd)

Consultant: Peter Bunyard, Founding Editor of *The Ecologist*

Printed and bound in Great Britain by BPCC Hazells Ltd

ISBN 1 85737 002 3

THE ILLUSTRATED DICTIONARY OF

ECOLOGY AND PLANT LIFE

Contributors
Martin Walters
Merilyn Holme

Merlion Publishing

Reader's notes

The entries in this dictionary have several features to help you understand more about the word you are looking up.

- Each entry is introduced by its headword. All the headwords in the dictionary are arranged in alphabetical order.

- Each headword is followed by a part of speech to show whether the word is used as a noun, adjective, verb or prefix.

- Each entry begins with a sentence that uses the headword as its subject.

- Words that are bold in an entry are cross references. You can look them up in this dictionary to find out more information about the topic.

- The sentence in italics at the end of an entry helps you to see how the headword can be used.

- Many of the entries are illustrated. The labels on the illustrations highlight all the key points of information.

- Many of the labels on the illustrations have their own entries in the dictionary and can therefore be used as cross references.

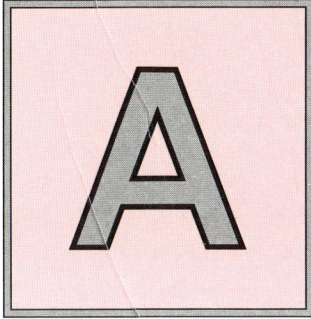

A

acacia   *noun*
An acacia is a small **tree** or **shrub**. There are about 1,200 **species** of acacia, which belong to the **pea** family. Many acacias are found in tropical and sub-tropical parts of Africa, Australia, North America and South America. Most species have yellow or white flowers that grow in clusters. Some acacias have sharp spines. Wattle is another name for acacia.
Some kinds of acacia produce a gum called gum arabic.

acid   *noun*
An acid is a **chemical** which dissolves in water to make an acidic solution. Acid solutions turn blue litmus paper red. Many acids are strong enough to dissolve metals.
Rain contains a weak solution of acid.

acid   *adjective*
Acid describes solutions of **acid**. Soils may have an acid reaction, and are called **acid soils**. Rain-fed peat bogs are usually acid. The opposite of acid is alkaline. Soils rich in minerals are usually alkaline.
The acid peat bog contained many insect-eating plants.

acid rain ► page 6

acid soil   *noun*
Acid soil is **soil** that contains minerals rich in hydrogen and aluminium. It has a **ph** of less than seven. Acid soil often has a high content of **peat**. The opposite of acid soil is **alkaline soil**.
Sphagnum moss grows well in acid soil.

acidification   *noun*
Acidification is the process by which **soils** or water become **acid**. Acidification happens when lakes, rivers or soils are affected by **acid rain**. It can also happen if minerals are carried, or **leached**, out of the soil by water passing through.
The fish in the lake died because the water had been affected by acidification.

acorn   *noun*
An acorn is a kind of **nut**. It is the fruit of an **oak** tree. Acorns are hard, oval-shaped nuts which grow on the twigs of an oak. Each acorn grows out of a cup-shaped base, called the acorn cup. Many animals, including pigs and squirrels, eat acorns.
They found plenty of acorns on the woodland floor.

adaptation   *noun*
An adaptation is a feature of an **organism** that allows it to survive in a particular **habitat**. In this way, many woodland plants develop and flower early in the spring. This is an adaptation to take advantage of the light, before the leaves grow on the trees above. Adaptation may be passed down by the parents or it may be learnt.
Organisms develop because those with useful adaptations survive best.
adapt   *verb*

aerial   *adjective*
Aerial describes the parts of plants which grow above the ground. The stems and leaves of most plants are aerial. The trunks and branches of trees are aerial. Some plants have **aerial roots** which hang down from the stems, or which grow up out of the ground or water.
They could see the aerial roots of the epiphyte trailing along the branch of the rain forest tree.

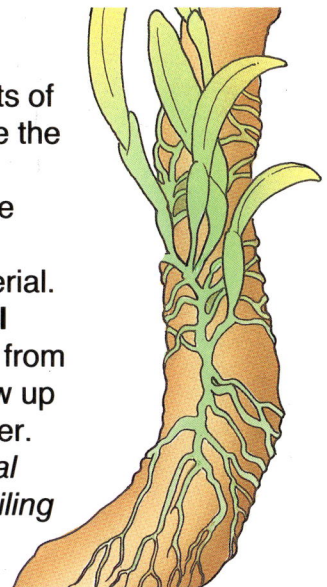

5

acid rain *noun*

Acid rain is rain which has been made more **acid** because of **chemicals** dissolved in it. Oxides of sulphur and nitrogen are the main chemicals which cause acid rain. These come from the burning of **fossil fuels** in factories and cars. Acid rain sometimes kills trees. It can also kill fish and other animals in rivers and lakes.

The forest was damaged by the effects of acid rain.

Sulphur dioxide and nitrogen oxide enter the air from coal-fired power stations and road vehicles. The sulphur dioxide and nitrogen oxide mix with moisture in the air to become sulphuric acid and nitric acid. These damage trees in the form of acid rain.

Acid rain causes damage to statues and buildings, as well as to living things.

Acid rain falling into a lake gradually kills most of the animals and plants living in the lake. Only a few species survive.

aerial root *noun*
Aerial roots are **roots** which grow down to the ground through the air. Many **climbing plants** have aerial roots, and so do some swamp plants, such as mangroves.
They had to push aside the aerial roots to clamber through the forest.

afforestation *noun*
Afforestation is the process of planting and growing **forests**. It usually takes place in areas that have lost their trees. Most afforestation in **temperate** countries is done using **conifers**. These trees grow quickly and provide a regular crop of soft **timber**.
The lower slopes of the hills were covered with trees due to afforestation.

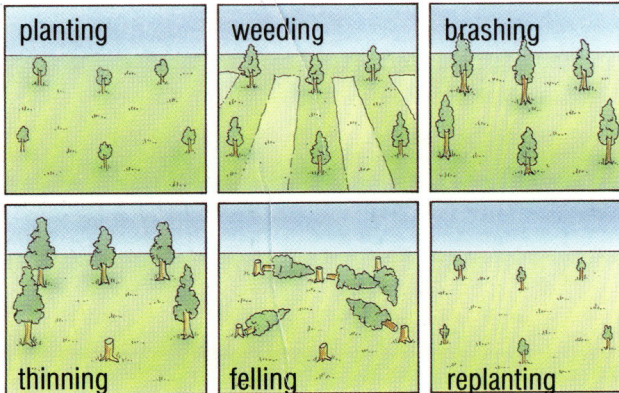

planting | weeding | brashing
thinning | felling | replanting

agriculture *noun*
Agriculture is the **cultivation** of the land to grow **crops** and rear farm animals. Agriculture provides shops with fruit, vegetables and meat. Agriculture is only possible in regions with fertile **soil** and regular **rainfall**, or **irrigation**.
The mid-west of North America is an area of intense agriculture.

agronomy *noun*
Agronomy is the science of land **cultivation**. It includes studying crop production and the management of soils to give the best yields of crops. It also includes the breeding of improved types of crop plant.
He studied agronomy before starting to farm the land with cereals.

air *noun*
Air is the mixture of **gases** that surround the Earth. The most common gases in air are **nitrogen**, **oxygen**, argon, **carbon dioxide** and water vapour. Plants and animals need the oxygen from air to live. Plants take in carbon dioxide during **photosynthesis**. Air becomes thinner and thinner away from the Earth. It disappears altogether in space.
The fast speed of the clouds showed that the air was moving quickly.

air pollution *noun*
Air pollution is **pollution** caused by smoke and other **chemicals** which are released from cars, houses and factory chimneys. Common chemicals causing air pollution are **sulphur dioxide** and **nitrogen** oxides. Serious air pollution can make the air poisonous to breathe and can kill plants. It also causes **acid rain**.
The air pollution made their throats sore.

alder *noun*
An alder is a kind of **deciduous** tree. There are 35 kinds of alder, found in Europe, Asia and America. Alders grow in damp or wet soil, sometimes at the edges of fens or bogs. Alders have oval or heart-shaped leaves. In the spring, alders have **catkins**, which are the male flowers. The female alder flowers are small **cones**.
The alder tree grew on the river bank.

alfalfa *noun*

Alfalfa is a **perennial** plant. It is a member of the **pea family**. Alfalfa is grown as a crop in many parts of the world. It is used mainly for feeding animals. The alfalfa plant has many slender stems, with **compound leaves** made up of three **leaflets**. It has purple flower **spikes**.
The leaves and stems of alfalfa are rich in minerals and vitamins.

algae (singular **alga**) *noun*

Algae are simple plants, which grow mostly in water. There are many thousands of species of algae. They grow in all parts of the world, especially in the sea, in lakes and in ponds. **Seaweeds** are algae, but many algae are tiny and can only be seen properly with a microscope. The largest algae are kelp. They live in shallow seas and can grow to hundreds of metres long.
He had to clean the algae from the sides of the aquarium.

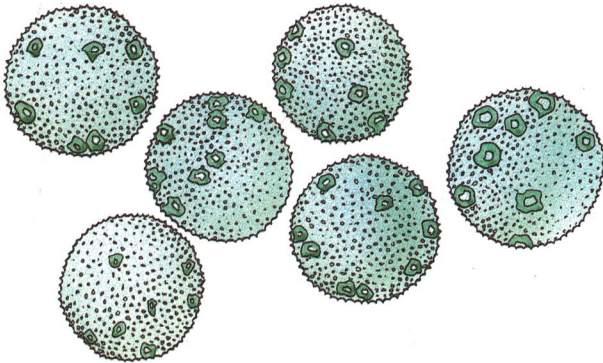

algal bloom *noun*

An algal bloom describes the way **algae** in the sea or a lake suddenly increase, or multiply, very quickly. In a bloom, the water may quickly turn green, or sometimes red, as the algae reproduce. Some algal blooms are very poisonous to fish and other **organisms**. An algal bloom may provide a sudden supply of food for plankton, and in turn for other marine animals.
The water turned a cloudy green, because of the algal bloom.

alien *adjective*

Alien describes a plant that does not grow naturally in a particular **habitat**. It is not **native** to the habitat, but has been introduced there.
The alien species of poppy grew well in the field.

alkaline soil *noun*

Alkaline soil is a soil that has a **pH** of more than seven. **Chalk** and **limestone soils** are alkaline soils.
A rich variety of plants grew in the alkaline soil.

alpine *adjective*

Alpine describes a mountain **habitat** or **climate**. Alpine areas are found on mountains, above the **tree-line**. The name comes from the Alp mountains of Europe, but is used for all such areas around the world. An alpine climate is cold for much of the year, with snow, ice and regular, strong winds. Alpine plants can grow in thin, stony soil and flower quickly in spring and summer.
The alpine plants grew well in the crevices of the rock garden.

amaryllis *noun*

An amaryllis is one of a **family** of flowering plants. There are more than 1,200 species in the amaryllis family. They have a long stem and many long, narrow leaves. The flowers have six petals and are trumpet-shaped.
Amaryllis flowers have a sweet scent.

angiosperm *noun*
Angiosperms are the flowering plants. They form the largest division of **vascular plants**. There are about 250,000 species of angiosperm. They include all the familiar **flowers**. They also include most **trees**, except the **conifers**. Angiosperms are divided into two classes, the **monocotyledons** and the **dicotyledons**. They are found in a wide variety of **habitats**. All angiosperms bear flowers and fruit, unlike the other group of plants, the **gymnosperms**.
About two-thirds of all angiosperms live in the tropics.

annual *adjective*
Annual describes a plant which completes its **life cycle** in a single year. Annuals grow from seed in the spring. They develop leaves and flowers in the summer and fruit in the autumn. They finally set seed and die at the end of the year. New annuals then grow from the seed the next year.
They planted seeds in the soil to provide a colourful show of annual flowers.

sweet peas

annual ring *noun*
An annual ring is a circular mark inside the trunk of a **tree**. When a tree is cut down, the annual rings can be clearly seen on the cut surface. Each ring shows the growth of the tree in one year. Trees can therefore be aged by counting the annual rings.
They counted over 150 annual rings on the stump of the old oak tree.

Antarctica *noun*
Antarctica is the Earth's most southerly continent. It surrounds the South Pole. Most of the land is covered by thick ice. Antarctica is the coldest continent on Earth.
The expedition headed off across the vast snowfields of Antarctica.

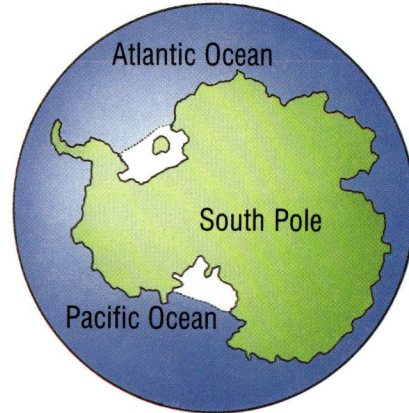

Atlantic Ocean

South Pole

Pacific Ocean

anther *noun*
An anther is part of a **flower**. It is part of the **stamen** in a flower. The anther produces **pollen grains**, which are the male sex cells of the plant. In some flowers, the anthers are large and hang out of the flower. In others, they are small and placed inside the flower. Insects rub their body against the anthers as they visit flowers to gather **nectar**.
The anthers were a bright yellow colour from the ripe pollen they contained.

anti- *prefix*
Anti- is a prefix meaning against or preventing.
An anti-bacterial substance stops the growth of bacteria.

apex *noun*
The apex is part of a growing **shoot**. The apex is the tip of the shoot where most of the growth of a young plant takes place. It contains the meristem, which is the place where cell division happens. The apex also produces **chemicals** which cause the stem to turn towards the light, or to twist. This is called **phototropism**.
The apex of the seedling grew quickly upwards from the seed.

apple *noun*
An apple is a kind of **tree**. The **fruits** of the tree are also known as apples. Wild apples are small and rather sour to taste. Hundreds of varieties of apple trees are grown in orchards. Famous varieties are Cox's Orange Pippin and Golden Delicious. Eating apples are sweet. Some apples are grown for cooking, and these are sour when raw.
The gardener used a ladder to harvest the apples from his orchard.

aquaculture *noun*
Aquaculture is the use of water for growing food. Plants and animals can both be grown using aquaculture. Some kinds of **algae** can be grown using aquaculture. Watercress is a common salad vegetable that is also grown by this method.
The farm had several large tanks which were used for aquaculture.

aquatic *adjective*
Aquatic describes a plant which lives in the water. Some aquatic plants have their roots in the soil under the water. Others grow completely in the water, or float at the surface. Many aquatic plants have spongy stems and leaves which support them well in the water. Aquatic plants are also known as water plants.
The shallows at the edge of the lake had a rich growth of aquatic plants.

arable *adjective*
Arable usually describes something to do with farming. It describes a type of farming in which crops are planted and harvested each year. A mild **climate** with dry summers is the most suitable for arable farming.
The hedgerows had been pulled up to make large fields for arable farming.

Arctic *noun*
The Arctic is the most northerly region of the world. It lies within the Arctic Circle. Northern Canada, much of Greenland and northern Russia lie within the Arctic Circle.
Eskimo people live in the Arctic.
arctic *adjective*

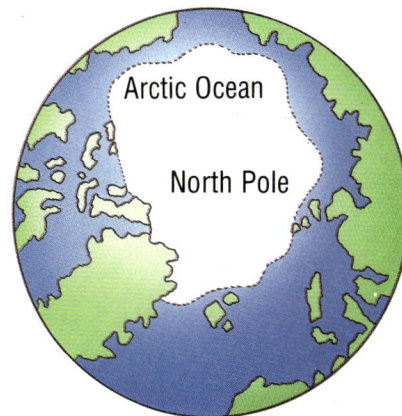

arid *adjective*
Arid describes regions which have a very dry **climate**, such as hot **deserts**. Arid regions either have very little rain, or lose most water that falls as rain by **evaporation**. Most arid regions lie in the tropics.
The soil was so arid that no crops would grow.

asexual reproduction *noun*
Asexual reproduction is reproduction without sex cells. Many plants use this form of reproduction. Some send out **suckers**, which then grow into new plants nearby. Others can set seed themselves, but without the need for **sexual reproduction**. The new plants that are made by asexual reproduction are exactly the same **genetically** as their parent.
The weed spread by asexual reproduction.

11

ash *noun*
Ash is a kind of **deciduous** tree. There are 65 kinds of ash. Ash trees are found mainly in temperate parts of Asia, Europe and North America. They grow tall, and are common in woodland. Ash trees have **compound leaves**. The fruits of the ash tree are known as keys. Ash wood is very tough and is good for making tool handles and furniture.
The boy sheltered under the large ash tree.

B

bacteria (singular **bacterium**) *noun*
Bacteria are tiny living things, or **organisms**. Each bacterium is a single cell. Most bacteria are harmless, but some can cause diseases when they invade other organisms.
A water drop contains thousands of bacteria.

badlands *noun*
Badlands are areas of rough country. They develop when the soil has been worn away, or **eroded**, leaving bare rock and gullies. Badlands are usually found in areas of low rainfall. The most famous badlands are in South Dakota and Nebraska in the United States of America.
Overgrazing turned the fertile soil into infertile badlands.

balsa *noun*
A balsa is a **tree** that grows in **tropical** regions of Mexico, Central America and South America. It has a long, slender trunk, simple, rounded leaves and very large, pink flowers. Balsa **wood** is extremely light. It is used for making some kinds of boat, life rafts and buoys, and model aeroplanes.
The flowers of the balsa tree are 12 centimetres long.

bamboo *noun*
Bamboo is a kind of giant **grass**. It can grow as tall as a tree. Bamboo grows wild in **tropical** climates and warm, **temperate** climates. It has long, narrow leaves and a straight, hollow stem with hard, thick joints. Bamboo has many uses. The young shoots can be eaten as vegetables.
The scaffolding was made from bamboo.

banana *noun*
A banana is a tropical **fruit**. There are several kinds of banana. Some are large and yellow when ripe. Others remain small and green or brown. Sweet bananas are very good to eat as fruit. Some kinds are less sweet and are used mainly as vegetables. Bananas are grown in many **tropical** countries. They are sent, or exported, all over the world. The banana plant has long, broad leaves and the fruits grow in thick bunches.
The farmer harvested the bunches of ripe bananas.

banyan *noun*
The banyan is a large, tropical **tree**. It is a kind of fig. Banyans grow in India and Pakistan. They have spreading branches and provide good shade from the Sun. Banyans support their branches by strong **aerial roots**.
The villagers sheltered beneath the banyan.

baobab *noun*
The baobab is a large **tree**. Baobabs are found in **tropical** parts of Africa. They have large, swollen trunks which are thicker at the base than the top. Baobabs can live for up to 2,000 years. Many animals make their homes in baobab trees, and eat their fruits. Bats and bushbabies **pollinate** the baobab flowers.
The monkeys gathered to feed in the baobab trees.

bark ▶ page 14

barley *noun*
Barley is a kind of **grass**. It belongs to the same **family** as **wheat, oats, rice** and **maize**. Barley is grown, or **cultivated**, as a cereal **crop** in **temperate** regions. Its seeds grow in spikes at the tops of the stems. They are harvested as **grain** and eaten by animals and people.
When they are ripe, barley seeds have long whiskers growing out of them.

barren *adjective*
Barren describes land which is **infertile**. Barren land has very poor **soil** and cannot support much **vegetation** or **agriculture**. If crops are grown year after year on poor land, the soil gradually becomes barren.
The crops failed because the soil was too barren.

basil *noun*
Basil is a member of the mint **family**. It has small, purple flowers and heart-shaped leaves with jagged edges. Basil is **cultivated** as a herb in many countries. It has an aromatic flavour and is used to season food.
He added some chopped basil leaves to the tomato salad.

bean *noun*
A bean is a kind of edible **seed**. Beans belong to the **pea** family. There are many kinds of bean, including haricot bean, broad bean and soya bean. Beans are very nutritious, and they are eaten all over the world.
They made a delicious soup, using several kinds of bean.

beech *noun*
A beech is a **broadleaf tree**. The beech family also includes **oaks** and **chestnuts**. Beeches grow up to 23 metres high and have a thick trunk and spreading branches. Their thin, papery leaves turn a golden colour in autumn before they fall. Beeches produce small nuts with a prickly case.
Beech wood is hard and tough, and is used to make furniture and tool handles.

begonia *noun*
A begonia is one of a **family** of flowering plants. Begonias grow wild in tropical regions, but many are **cultivated** as **garden plants**. Most kinds have shiny leaves and brightly-coloured flowers. Some begonias develop from a thick, undergrown stem called a **rhizome**. Others grow from **tubers**.
A rex begonia has leaves which are coloured in shades of white, red or silver.

bark *noun*

Bark is the outer covering of the trunks and stems of **trees** and **shrubs**. Bark may be hard, soft or flaky depending upon the species of tree. Sometimes bark has bumps or ridges, but it can also be smooth. Bark is made up of dead **cells** produced by the growing cells beneath. Bark protects trees from very cold or very hot temperatures, from fire damage and from animal attack.
The bark of the redwood tree is soft and spongy.

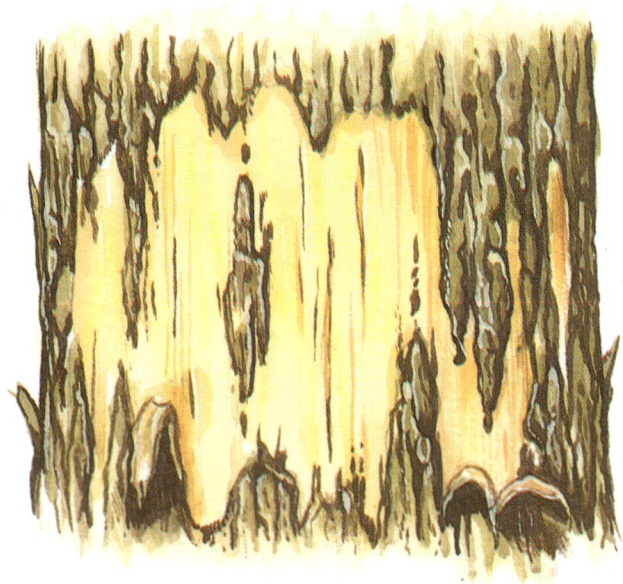

Animals, such as deer and squirrels, strip the bark off trees to eat. This can damage the trees and some may eventually die.

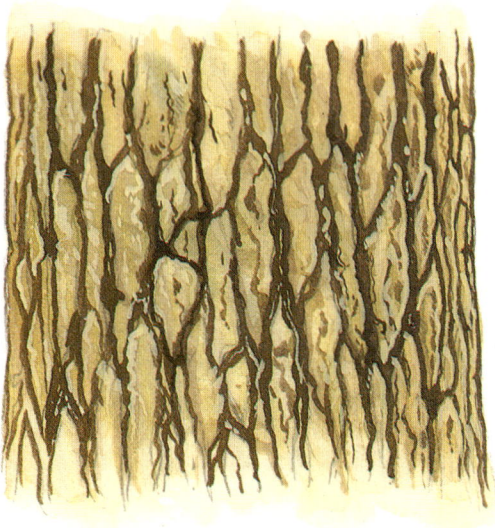

The horse chestnut tree has hard, rough bark, with ridges.

outer bark

wood

inner bark

The bark of the silver birch tree is smooth, thin and papery. It peels easily.

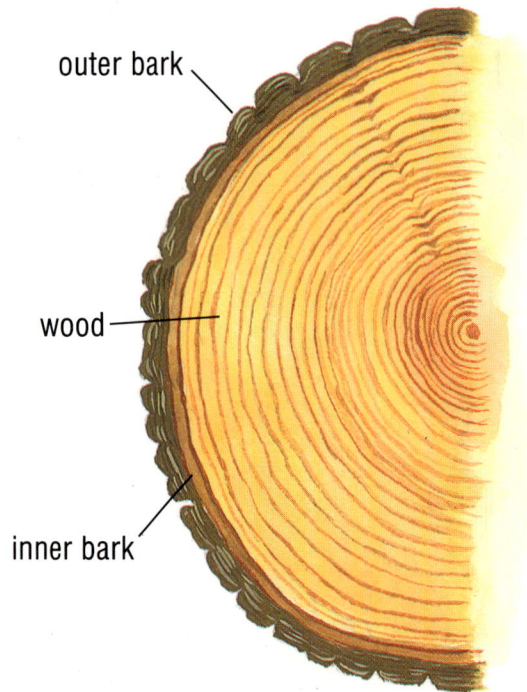

Bark is made up of inner bark and outer bark. The inner bark is living tissue that carries and stores food. The outer bark is dead tissue that forms a thick, protective covering for the tree.

tyre

Wellington boots

rubber gloves

eraser

elastic bands

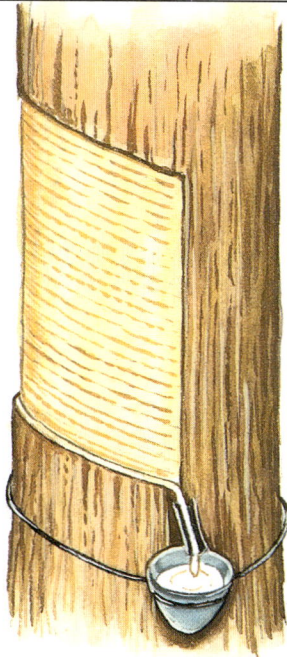

The bark of the rubber tree is cut to allow latex to flow out. Latex is a kind of sap that is used to make rubber products.

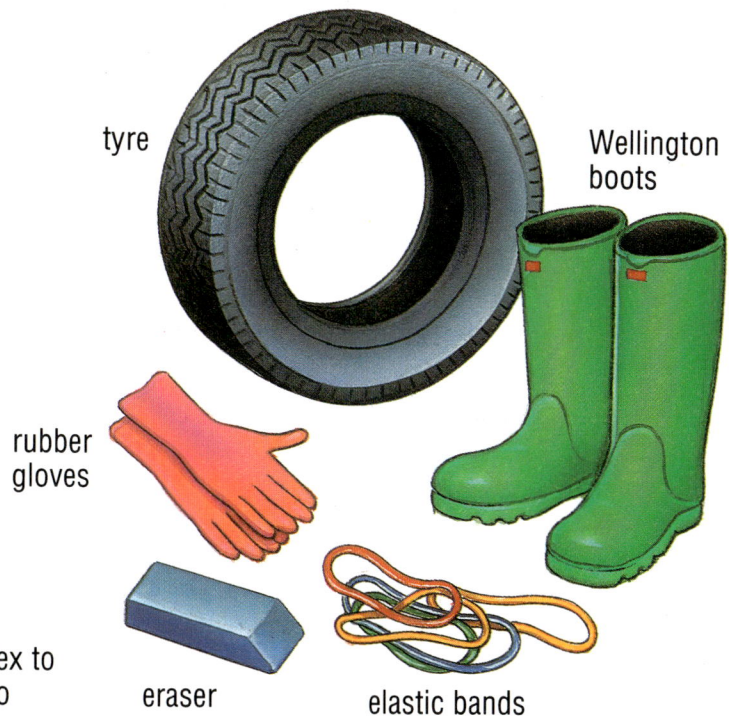

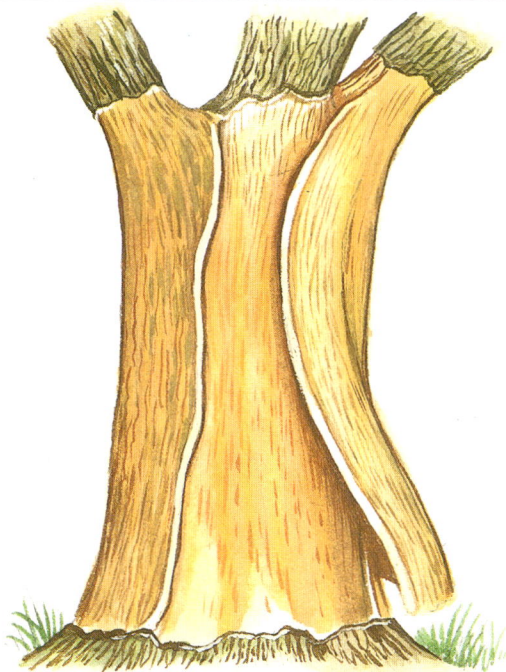

notice board

tiles

shoes

bottle corks

washers

The bark of the cork oak tree is stripped and used to make many cork products.

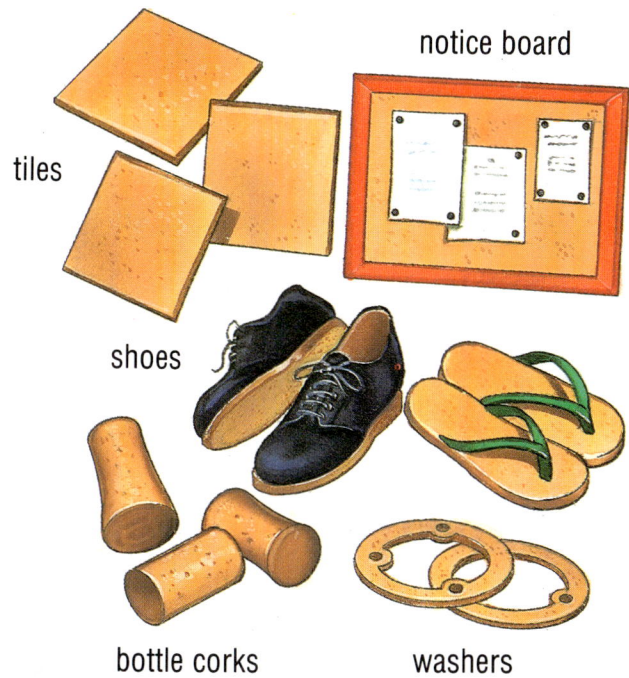

bellflower *noun*
A bellflower, or campanula, is one of a **family** of flowering plants. Bellflowers are found mainly in the northern part of the world. Some bellflowers grow as tall as 1.8 metres, but others creep along the ground. Most bellflowers have bell-shaped blossoms which are pink, blue, purple or white.
Harebells and bluebells are bellflowers that grow wild in the British Isles.

benthos *noun*
Benthos is the name used for the plants and animals living on the sea-bed, or in the benthic zone. The benthos includes **seaweeds**, and sea animals such as crabs, shellfish and flatfish.
The benthos of the continental shelf is very varied.

berry *noun*
A berry is a kind of **fruit**. It is a soft fruit containing many **seeds**. Many berries have brightly-coloured flesh. This attracts mammals and birds, which eat the berries and disperse the seeds.
Tomatoes and grapes are berries.

mulberries

rowan berries   **blackcurrants**

biennial *adjective*
A biennial is a kind of flowering plant. Biennials usually grow for two years. In the first year, they grow leaves and stems. In the second year, they flower and set seed. After setting seed, the biennial dies and grows again from seed the following year.
Many crop plants, such as carrots, are biennials.

binary fission *noun*
Binary fission is a type of **asexual reproduction** in plants or animals. In binary fission, a one-celled, or **unicellular**, plant or animal reproduces by splitting in two.
Binary fission is the simplest form of reproduction.

bio- *prefix*
Bio- describes anything to do with living things.
Biotechnology finds out how people can use living things to make medicine, food and fuels.

biodegradable *adjective*
Biodegradable describes substances which **decay** naturally when thrown away. **Bacteria** in the soil or water break down biodegradable material into simpler substances.
The plastic remained in the soil for a long time because it was not biodegradable.

biofuel *noun*
A biofuel is a kind of fuel which is made from natural materials or waste. Charcoal and **biogas** are biofuels which can be burned to release energy.
Motor cars which run on biofuel cause less pollution than those which use petrol.

biogas *noun*
Biogas is a gas given off when waste materials break down, or **decompose**. The main gas produced in this way is **methane**. Methane can be collected and burned to provide heat energy.
Manure and food waste are good sources of biogas.

biological *adjective*
Biological describes anything to do with living **organisms**. For example, biological science is the study of living things.
The region's unusual animals and plants proved to be of great biological interest to the scientist.

16

biological control *noun*

Biological control is the control of pests and diseases using other organisms. It is often safer than **chemical** control as it causes no **pollution**. It can also be used against a single pest. Ladybirds eating aphids is an example of biological control.
Biological control was the only successful way of controlling the prickly pear in Australia.

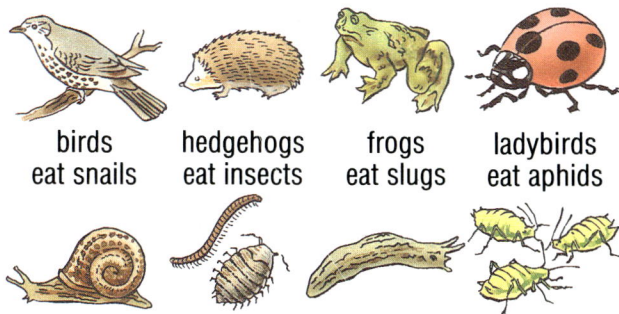

birds eat snails hedgehogs eat insects frogs eat slugs ladybirds eat aphids

biomass *noun*

Biomass is the term used for the total weight of living things, or **organisms**, in a particular area, such as a stretch of grassland, or woodland.
The patch of tropical rain forest had a large biomass.

biome *noun*

A biome is a **community** of plants and animals. Each climatic region of the world has its own particular biome, or set of biomes. The **tundra** biome is found in the Arctic region, the tropical forest biome is found in the tropics, and the broadleaf forest biome in parts of the temperate regions.
The coniferous forest biome stretches out to the south of the tundra biome.

biosphere *noun*

The biosphere is the name given to the parts of the Earth where living things are found. The biosphere is also called the global ecosystem.
The atmosphere, the sea and the surface of the Earth all make up the biosphere.

biosphere reserve *noun*

A biosphere reserve is a special kind of protected area. There are around 250 biosphere reserves, in all parts of the world. Together, these reserves make up a network of natural reserves. They protect examples of all the main **ecosystems** of the Earth. Each biosphere reserve has an inner, protected **core area**, and an outer **buffer zone**. In the buffer zone, some human activities are allowed.
A biosphere reserve is given special protection from development because of its unique flora and fauna.

birch *noun*

A birch is a **deciduous tree**. There are about 40 species in the birch **family**. They grow in North America, Europe and northern Asia. Birches are tall, slender trees with delicate branches. They produce long **catkins**.
Birch trees have thin, peeling bark.

blade *noun*

The blade is the main part of a **leaf**. It is usually flat and thin. This shape allows the blade to absorb large amounts of sunlight.
The blade was attached by a long stalk to the stem of the plant.

blanket bog *noun*

A blanket bog is a kind of peat **habitat**. Blanket bogs are large areas of wet peat which cover the ground. They form in cool, **temperate** regions with high **rainfall**. In a blanket bog, the **mosses** at the surface are growing. Further down, the dead remains of the mosses form peat. Most blanket bogs are **acid**.
The lower hill slopes were covered by dark brown blanket bogs.

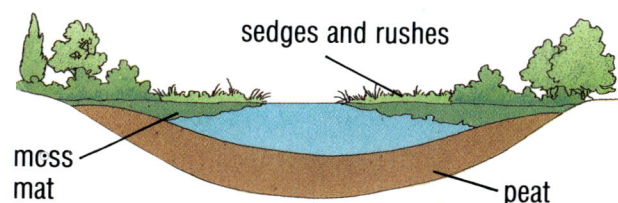

sedges and rushes
moss mat
peat

blight   *noun*
A blight is a **disease** that causes whole parts of plants to wilt and die. The diseased parts do not actually fall off. Most blights are caused by **fungi**.
The whole potato crop was destroyed by blight.

bloom   *verb*
Bloom describes the flowering of a plant.
In the northern hemisphere of the Earth, many plants bloom in the spring.
bloom   *noun*

blossom   *noun*
A blossom is a **flower**. It is especially the flower of a plant that produces fruit, such as an apple tree.
The cherry trees in the orchard were covered in pink blossom.
blossom   *verb*

bog   *noun*
A bog is an area of marshy ground where the soil is made up of wet **peat**. Bogs are made of many thousands of **moss** plants. These grow in water and are known as bog mosses. As the older moss plants die, their remains gradually decay, or **decompose**, forming peat. In most bogs, a new layer of plants grows on top of the dead peat.
The soil in the bog was very acidic and few plants could grow there.

bole   *noun*
A bole is another word for the **trunk** of a tree.
The oak tree had lichen growing on the lower half of its bole.

bonsai   *noun*
Bonsai is the art of growing trees on a very small, or miniature, scale. Bonsai trees are grown from **seed cuttings** or **seedlings** in a pot or tray. Their roots and branches are cut, or **pruned**, regularly to keep the trees small.
The art of bonsai was first practised in Japan and China about 1,000 years ago.

borage   *noun*
Borage is a **family** of flowering plants that grows naturally in southern Europe. Many species of borage are **herbs**, which are used in cooking and in medicine. They have hairy stems and leaves, and bright blue or purple leaves.
Heliotrope and forget-me-not are two kinds of borage.

boreal   *adjective*
Boreal describes a region of the Earth. The boreal region lies south of the **Arctic**. In the boreal region, the main type of **vegetation** is the boreal forest, or **taiga**. Boreal forests are made up mostly of coniferous trees.
The boreal forests of Siberia stretch for thousands of kilometres.

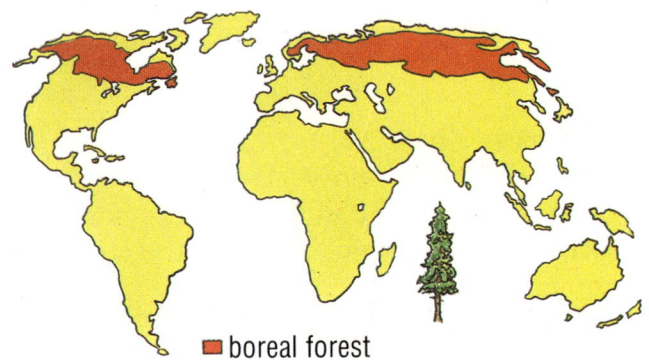

■ boreal forest

boreal forest ▶ **taiga**

botanist   *noun*
A botanist is a person who studies or practises **botany**.
The botanist made a study of all the mosses in the wood.

botany   *noun*
Botany is the study of plants. It includes plant ecology, plant physiology and plant biochemistry. Botany is important because many raw materials come from plants. Plants are under threat around the world and need to be studied before many of them become extinct.
She decided to study botany because she was interested in plants.

18

box *noun*

Box is a kind of **evergreen** broadleaf tree or bush. Box wood is very hard and heavy. It is used for carving items such as furniture and musical instruments. Box is also planted in gardens to make hedges.
They ran through the maze, which was made of box hedges.

bracken *noun*

Bracken is a kind of **fern**. It grows quickly and covers large areas of land on hills and heavy soils. Bracken spreads mainly by **vegetative reproduction**. It is poisonous to animals. Green, yellow and black **dye** can be made from bracken.
The birds disappeared into the thick clump of bracken.

bract *noun*

A bract is a kind of **leaf**. Bracts are found just below the flowers on the plant. In some flowers, like **grasses**, the bracts are delicate and pale. In others, they are bright and look like petals. Petal-like bracts help to attract insects to the flower for **pollination**.
The poinsettia flower has bright red bracts surrounding its flowers.

branch *noun*

A branch is a woody **stem** in a shrub or tree. The main **trunk** of a tree divides into several branches. Each branch then divides further into **twigs**. The branches help to keep the tree upright and to give it its shape.
The creeper trailed over the tree branch.

brashing *noun*

Brashing is the removal of the lower branches of a **tree**. It is one of the stages in the care of trees that are being grown for **timber**. Brashing is carried out when the trees are about 10 years old. It helps to reduce the number of **knots** when the timber is fully grown, or **mature**.
The branches that are cut off during brashing are used to make wood pulp.

broadleaf tree *noun*

A broadleaf tree is a tree which has flat, wide leaves. The other main type of tree is the **needleleaf tree**. Broadleaf trees grow in woods and forests, especially in **temperate** and **tropical** regions. Most broadleaf trees are **deciduous**, but a few are **evergreen**, such as the **holly** and the **box**.
Oaks are some of the most common broadleaf trees.

avocado

bromeliad *noun*

A bromeliad is a **tropical** plant. There are about 1,500 species of bromeliad. They are found mainly in the tropical forests of North America, Central America and South America. Many species of bromeliad are **epiphytes**, or air plants. They grow on the branches of trees in **rain forests** and their **aerial roots** take in moisture from the air. Most bromeliads have long, sword-shaped leaves that form tight clusters. Flowers grow amongst these, or on spikes.
The pineapple is a species of bromeliad.

bryophyte *noun*
A bryophyte is a kind of plant. There are about 25,000 species of bryophyte. They are the **mosses** and the **liverworts**. Bryophytes live in damp or wet habitats. They are low-growing and live on the surfaces of wet rocks, logs or on the ground. The **tundra** and **bogs** are rich in bryophytes.
The stones by the waterfall had a covering of bryophytes.

buckwheat *noun*
Buckwheat is a family of plants grown for its seeds. These are used to make flour. Buckwheat has heart-shaped leaves on a straight stem. Its flowers are white, pink, red or greenish-coloured.
Buckwheat is grown in North America.

bud *noun*
A bud is part of a plant. The bud protects the delicate parts of the plants that are growing during the resting season. Many plants develop buds which then rest during the winter. When the warm weather comes, the buds open out to reveal flowers or fresh stem growth. Inside the bud, there are tiny leaves or petals, ready to grow when the warm weather returns.
In the spring, the buds begin to open.

bud scale *noun*
A bud scale is a part of a **bud**. It is a type of simple leaf that protects the soft parts of the bud inside. The buds of most woody plants are covered by overlapping bud scales.
The buds of horse chestnut trees have sticky bud scales.

buffer zone *noun*
A buffer zone is part of a **nature reserve**. It is the outermost part of the reserve. In the buffer zone, some human activities, such as hunting, or careful tree-felling, may be allowed. The buffer zone helps to protect the inner **core area** of the reserve.
The large forest reserve was surrounded by a wide buffer zone.

bulb *noun*
A bulb is part of a plant. It is a storage **organ** that allows a plant to survive a dry or cold season. Bulbs are common in members of the **lily** family. Each bulb is made up of swollen leaves, pressed firmly together. At the beginning of the **growing season**, the food stored in the bulb is released.
The daffodils emerged from their bulbs.

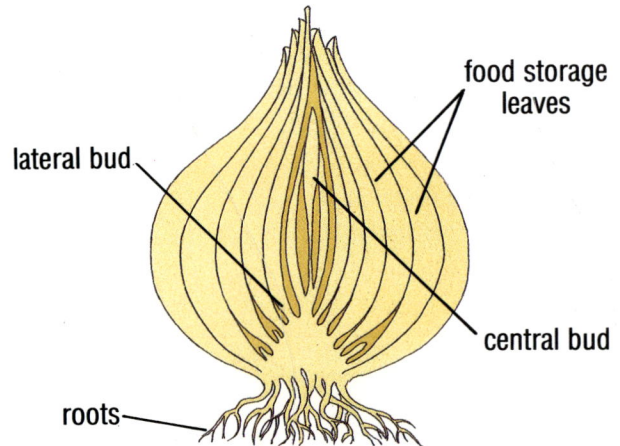

food storage leaves

lateral bud

central bud

roots

bulbil *noun*
A bulbil is a fleshy type of **bud** that a plant produces above the ground. It has a store of food and can develop into a new plant.
The bulbils of the crow garlic fell to the ground and grew into new plants.

burr *noun*
A burr is a kind of **fruit**. In a burr, the outermost part of the fruit is covered in hooks. These hooks catch in the fur of passing animals. In this way, the plant can **disperse** its seeds.
The burdock plant has burrs.

bush *noun*
A bush is a low, rounded woody plant. Most bushes grow to only a few metres high. Hawthorns and gorse are examples of bushes. Bush is also the name used for some habitats which are **dominated** by low shrubs and bushes. This term is used especially in southern Africa and in Australia.
Many eucalyptus trees grow in the Australian bush.

buttercup *noun*
Buttercup, or crowfoot, is a **family** of flowering plants. Buttercups are found in most **temperate** regions. They have bright yellow flowers, usually with five rounded, shiny petals. Most buttercup leaves are divided into three main parts and look a little like birds' feet.
Most buttercups grow best in damp ground.

buttress root *noun*
A buttress root is a kind of tree **root**. Many rain forest trees have buttress roots. These look like fins, growing out from the base of the trunk. Buttress roots help to support the whole tree and to keep it upright in high winds.
The explorers had to climb carefully around the buttress roots in the tropical forest.

C

cacao *noun*
Cacao is an **evergreen** tree that grows in **tropical rain forests**. It reaches a height of up to 12 metres and produces large flowers on its trunk. The flowers develop into **pods** which contain seeds, or beans. These are used by people to make chocolate and cocoa. Cacao trees are **cultivated** in Central America and South America, the East Indies, West Indies and West Africa.
Cacao pods range in colour from light brown to purple and can be as long as 30 centimetres.

cactus ► page 22

calyx *noun*
The calyx is a part of a **flower**. It is the name for the ring of **sepals** which grows just below the **petals** of a flower. Sometimes the sepals in a calyx are joined together, sometimes they are separate. The calyx is usually green in colour. It protects the rest of the flower as it develops. The calyx is the first part to form in most flowers.
Beneath the petals could be seen the shiny calyx.

cambium *noun*
The cambium is a layer of growing **cells** in a plant. The cambium forms a ring of dividing cells in the **stem** of a plant or in the **trunk** of a tree. More and more new cells form in the cambium as the plant grows. Cambium near the surface of a tree trunk produces cork cells to make the **bark**.
They stripped the bark away to show the cambium.

cactus (plural **cacti**) *noun*

Cactus is a family of plants that usually have clusters of **spines**. There are about 2,000 species of cactus. They are **native** to North America and South America, but many are found in hot, dry parts of other continents. Most cacti have special features to help them survive in dry climates. They have thick, fleshy stems which hold water.

Most cacti have a waxy skin that stops water evaporating from the plant.

The prickly pear grows in many dry, hot parts of the world. It has pear-shaped fruits that are good to eat.

The giant saguaro can grow to a height of 18 metres.

The pincushion cactus produces bright pink or yellow flowers.

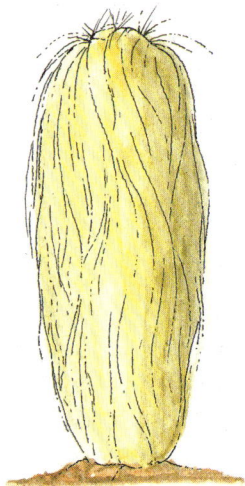

The old man cactus has a coat of white hair that protects it from the Sun.

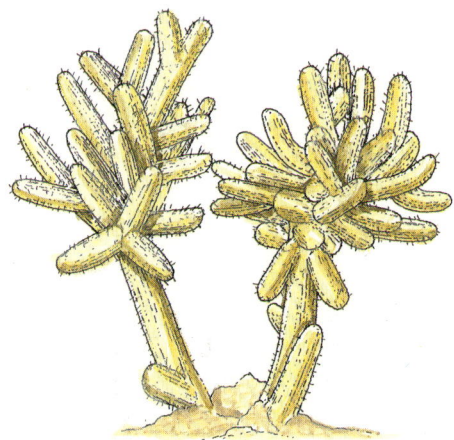

The jumping chola's thorny branches break off so easily they seem to 'jump' at passers-by.

camouflage   *noun*

Camouflage is the way some plants grow to look like their background, so they are not eaten by animals. Stone plants are desert **succulents** that look like the pebbles that surround them.
Camouflage is one defence that plants have against being eaten by animals.

canopy   *noun*

The canopy is part of a **forest**. It is the upper layer in a forest, formed by the main branches of the tallest trees. In the canopy, the branches of nearby trees come close together, to make a dense layer. Many birds and insects live in the canopy. It can be more than 30 metres above the ground.
Plants called epiphytes are found in the canopy.

capsule   *noun*

A capsule is a kind of **fruit**. Capsules are dry when ripe. They release the seeds inside by splitting open, or by shaking.
Many plants, such as poppies and water lilies, have capsules.

foxglove

water lily

scarlet
pimpernel

carbohydrate   *noun*

Carbohydrate is a substance that is found in plants. It is produced by **photosynthesis**. Carbohydrates are made up of carbon, hydrogen and oxygen. They provide energy for the growth of **cells**.
Sugar, starch and cellulose are all carbohydrates.

carbon cycle   *noun*

The carbon cycle describes the movement of the element carbon in nature. Carbon atoms are the basis of the bodies of all plants and animals. Carbon moves between living plants and animals and the air, water and soil. In the carbon cycle, plants take in **carbon dioxide** during **photosynthesis**. Plants and animals give out carbon dioxide during **respiration**.
The carbon cycle is a central part of all ecosystems.

carbon dioxide   *noun*

Carbon dioxide is a colourless **gas** which has no smell. It is formed when substances containing carbon are burned, and when animals and plants breathe. Carbon dioxide makes up a tiny fraction of the air. It is also the main gas that causes the **greenhouse effect**. Carbon dioxide absorbs some of the Sun's heat and prevents this heat from escaping out into space.
Plants make their food from carbon dioxide.

carbon monoxide   *noun*

Carbon monoxide is a colourless **gas** which does not smell. It is very poisonous to breathe, because it stops the blood taking in oxygen. Carbon monoxide is formed when substances containing carbon are burned, but are not burned completely.
Exhaust from motor cars contains a mixture of poisonous gases, including carbon monoxide.

carnivorous plant ▶ **insectivorous plant**

carotene   *noun*

Carotene is a substance that gives a yellow, orange or red colour to certain plants. It is a **pigment**. If an animal eats a plant containing carotene, its body changes it into vitamin A which is an important **nutrient**. Dandelions, apricots and carrots all contain carotene.
Carotene gives carrots their bright orange colour.

carpel *noun*
A carpel is part of a **flower**. It is that part which surrounds the **ovules**. The carpel is made up of the **ovary**, the **style** and the **stigma**. Carpels are joined, or fused, together in some kinds of flower. In other kinds of flower there may be large numbers of separate carpels.
The magnolia flower had many carpels, arranged in a spiral pattern.

catkin *noun*
A catkin is a kind of **flower**. Catkins are made up of many tiny flowers, usually without any petals. Catkins hang down and wave in the wind. Male catkins produce dust-like **pollen** which is carried away in the air. Female catkins have long, hairy **styles** and **stigmas**, to catch the pollen. Trees, such as **birches**, **alders** and **hazels**, have catkins.
In the growing season, the hedge was laden with yellow catkins.

cedar *noun*
Cedars are **conifers**. The true cedars include the cedar of Lebanon of the Middle East and the deodar of the Himalayas. Cedars grow tall and have spreading branches.
Cedar wood has scented oil which is used to make perfumes.

cell *noun*
A cell is a single, tiny part of all living things. It has a **cell wall** which surrounds the protoplasm and a nucleus, where the **genes** are found. Some simple **organisms** are made up of only a single cell. Most animals and plants are made of tissues that contain millions of cells.
She looked through the microscope to see the cells in the leaf.

cell membrane *noun*
The cell membrane is the outer covering of a **cell**. It allows some substances, like water, to pass in and out of the cell. Inside the membrane lie the cell's contents, such as the **nucleus** and the **cytoplasm**.
They could see each cell surrounded by its cell membrane.

cell wall *noun*
The cell wall is part of a **cell**. In plants, the cell wall covers the cell and is made of tiny fibres. These fibres are mainly made of **cellulose**. They make the cell wall firm. When a plant cell fills with water, the cell wall holds it firm. This gives support to the plant.
Under the microscope, the cell wall showed clearly.

cellular *adjective*
Cellular describes a part of a plant or animal which is formed from **cells**.
A plant's leaves are cellular.

cellulose *noun*
Cellulose is a **chemical**. It is made up of the sugar glucose. Cellulose is the main substance found in the **cell walls** of plants. It is one of the substances that is found in the largest quantity in living things.
Leaves and grasses contain large amounts of cellulose.

cereal *noun*
A cereal is a kind of **grass** planted for its crop of **grain**. Many of the world's major crops are cereals. Wheat, rice, oats, barley, millet and maize are all different kinds of cereal.
The fields had been planted with cereals.

chalk soil *noun*
Chalk soil is a type of **alkaline soil**. It is shallow and well-drained, which means it does not become filled with water, or waterlogged. Chalk soil is rich in **organic** matter.
A variety of plants grew in the chalk soil.

24

chaparral *noun*

Chaparral is a kind of **vegetation**. It is the scrub vegetation found in the coastal region of California. It develops under a Mediterranean type climate, with hot, dry summers and warm, wet winters.
They saw spiny bushes in the chaparral.

chemical *noun*

A chemical is any one of the single, pure substances from which all materials are made. The simplest chemicals are the elements. Elements join together to make more complicated chemicals called compounds.
The scientist found out which chemicals were stored in the root of the plant.

chestnut *noun*

Chestnuts are **deciduous** trees. There are 12 kinds of true chestnut, found in Europe, Asia and North America. The sweet chestnut of southern Europe has edible nuts. The wood is used for making fences, gates and railway sleepers.
The horse chestnut is a common chestnut that grows in temperate regions.

chlorophyll *noun*

Chlorophyll is a **chemical** mixture, or compound. It is found in the **chloroplasts** of plant cells and gives plants their green colour. Plants use chlorophyll to change the energy of sunlight into food, in the process of **photosynthesis**.
Leaves are green because of chlorophyll.

chloroplast *noun*

A chloroplast is a structure within the **cells** of green plants. It contains **chlorophyll**. A chloroplast is where the chemical reactions involved in **photosynthesis** take place. Cells which are exposed to the light develop large numbers of chloroplasts, and turn the plant a dark green colour.
We could see the many chloroplasts under the microscope.

chromosome *noun*

A chromosome is a string-shaped structure found inside the nucleus of a **cell**. The chromosomes contain the **genetic** material of each cell, made up largely of DNA. Each chromosome is a linked pair of two strands which are exactly alike. Each species of **organism** has a particular number of chromosomes.
Chromosomes become visible under a microscope when a cell divides.

citric acid *noun*

Citric acid is an **acid** found in plant **cells**. It forms the basis of a series of complicated reactions, known as the citric acid cycle. These reactions are an essential part of the life of cells.
Citric acid makes lemons taste sour.

citrus *adjective*

Citrus describes certain kinds of **fruit**. Citrus fruits are oranges, lemons, grapefruits, tangerines and their relatives. They contain large amounts of **citric acid** in their cells.
Citrus fruits grow best in warm climates.

grapefruit
mandarin
orange
lemon

25

class *noun*
Class is a group, or rank, in the
classification of plants. The class lies
between the **division** and the **order**.
Angiosperms and **gymnosperms** are both
classes of plants within the order
Tracheophyta.
*The angiosperms are the largest class of
vascular plants.*

classification *noun*
Classification is the process used by
scientists to sort, or classify, plants. In a
classification, each **species** is put into a
larger category, the **genus**. Each genus, in
turn, belongs in a larger category, the **family**.
The higher categories above the family are
order, **class** and **division**. At the top of the
scale is the plant **kingdom**. All plants are in
the plant kingdom.
*Classification placed the genus in the rose
family.*
classify *verb*

clay *noun*
Clay is a mud-like substance formed from
tiny particles of minerals. Clay minerals are
mostly made up of sheets of silicates. Clay
cracks when dry. It takes in, or absorbs,
water easily, and becomes sticky and soft.
Clay is used to make pottery and
earthenware.
*The clay on the river bed stuck to their boots
as they waded across to the other side.*

clear felling *noun*
Clear felling is a kind of **forestry**. In clear
felling, the trees of a patch of woodland or
forest are all removed at the same time. This
leaves a bare patch with no trees remaining.
Areas which have been clear-felled may take
a long time to grow back, or **regenerate**.
Saplings may be planted to speed up the
regeneration.
*The hillside showed large open spaces
where the evergreen forest had been
clear-felled.*
clear-fell *verb*

climate *noun*
Climate is the overall weather of a site or
region. **Temperature**, **rainfall**, altitude and
distance from the sea all affect the climate.
Polar, temperate, oceanic, tropical, arid and
Mediterranean are some of the major kinds
of climate.
*Countries close to the equator have a
tropical climate.*

climatic change *noun*
Climatic change is the slow change that
takes place in the Earth's climate. It is not
known exactly what causes climatic change.
A possible cause is changes in the amount
of energy given off by the Sun. Other
reasons may be continent movement, or
changes in how the atmosphere is made up.
*Carbon dioxide pollution of the atmosphere
may be one cause of climatic change.*

climax community *noun*
A climax community is part of **ecological
succession**. The climax is the **community**
which remains at the end of a succession.
The climax community remains the same, or
similar for a long period. It is given its
character by the **soil** and **climate**. **Tropical
rain forest** is the climax community for many
lowland sites in the wet tropics.
*The scrub turned gradually into the climax
community of oak woodland.*

climbing plant *noun*
A climbing plant is any plant which climbs as
it grows. **Vines** are climbing plants. Climbing
plants may climb by twisting their stems
around other plants. They may hold on with
the help of special pads called **suckers**.
Virginia creeper is a famous climbing plant.

clone *noun*
A clone is a group of plants that are exactly
alike, or identical. Many plants increase their
numbers by **vegetative reproduction**. This
produces a clone of identical single plants.
*The disease spread rapidly through the
whole clone.*

club moss *noun*
Club moss is a kind of **pteridophyte**. There are about 900 species of club moss, in the same **class** as **quillworts**. Most club mosses are found in **tropical** and **sub-tropical** regions, but some live in **temperate** and cold areas. They usually creep or trail on the ground, but some have stems that grow upwards. Most club mosses have small leaves that are arranged in a spiral. They produce **spores** which are scattered, or **dispersed**, by the wind.
Stag's horn club moss has long, white stalks with two cones on the end of each stalk.

cocoa ► cacao

coconut *noun*
Coconuts are the **seeds** of the coconut palm. Coconut palms grow all over the world, in **tropical** climates. The large leaves are used for shelter and the wood for building. The coconut is a large fruit. The single seed is surrounded by a shell, or husk. The fibres from the husk are used to make mats and rope. The seed has a sweet juice known as coconut milk. Coconuts have white flesh that is good to eat.
The beach was covered with fallen coconuts.

colony *noun*
A colony is a group of plants living close together. In **algae**, a colony may be made up of many similar cells living together in a group.
The waste ground was soon covered by a colony of weeds.

commensal *noun*
A commensal is a living thing, or **organism**, that lives with another and shares its food. The sharing does no harm to either organism. Sometimes, commensal plants gain, or benefit, from their life together.
Some fungi are commensal with certain trees.
commensal *adjective*

community *noun*
A community is a group of plants living together in the same **habitat**. A **salt marsh** is one type of plant community, temperate **woodland** is another. **Botanists** also recognize smaller, more detailed communities within the larger ones. Examples of these are acid lowland bog and Scots pine forest.
The main, or dominant, species of plant growing in the highland heath community was heather.

composite family *noun*
The composite family is the largest and most highly developed **family** of flowering plants. There are more than 20,000 species of **herbs** and **shrubs** in the composite family. Composite flower heads are made up of many small flowers. These are usually both **disc florets** and **ray florets**. Members of the composite family have efficient methods of reproduction. They produce many seeds and have many ways of scattering the seeds.
The composite family of flowers includes some vegetables as well as flowers.

compost *noun*
Compost is a kind of young **soil**. Compost forms when leaves, bark and other organic matter begin to break down on the ground. Many gardeners make their own compost, using waste vegetables and garden rubbish. Compost is very **fertile** and is good for the soil.
He dug a layer of compost into the vegetable garden.

compound fruit   *noun*

A compound fruit is a **fruit** belonging to one of the two main groups of fruit. The other group is **simple fruit**. Compound fruits develop from two or more **ovaries**. They are made up of a cluster of tiny fruits, each of which contains a **seed**.
Strawberries, blackberries, figs, mulberries and pineapples are all compound fruits.

compound leaf   *noun*

A compound leaf is a type of **leaf** shape. In a compound leaf, the leaf is made up of a few or several **leaflets**. In the **horse chestnut**, each compound leaf is shaped like a hand, with finger-like leaflets.
The compound leaf of a clover is divided into three leaflets.

maple

horse chestnut

cone   *noun*

A cone is a kind of **flower** or **fruit** in which the seeds are not protected by an **ovary**. The **gymnosperms** are the main plants with cones. Trees with cones are often called **conifers**. Cones are hard, woody structures, usually brown in colour. The fruits of the alder are also known as cones.
The hard cones fell onto the forest floor.

conifer   *noun*

A conifer is a tall, straight tree which develops **cones**. Examples of conifers are **pines**, **spruces** and **firs**. Conifers have soft wood which is good for building. Most conifers have needle-shaped leaves which are constantly replaced when they fall, and not lost all at once.
We could see the dark foliage of the conifers in the distance.

coniferous forest   *noun*

A coniferous forest is a **forest** in which most of the trees are **conifers**. Many coniferous forests are found in the **boreal** region. This lies to the south of the Arctic. The coniferous forest of Siberia is also known as the **taiga**. The main trees of coniferous forests are **spruce**, **fir**, **pine** and **larch**. Their dark colour helps them shed snow in the spring.
The coniferous forests are dark and shady throughout the year.

conservation   *noun*

Conservation describes the protection of the natural resources of the Earth, including landscapes and wildlife. Conservation of the natural surroundings, or environment, is important for future generations of people.
They sent money to help the conservation of the tropical rain forests.
conserve   *verb*

coppicing   *noun*

Coppicing is a way of looking after **trees**. In coppicing, trees are cut back to near ground level every 10 to 15 years. The trees which have been coppiced then produce thin shoots. These shoots are harvested as poles, for firewood, or for charcoal burning. Many woods, especially in Europe, have been coppiced for hundreds of years.
They could see from the shape of the trees that coppicing had been practised in the ancient wood.

core area *noun*
A core area is a part of a **nature reserve**. In some nature reserves, the centre of the reserve is carefully protected, so that the plants and animals can thrive without disturbance from people. This central area is called the core area. The core area is surrounded by a **buffer zone**, which is less heavily protected.
The core area of the reserve contained many rare species.

cork *noun*
Cork is part of the **bark** of trees. It forms in the outer layer of the bark. Cork is strong, but light and squashy. It protects the trunk of the tree from drying out, and perhaps also from attack by insects. Some trees, notably the cork oak, have unusually large amounts of cork in their bark. Cork is stripped from the cork oak to make many products, including corks for bottles.
He pulled a large chunk of cork from the trunk of the tree.

corm *noun*
A corm is a kind of underground **stem**. It is a swollen stem which contains stores of food. Plants such as crocuses have corms. In the **growing season**, buds on the corm develop and sprout, producing leaves and flowering stems. At the end of the season, new corms form at the bases of the flowering stems. These remain **dormant** during the cold season. They then develop into new plants during the next growing season.
The gardener gathered in the corms to keep for planting next season.

corolla *noun*
The corolla is part of the **flower** of a plant. It is the name for the ring of **petals**. In some flowers, the corolla forms a tube of joined petals. In others, the corolla is made up of several, separate petals.
The bee climbed deep inside the corolla of the flower to gather the nectar contained inside the flower.

cortex *noun*
The cortex is part of the **stem** or **root** of a plant. It is the part between the **epidermis** and the stele in a stem or root.
The cross-section of the root showed the cortex clearly.

corymb *noun*
A corymb is a type of flower head. It is a flat-topped cluster of flowers. In a corymb, the outer flowers blossom before the inner ones. The small flowers grow on short stems from a longer, central stem, making a flat, round shape.
Cherry blossoms are corymbs.

cotton *noun*
Cotton is a flowering plant. It is grown as a **crop** for its white, fluffy seed heads. These are harvested and then spun to make cotton fibres. Oil and cattle-feed is also made from the cotton plant. Cotton is grown in warm regions of China, Asia and America.
He watched the cotton being harvested.

cotyledon *noun*
A cotyledon is a kind of **leaf**. Cotyledons are the very first leaves to form as a **seed-bearing plant** grows. The **monocotyledons** have a single cotyledon. The **dicotyledons** have two cotyledons. **Gymnosperms** may have several cotyledons. In some seeds, the cotyledons remain inside the seed. In others, they come out as the first leaves.
As the pea grew, the cotyledons unfolded.

creeper *noun*
A creeper is any plant which grows by creeping. Some creepers grow along the ground, others grow along the twigs and branches of other plants. Some creepers can grow up vertical rock faces or up the walls of buildings.
We decided to plant a creeper to cover the bare walls.

crop *noun*
A crop is a kind of plant grown by farmers to provide food or some other product. Rice, wheat, sugar-cane, cotton and potatoes are all crops. Crops are harvested each season.
The farmer planted his crops in the fertile valley soil.

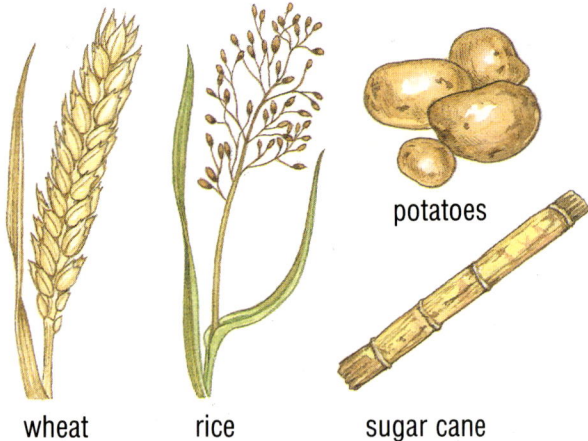

potatoes

wheat   rice   sugar cane

crop rotation *noun*
Crop rotation is a method of **agriculture**. In crop rotation, a different crop is grown each season on the same piece of land. So one year, the farmer might grow a **cereal** crop. The next season, he might grow beans, and the next season potatoes. Crops take out and add different chemicals to the soil, and rotation helps them to grow better. Diseases also find it more difficult to take hold under crop rotation.
The farmer practised crop rotation, changing crops each year.

cross-pollination *noun*
Cross-pollination is a type of **pollination**. In cross-pollination, **pollen** from one flower travels to the **stigma** of any other flower of the same **species**. Flowers can be cross-pollinated by the wind or by insects and other small animals. **Self-pollination** is the other type of pollination.
Cross-pollination by a bee allowed the foxglove to produce seeds.
cross-pollinate *verb*

crown *noun*
1.   A crown is a part of a **tree**. It is the point from which most of the main branches grow.
The crown of the mahogany tree soared into the canopy of the rain forest.
2.   A crown is the part of a plant where the **stem** joins the **root**.
The crown of the dandelion lay just under the soil.

crude oil ► **petroleum**

cucumber *noun*
Cucumbers are long, green **fruits**. They are related to **melons**, but they are not sweet. Cucumbers grow on trailing **vines**. They are used as vegetables and in salads. Young cucumbers are often called gherkins and are pickled in vinegar.
She sliced the cucumber and put it in a sandwich.

cultivar *noun*
A cultivar is a kind of plant. Cultivars are varieties of a **species** which people have developed under **cultivation**. In this way, the wild plants, such as the rose, have been bred in gardens into huge numbers of cultivars. Cultivars can usually breed with each other, but their varieties are mostly kept separate by taking **cuttings**.
There are many thousands of cultivars of crop and garden plants.

cultivate *verb*
To cultivate is to grow plants in gardens or on farms. It involves preparing the ground by digging or ploughing, planting the crops, watering and fertilizing them, and then harvesting. It is only possible to cultivate on good, **fertile** soils, and in **climates** with regular **rainfall** or good **irrigation**.
After removing the trees from the land, the farmers began to cultivate it.
cultivation *noun*

cushion plant *noun*
A cushion plant is a kind of plant that grows in cold **habitats**, such as mountains and tundra. Its leaves grow low on the ground, packed tightly together to form a dense cushion. A cushion plant traps air amongst its leaves. This creates a **microclimate** for the plant, which is much warmer than the surrounding air. Many **alpine** plants are cushion plants.
Cushion plants often have brightly-coloured flowers to attract the few insects that live in cold regions.

cutting *noun*
A cutting is a stem or a branch of a plant that is cut off to grow into a new plant. Some kinds of plant can be **propagated** in this way. The cutting is planted in soil and grows roots of its own.
He took a cutting of the geranium plant to grow a new plant.
cut *verb*

cycad *noun*
A cycad is a kind of plant. Cycads are **gymnosperms** belonging to the **order** Cycadales. There are about 70 different species of cycad, found in Central America, southern Africa, eastern Asia and Australia. Cycads grow like a **palm**, with a single, thick trunk and a circle of feathery leaves. The tallest cycads grow to about 15 metres.
She went into the tropical greenhouse to look at the cycads.

cycle *noun*
A cycle is a process in which any material moves round a system. In the water cycle, water moves from the sea into the air by **evaporation**. It then returns to the sea via the rivers, after falling as rain on the land.
Rainfall is an important part of the water cycle.

cytoplasm *noun*
Cytoplasm is the substance that makes up all the living part of a **cell**, except the nucleus.
A cell wall made of cellulose surrounds the cytoplasm.

D

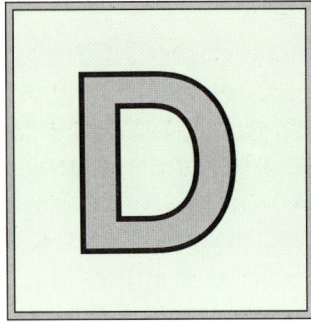

date palm *noun*

A date palm is a kind of **palm** tree. Date palms grow in North Africa and Arabia, and they are also grown as a **crop** in California. They produce **fruits** called dates, which are sweet and nutritious. The leaves of the date palm are used to make thatch and matting.
The camels sheltered under the date palms.

DDT *noun*

DDT is a chemical mixture, or compound, used to kill insect **pests** on crops. It is a hydrocarbon and contains chlorine. DDT is now banned in many places because it builds up in other animals and kills them.
The plane sprayed DDT onto the field to kill the pests.

debris *noun*

Debris is a collection of tiny particles which gather together in one area. A river-bed has a layer of debris, formed from tiny particles of rock and soil. Debris also covers the sea-bed. This is made up of the skeletons of millions of sea plants and animals.
The diver could see the wreck clearly after removing the debris.

decay *verb*

Decay describes how things break down into smaller parts. When plants and animals die, their bodies decay in the soil and break down into simpler substances. **Humus** in the soil forms when leaves and other organic substances decay.
The farmer ploughed the straw into the soil, so that it would decay.
decay *noun*

deciduous forest *noun*

A deciduous forest is a **forest** made up mainly of deciduous trees. These trees lose their leaves during part of the year. The trees in a deciduous forest only have leaves during the **growing season**, which is usually in the spring and summer. The leaves fall in the autumn and the forest is bare through the winter. Before they fall, the leaves of many deciduous trees turn shades of gold, red and brown.
The lower hill slopes were covered with a deciduous forest of oak.

deciduous tree ▶ **deciduous forest**

decompose *verb*

Decompose describes the breaking up of a chemical substance into simpler substances. When animals and plants decompose, their complicated organic chemicals break down into simpler chemicals in the ground.
The dead trees gradually decomposed.
decomposition *noun*

decomposer *noun*

A decomposer is a living thing that helps in the process of decomposition of a dead plant or animal. Decomposers help to break down the remains of the bodies into simpler materials. These materials are then absorbed into the soil and make it richer.
Decomposers are an important part of an ecosystem.

defoliant *noun*

1. A defoliant is a **chemical** which kills leaves on plants. Some defoliants kill **weeds** outright. Others destroy trees by killing their green leaves and twigs. Defoliants are sometimes used to kill weeds amongst **crops**. Many defoliants are poisonous to animals as well and their use has to be carefully controlled.
The aeroplane sprayed defoliant onto the field.
2. A defoliant is any **fungus** or animal which infects or feeds on the leaves and stems of plants.
Many caterpillars and locusts are defoliants.
defoliate *verb*

deforestation *noun*
Deforestation is the clearing of natural **forest**. The forest trees are felled, so that the land can be used for growing **crops** or for building. In areas of high rainfall, deforestation may be followed by **erosion** of the soil. Deforestation is a particular problem in the **tropical rain forests**.
Deforestation had left huge, bare patches on the hillsides.

delphinium *noun*
A delphinium, or larkspur, is a flowering plant. The delphinium **genus** belongs to the crowfoot family. Delphiniums grow in cool regions of both the northern and southern hemispheres. They range in height from about 30 centimetres to 2 metres. Delphiniums have several small, trumpet-shaped flowers growing up the stem. These may be blue, white, pink or reddish-purple.
Many kinds of delphinium are grown as garden flowers.

dendrochronology *noun*
Dendrochronology is the study of tree **rings**. It may be used to work out the age of a tree. Dendrochronology can also give information about past events, such as changes in climate.
The scientist used dendrochronology to find out the age of the fossil tree.

deplete *verb*
Deplete describes how the amount of a substance is reduced. The layer of the chemical ozone in the **ozone layer** is being gradually depleted because of the build-up of chlorofluorocarbons in the atmosphere. Many plants are being depleted due to destruction of their **habitats**.
The trees in many forests are being depleted by the effects of acid rain.
depletion *noun*

desert *noun*
A desert is a dry, open area of land, where few plants can grow. Deserts mostly have less than 25 centimetres of rain a year. Some deserts, like the Sahara in North Africa, are hot. Others, like the Gobi in Asia, may be cold. The polar deserts of the **Arctic** and **Antarctica** are covered in ice.
The only plants we found in the desert were a few thorny shrubs.

desertification *noun*
Desertification describes how a **desert** spreads. If there are too many animals, they will destroy the **vegetation** in dry areas. Without the plants as protection, the soil may be eroded and turn into desert.
The Sahara of North Africa is becoming larger because of desertification.

diaspore *noun*
A diaspore is any part of a plant that can be **dispersed** and grow into a new plant. **Seeds**, **bulbils** and **spores** are diaspores.
Plants produce diaspores after fertilization.

diatom *noun*
Diatoms are tiny **monera**. They may be **unicellular** or live in **colonies**. There are about 10,000 species of diatom, found in the sea, in fresh water or on wet mud. They are very common in the **plankton** of the ocean, where they are at the base of the **food chains**, along with **algae**.
Many diatoms are extremely beautiful under the microscope.

dicotyledon *noun*
Dicotyledons are the main group of flowering plants. The other group are the **monocotyledons**. There are about 250 families in the dicotyledons. The **embryo** of a dicotyledon has two tiny leaves, or **cotyledons**. Dicotyledons also have broad leaves with branching veins, and complicated flowers.
Familiar flowers such as roses and wallflowers are dicotyledons.

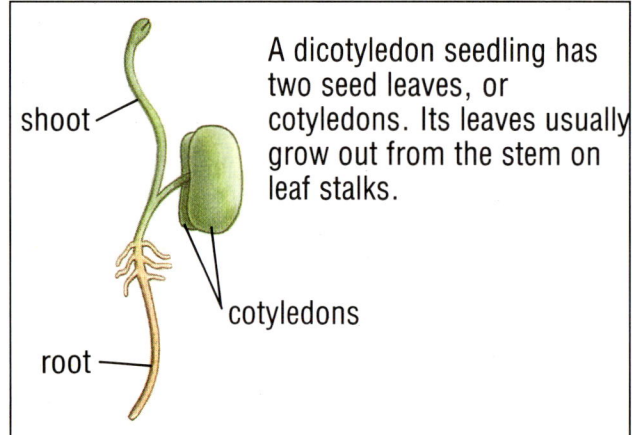

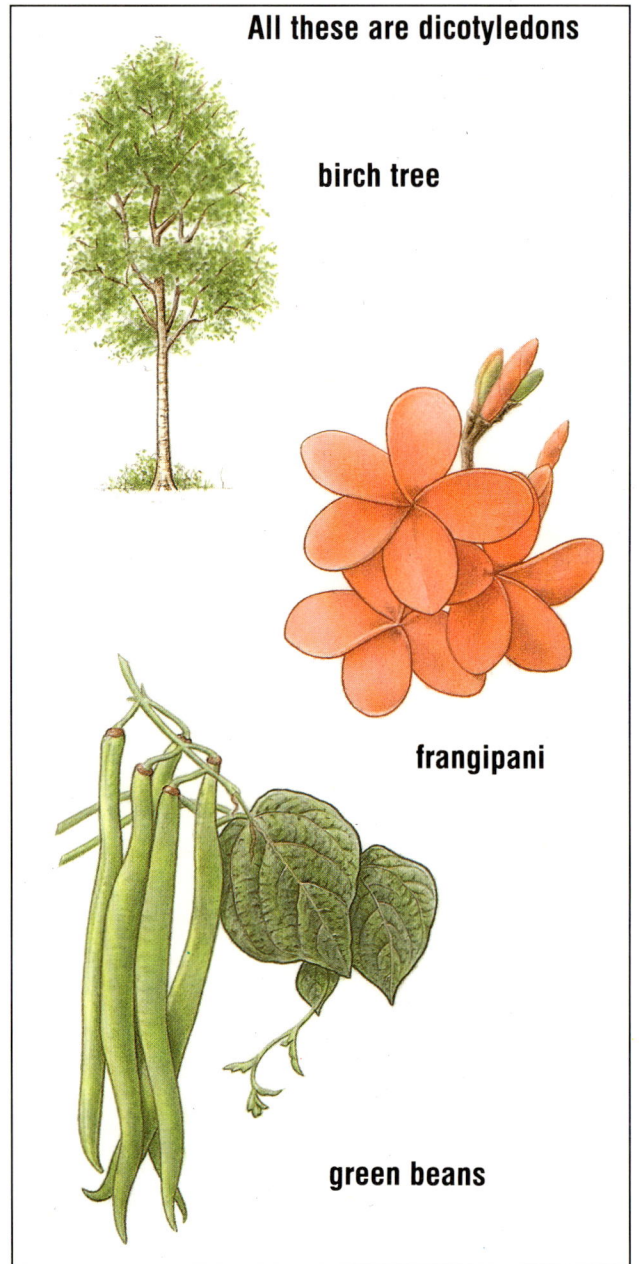

A dicotyledon seedling has two seed leaves, or cotyledons. Its leaves usually grow out from the stem on leaf stalks.

shoot

cotyledons

root

five-petalled flower

buttercup

net-veined leaf

tap root

secondary root

All these are dicotyledons

birch tree

frangipani

green beans

dicotyledon ► page 34

dioxin *noun*
Dioxin is a **chemical**. It is very poisonous to animals and also to people. Dioxin is a by-product of the manufacture of some **herbicides** and **defoliants**. It can cause damage to the skin and also diseases such as cancer.
The explosion at the factory released dangerous dioxin into the air.

diploid *adjective*
Diploid describes a plant that has two basic sets of the cells called **chromosomes**. One set comes from the **female** parent plant, the other from the **male** parent plant. **Gamete** plants have only one set of chromosomes.
Diploid cells have the same number of chromosomes as their parent cells.

disaster *noun*
A disaster is a bad accident or natural event. Natural disasters include earthquakes, typhoons, floods and droughts. Some disasters, such as fires at nuclear power plants, are caused by people.
A disaster happened because the earthquake was centred near to a city.

disc floret *noun*
A disc floret is one of a group of small flowers that make up the central part, or disc, of a flower in the **composite family**, such as a **daisy**.
Disc florets are usually shaped like a trumpet.

disease *noun*
A disease is an illness or unhealthy state of an **organism**. Diseases are caused when other organisms attack the body of a plant or animal. Many diseases are caused by **bacteria** and by **viruses**. They may also be caused by the lack of an essential mineral, such as iron or calcium.
The farmer sprayed his crop to reduce the disease.

dispersal *noun*
Dispersal is the process by which **seeds** are spread by the parent plant. In some plants, the seeds are very light and dispersal is by wind. Some seeds are dispersed by animals which eat the flesh of the **fruits**.
In many aquatic plants, dispersal is by water.
disperse *verb*

reedmace   **poppy**   burrs sticking to animal fur

diversity *noun*
Diversity is a measure of the numbers of **species** in a **habitat**. Habitats with a high diversity contain many species. Habitats with a low diversity contain fewer species.
The desert had a very low diversity.
diverse *adjective*

division *noun*
1. Division is part of the process by which plants grow. In a growing plant, the cells first divide. They then take on different forms to make the new tissues of the growing plant.
The meristem is the site of plant cell division.
2. A division is the second largest group, or rank, in the **classification** of plants.
Angiosperms are a division of plants.

dominant *adjective*
Dominant describes a plant **species** that is the largest or most widespread of all the **vegetation** in an area. The dominant species gives the area its overall appearance.
Bracken dominated the hillside.
dominate *verb*

dormant *adjective*
Dormant describes something which is in a resting state. The **seeds** of many plants lie dormant for several months before they are ready to **germinate**.
When the land was ploughed up, many dormant seeds came to the surface.

downland *noun*
Downland is a kind of chalk **grassland**, which has been grazed for many years by sheep and rabbits.
Downland is common in southern England.

drainage *noun*
Drainage describes the way water runs away through the **soil** or rocks. If a soil has good drainage, it will dry out quickly after rain. Soil with bad drainage quickly becomes full of water and is difficult to use.
He improved the drainage by digging a ditch below the field.

drought *noun*
A drought is a long period with no **rainfall**. Where droughts are normal, **deserts** develop. Wild plants and animals can often survive short droughts, but crops may suffer.
The farmer's crops failed in the long drought.

drupe *noun*
A drupe is a kind of **fruit**. In a drupe, the **seed** or seeds are surrounded by a hard stone and also a soft, fleshy part. Plants with drupes include cherries and plums.
The botanist explained that the cherry fruit was a drupe.

dune *noun*
A dune is a large hill of **sand**. Dunes are moved and shaped by the wind. Some dunes are shaped like a half-moon, or crescent. Others are long lines of ridges. Sandy **deserts** have large areas of dunes. Dunes are also found near the coast, behind sandy beaches.
They found it hard to walk over the soft dunes.

dust bowl *noun*
The dust bowl is the name given to part of the central **plains** of the United States of America. It is centred on Kansas and Texas, and has occasional dust storms. In the 1930s, dry weather and storms destroyed much of the farmland of the dust bowl.
He was used to seeing dust storms, because his farm was in the dust bowl.

dwarf *adjective*
Dwarf describes a **species** of plant that is much smaller than the plants to which it is closely related. Some dwarf species have become small because they have **adapted** to difficult conditions, such as extreme cold.
There are many dwarf trees in the Arctic.

dye *noun*
A dye is a strongly-coloured **chemical**. Dyes are usually **organic** chemicals. Most dyes originally came from plants. For example, the blue dye indigo comes from a tropical shrub. When a dye is boiled up with cloth, the colour moves, or transfers, to the cloth.
They gathered the lichens to make dye.

plum

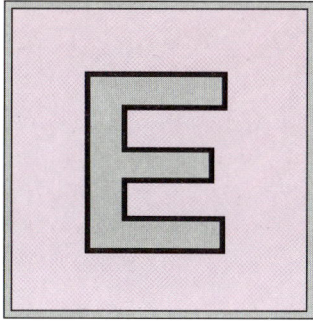

E

ear *noun*
An ear is the name used for the **fruit** of some **cereals**. The **grains** of cereals, such as wheat and barley, grow clustered together in ears.
He shook the ripe wheat to remove the grain from the ears.

Earth *noun*
The Earth is the name of our planet. It is the third planet from the Sun. The Earth takes about 365 days to circle, or travel in its orbit, around the Sun. It is the only planet known to support life.
The climate of the Earth has changed many times during the 4.5 billion years of its life.

ebony *noun*
Ebony is a **tropical tree**. It has very hard wood which is used for making furniture. It has a dark brown or black **heartwood**. One kind of ebony grows in India and Sri Lanka. Others grow in Africa, South-east Asia, and Central America.
The carved walking stick had a dark handle of ebony.

eco- *prefix*
Eco- is a prefix that means to do with living things and their **environment**.
Ecocide is the total destruction of an area of natural environment.

ecological succession ► **succession**

ecologist *noun*
An ecologist is a person who studies **ecology**. A plant ecologist may study the flowering of plants in a wood. A bird ecologist might study the feeding habits of seabirds.
The ecologist took a sample of water in the pond to list the animals living in it.

ecology *noun*
Ecology is the study of living things in their natural **environments**. An understanding of ecology is vital for the **conservation** of wildlife around the world.
She studied ecology to understand how the forest trees developed.

ecosystem ► page 38

ectotrophic *adjective*
Ectotrophic describes a plant that finds food from outside. For example, some **fungi** are ectotrophic. They surround roots of other plants and take out, or extract, nourishment from them. Some ectotrophic organisms give their **host** plants nourishment, as well as taking it. The opposite of ectotrophic is **endotrophic**.
Ectotrophic fungi provide birch trees with important nutrients.

elm *noun*
Elms are **deciduous trees**. There are several different kinds of elm, all growing in **temperate** parts of Europe, Asia and North America. Most elms grow tall. They grow in woods and are also planted in streets and gardens. Elm trees have small, **simple leaves**.
The carpenter used elm wood to make the chair.

ecosystem *noun*

An ecosystem is the name given to the whole **community** in which plants and animals live together. Tropical rain forest, with its trees, undergrowth and animals, makes up an ecosystem.
The oil spillage affected the whole marine ecosystem.

In a land-based, or terrestrial, ecosystem, predators such as the fox and the eagle are at the top of the food chain. They prey on small animals such as rabbits and squirrels. These in turn eat plants. The plants depend on the decomposers at the bottom of the chain to enrich the soil the plants grow in.

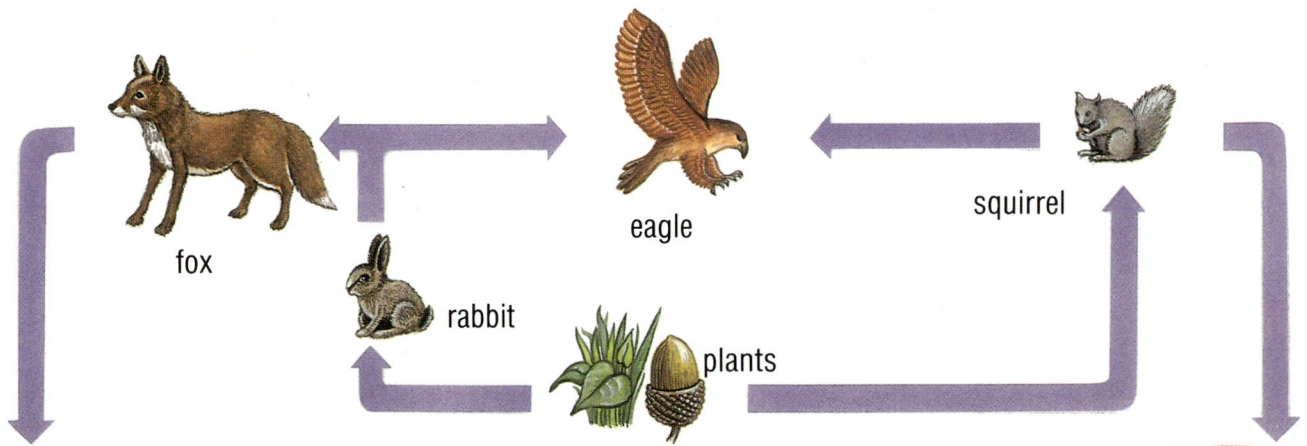

fox

eagle

squirrel

rabbit

plants

In a water-based, or aquatic, ecosystem, the predators are large fish and birds such as pikes and herons. They eat smaller fish and young birds. The smaller fish feed on water insects and plants. Decaying matter at the bottom of the river bed forms a rich base for the plants.

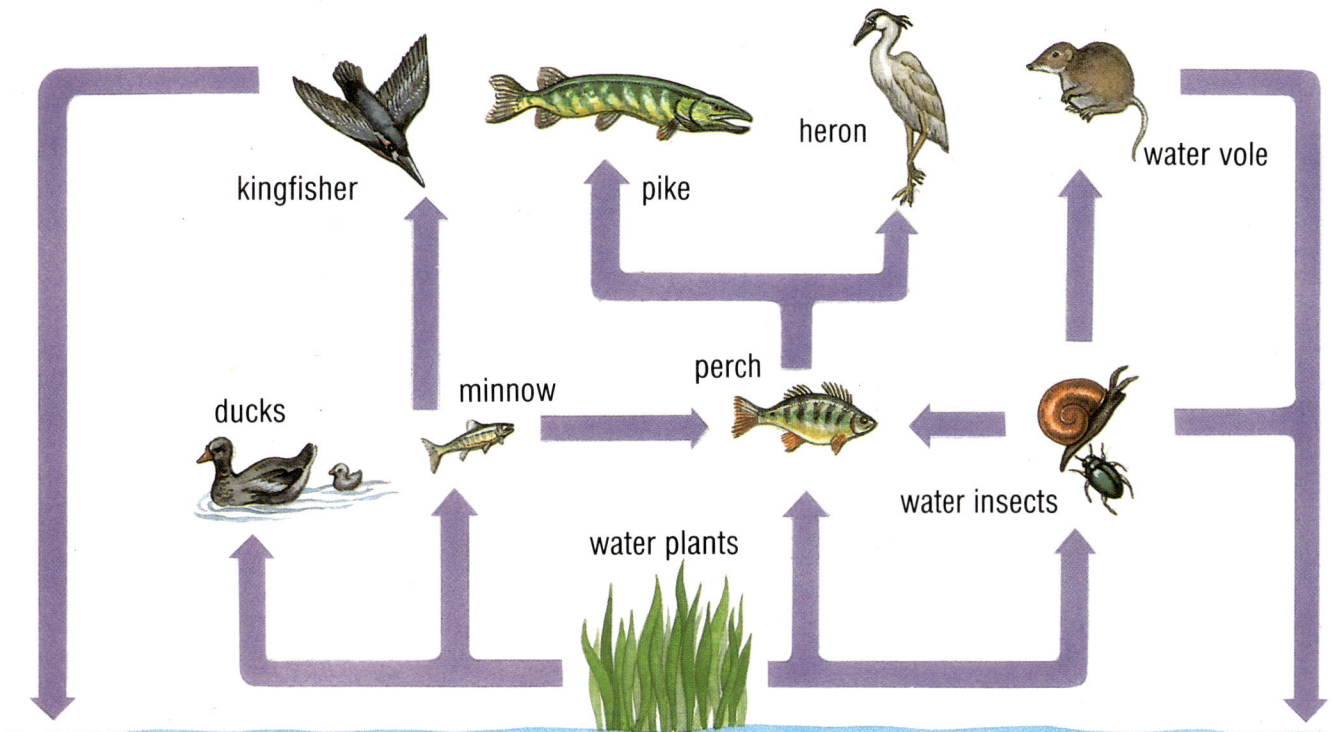

kingfisher

pike

heron

water vole

ducks

minnow

perch

water insects

water plants

endangered species *noun*

An endangered species is one which is thought to be in danger of becoming **extinct** in the near future. When the population of a species becomes very small, it may be endangered.

The botanist explained that the rafflesia is now an endangered species.

The wood cycad is one of the world's rarest plants. The female of the species has never been found.

About half of the 70 species of slipper orchid are seriously threatened by logging, agriculture and collecting.

Knowlton's cactus is one of many species of cactus that are being stolen from the Arizona and Mexican deserts. The cacti fetch high prices in the illegal plant trade.

The giant rafflesia has the largest flower in the world. It measures up to 90 centimetres across and weighs as much as seven kilograms. It lives in the rain forests of Sumatra, which are fast disappearing.

The snakeshead fritillary used to be a common plant of water meadows in southern England. It is now rare, due to the disappearance of most of its habitats.

The 'Symphonia nectarifera' is a tree found only in the rain forests of Madagascar. The population of Madagascar will double by the year 2020. Unless the rain forests are protected, they will be destroyed to provide farmland for the growing population.

emergent *noun*
An emergent is a forest tree that grows so tall that its top, or **crown**, is higher than the rest of the trees. It emerges above them.
Most of the emergents in the rain forest were broadleaved evergreens with waxy leaves.
emerge *verb*

endangered species ▶ page 40

endemic *adjective*
Endemic describes a plant that is found only in a particular area or region. Many tropical islands contain endemic species, which live on that island, but are found nowhere else in the world.
The island was made into a reserve because it contained so many endemic species.

endosperm *noun*
The endosperm is part of the **seed** of a plant. The endosperm contains the food stores of the seed. When a seed grows, it uses up this food, until it is large enough to make its own food. The food stored in the endosperm may be starch, proteins, oil or fat.
Cereal grains have large endosperms with stored food.

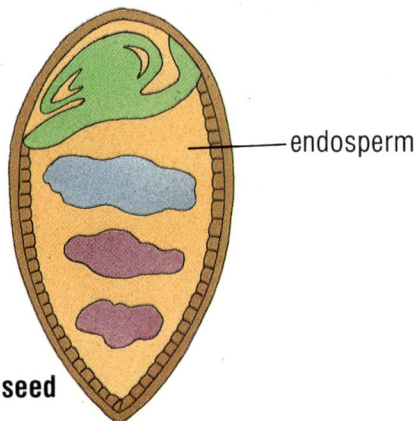

— endosperm

cross-section of seed

endotrophic *adjective*
Endotrophic describes a plant that finds its food from inside. Many **fungi** are endotrophic. They pierce the roots of their **host** plant and take in nourishment from them.
The opposite of endotrophic is ectotrophic.

energy *noun*
Energy is the ability to do work. There are many kinds of natural energy. These include heat from rocks underground, energy from water power and solar energy from the Sun. These sources of energy can be turned into electric energy. Plants use solar energy to make their own food during **photosynthesis**.
The plants died because they could not get enough sunlight for energy to make food.

environment *noun*
Environment describes a living thing's surroundings. It includes the other plants and animals. It also includes the climate, rocks and soil. **Pollution** of the environment is a growing problem in the world.
The factory was fined because it released poisonous waste into the environment.

enzyme *noun*
An enzyme is a natural **chemical** mixture, or compound, found in plants and animals. Enzymes are **proteins**. They break down other chemicals by controlling chemical reactions. Plants and animals use enzymes to break down complicated chemicals into simpler ones, and also the other way round.
Processes such as photosynthesis in plants are controlled by enzymes.

ephemeral *adjective*
Ephemeral describes a plant with a short **life cycle**. Ephemeral plants grow quickly from seed, then come into flower and fruit very fast, before setting seed and dying within a season. Many **weeds** are ephemeral.
The bare soil was quickly covered by ephemeral plants.

epidemic *noun*
An epidemic is a rapid spread by an **organism** through a population of host plants or animals. Organisms which cause **disease**, such as **bacteria**, sometimes have epidemics.
The epidemic of aphids quickly infected the whole field of flowers.

epidermis *noun*
The epidermis is a layer of **cells**. It is the outermost layer of cells in a plant. The epidermis protects the inner cells from harsh conditions outside and prevents the plant from drying out. It also helps to stop **diseases** from entering the plant.
The fungus spread over the plant's epidermis.

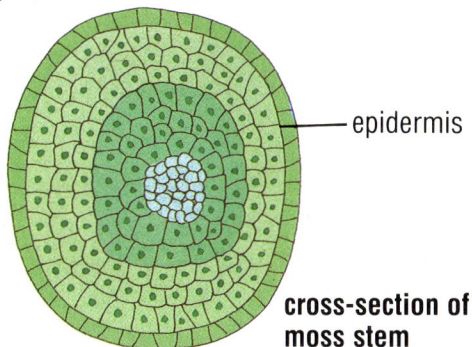

— epidermis

cross-section of moss stem

epiphyte ► page 44

erosion *noun*
Erosion is the wearing down of rocks or **soils**. It is caused by the action of water, wind or ice. Erosion can also be caused by living **organisms**. Natural **vegetation** protects the soil underneath from erosion.
Areas with high winds or heavy rainfall are likely to show signs of erosion.
erode *verb*

escape *noun*
An escape is a plant that has spread from a garden or park where it is **cultivated**, into the surrounding, uncultivated land.
He was surprised to find several Chinese delphiniums growing in the field.

ethanol *noun*
Ethanol is a colourless liquid. It is an alcohol which mixes with water. Ethanol burns easily and has a sweet smell. It is produced naturally when **yeast** grows in **sugar**, in the process of fermentation. In some countries, ethanol is made from **sugar cane**.
The car was able to run on a mixture of petrol and ethanol.

eucalyptus *noun*
A eucalyptus is a tall, **evergreen tree**. It belongs to the myrtle family and grows mainly in Australia. Eucalyptus trees can grow as tall as 100 metres. They have long, narrow, leathery leaves and flowers that are filled with **nectar**.
Eucalyptus trees provide people with oil, gum and timber.

eutrophication *noun*
Eutrophication is the process by which water or soil becomes rich in minerals, such as **nitrogen** and **phosphorous**. It can happen when chemicals, such as **fertilizers**, find their way into streams, lakes and ponds. The eutrophied water becomes much more fertile. This often means the animal and plant communities change. **Algae** may increase and form an **algal bloom**. Sensitive plants and animals may die out.
The vegetation of the lake changed over the years because it was affected by eutrophication.
eutrophy *verb*

evaporate *verb*
Evaporate describes the changing from liquid to gas. Water evaporates when it enters the air as water vapour. In the **water cycle**, water evaporates from the land and from plants, before returning as rain.
The road soon dried in the hot Sun as the rain began to evaporate.
evaporation *noun*

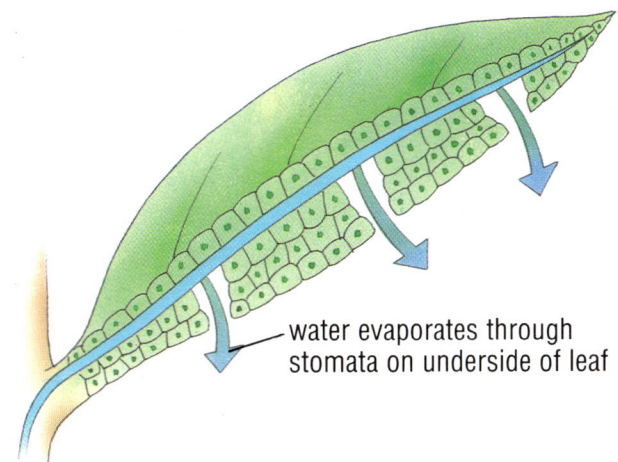

water evaporates through stomata on underside of leaf

43

epiphyte *noun*

An epiphyte is a plant which grows on another plant, not on the ground. Some epiphytes take in moisture and minerals from the air. Others feed from pockets of **humus** and **soil** trapped in the bark of the supporting plant. Some epiphytes trap rain amongst their leaves and then take in the water through their roots.

Many of the trees in the rain forest had epiphytes growing on them.

bromeliad

orchid

Epiphytes, such as the bromeliad and orchid, have aerial roots which they use to take in moisture from the air.

Ferns, mosses and bromeliads grow along the branch of a tree in the understorey of a rain forest.

evening primrose   *noun*

An evening primrose is a **wildflower** that grows in North America. There are several **species** of evening primrose that grow between 30 and 180 centimetres high. They have hairy leaves and saucer-shaped flowers. The flowers are white, pink or bright yellow and grow among the upper leaves of the plant. Evening primroses also grow in other countries as **cultivated** flowers.
Evening primroses produce an oil which is used in medicine and face creams.

evergreen forest   *noun*

An evergreen forest is a **forest** that is made up mostly of evergreen trees. There are many different kinds of evergreen forest. The northern evergreen forests are **dominated** by **conifers**. The Mediterranean regions were once covered in evergreen oak forests. Most tropical forests are evergreen forests.
The floor of the evergreen forest was always shady.

evolution   *noun*

Evolution is the process by which all **organisms** change over time. It is based on gradual change and **natural selection**. **Sexual reproduction** produces offspring which differ slightly from their parents. Those better fitted to the environment survive longer. They pass on these characteristics to their young, and so the species evolve.
All the species we see today have been produced by the process of evolution.

exhaust   *verb*

Exhaust describes using up the reserves of something. A piece of land can be exhausted after many crops have been grown upon it. Each crop takes **nutrients** from the soil, until the soil becomes too poor for the crops to grow well.
When the ground became exhausted, the farmers ploughed up a fresh strip.

exotic   *adjective*

Exotic describes an animal or plant which is not native. Exotic species are **species** that have been introduced from another country or region. Sometimes, exotic species reproduce very fast and become a nuisance. That is because they have fewer natural enemies.
Many weeds are exotic species.

exploit   *verb*

Exploit describes making use of something. People exploit the forests and other communities to feed and clothe themselves. People exploit the seas by catching fish and whales. Exploitation may cause a habitat or species to become **depleted**.
Exploited habitats must be allowed to recover or many will soon be destroyed.
exploitation   *noun*

exterminate   *verb*

To exterminate is to remove a plant or animal completely from an area. **Pest** species are sometimes exterminated when they affect crops or damage other habitats. It is often very difficult to exterminate a species completely.
They managed to exterminate the weeds from the field.

extinct   *adjective*

An extinct species of plant or animal is a **species** that has disappeared completely from the Earth. When it is extinct, it cannot be replaced in its original form.
The dinosaurs were once common, but are now extinct.

extinction *noun*
Extinction is the process by which **organisms** become **extinct**. It may be caused by hunting or collecting species of plant or animal, or by the destruction of their **habitats**.
The extinction of the species was certain after the forest where it lived had been destroyed.

F

fairy ring *noun*
A fairy ring is a kind of **fungus**. Fairy ring fungi commonly grow on pastures and lawns. The toadstools grow outwards in the shape of a ring, leaving a circle in the grass.
The lawn was covered with circular fairy rings.

fallow *adjective*
Fallow describes land which has been left uncultivated. Sometimes, farmers grow **crops** for several years and then leave the land fallow. This allows **nutrients** to return and the land to become **fertile** again. Farm animals may be allowed to feed on the fallow land. Their droppings form **manure** for the land.
Weeds and grasses grew in profusion on the fallow field.

family *noun*
A family is part of the **classification** system. All plants belonging to the same family share certain characteristics. Each family contains one or more **genera**. The family lies between **order** and genus in the classification system.
Peas and beans both belong to the legume family.

famine *noun*
A famine is a very serious food shortage. When a large area suffers crop failures and food supplies are all used up, a famine may result. Many people die every year in famines. Famines may be caused by drought, by floods, and also by wars.
The relief workers flew in extra supplies of wheat during the famine.

fen *noun*
A fen is a kind of wetland **habitat**. In a fen, the soil is usually made of peat which is rich in minerals. The **vegetation** of a fen has many **sedges**, with **reeds** in wetter sites. Older fens develop into drier land called carr, with bushes. Fens often form at the shallow fringes of rich lakes.
The fen was protected as a nature reserve.

fern *noun*
A fern is a kind of plant. Ferns form part of the **pteridophyte** division. They are feathery, green plants which mostly grow in wet or damp places. There are over 10,000 species of fern found all over the world. The damp tropical regions have the greatest numbers of ferns. Ferns produces **spores** on the underside of their leaves in order to reproduce.
In the wet woodland we found many ferns.

royal fern   polypody fern

fertile *adjective*
Fertile describes soil which is rich in **nutrients** needed by plants for healthy growth. The most fertile soils are usually those under woodland or grassland.
Soils in mountain valleys are usually fertile due to minerals washed out from rocks.

fertilizer *noun*
Fertilizer is a **chemical** or mixture of chemicals added to **soil** to make it more **fertile**. **Compost** and **manure** are forms of natural fertilizer. Most fertilizers contain the element **nitrogen**.
The farmer added fertilizer to make the crops grow better.

fibre *noun*
A fibre is a kind of plant **cell**. Fibres are long cells found in the stems of plants. They are common in the **xylem** and **phloem**. Plant fibres are used to make clothes and also to make rope and baskets. Examples of fibre plants are sisal, cotton, flax, jute and hemp.
They grew a crop of jute and harvested it for the fibres.

field *noun*
A field is an area of farmland. Many fields are surrounded by hedges or fences, to keep animals from roaming outside. Some fields are sown with **grasses** and may be grazed by animals, such as cows. Other fields are planted with **crops**, such as **cereals**.
Cultivated fields surrounded the farm.

field layer *noun*
A field layer is a part of a **forest**. It is the lowest level of plants, below the **canopy** and **understorey**. A field layer is made up of **herbaceous** plants, **mosses**, **lichens**, and small, woody plants.
The field layer of the forest was carpeted with bluebells.

figwort *noun*
Figwort is a **family** of flowering plants. There are about 3,000 species of **herbs**, **shrubs** and small **trees** in the figwort family. They are found mainly in **temperate** regions. Figworts have bell-shaped flowers that are divided into two lips.
Some figworts are medicinal plants.

filament *noun*
A filament is part of a **flower**. It is the long, thin stalk of the **stamen**. The filament swells at its tip to form the **anther**. Filament is also the name used for the thin strands of certain kinds of algae.
The filaments grew out from the centre of the flower.

fir *noun*
A fir is an **evergreen tree** that belongs to the **pine** family. Firs grow in the shape of a pyramid, up to about 70 metres tall. They have needle-shaped leaves that grow evenly all around the branch. Firs have **cones** that grow upright on the branches.
The bark of young fir trees contains a resin called balsam.

flagellum (plural **flagella**) *noun*
A flagellum is a tiny, whip-like tail. It is attached to some single-celled **organisms**. The organisms move around by lashing their flagellum.
The gamete moved by whipping its flagellum from side to side.

flash flood *noun*
A flash flood is a sudden flood. Flash floods happen occasionally in areas with irregular, heavy rains. A flash flood can be very damaging and cause **erosion**, by carrying away the soil and vegetation.
The crops were completely destroyed by the flash flood.

flax *noun*
Flax is a **crop**. It is grown for its **fibres** and also for its oil and seed. Flax has blue flowers and smooth, shiny leaves. The fibres are used to make linen. The seeds contain linseed oil. Cattle food is also made from flax seeds.
The flowering flax turned the field bright blue.

flora *noun*
Flora is the plant life of a region or **habitat**. It includes the tiny **mosses** and **liverworts**, as well as larger plants, such as **shrubs** and **trees**. The flora of an area depends on its soil and climate, and on its history. People have changed the natural flora over much of the world. The animal life of a region is called fauna.
The original flora of much of lowland Europe was a mixed, deciduous forest.

floret *noun*
A floret is a kind of **flower**. The florets in a flower head may look different from each other, so that the whole collection of florets looks like a single, larger flower. Florets are found especially in the dandelion family and grasses. The flower head of a dandelion looks like a single flower, but it is a collection of florets. In a dandelion flower head, the outer petals are called **ray florets** and those at the centre are called **disc florets**.
Under the magnifying glass, he could see the separate florets.

flower ► page 50

fodder *noun*
Fodder is a kind of food. It is food which is prepared for farm animals. **Crops**, such as clover, lucerne, broad beans, kale, rape and maize, are often made into fodder. Fodder is sometimes cut and dried and turned into hay. Sometimes, it is preserved in a moister form as **silage**.
In the cold season, the farmer fed his cows on fodder.

foliage *noun*

Foliage is the name used for the green parts of **trees**, **shrubs** and **herbs**. It includes the leaves and fresh twigs produced each season by the main branches of a tree. Many forest insects, such as caterpillars, feed on the foliage of trees.

Many plants that are grown in gardens have decorative foliage.

food *noun*

Food is any substance which is used as a source of **energy** by a living **organism**. Green plants make their own food out of water and carbon dioxide by using the energy of the Sun. Animals use plants or other animals as food.

The main food of the tawny owl was small mice and voles.

food chain *noun*

A food chain is the name given to a group of plants and animals which feed upon each other in an **ecosystem**. **Energy** is passed up the food chain. So in one kind of food chain, plants are eaten by caterpillars, the caterpillars are eaten by birds, which in turn are killed for food by larger birds. Large carnivores, such as lions, are normally at the very top of the food chain. At the very bottom of the food chain are the **decomposers**.

The ecologist explained how the animals and plants depended on each other in the food chain.

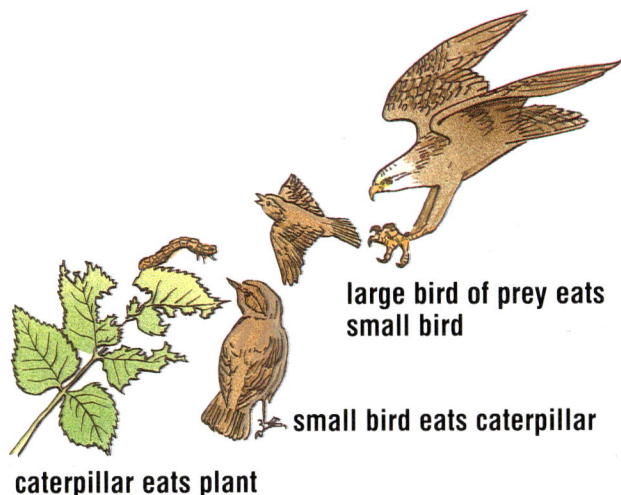

food preservation *noun*

Food preservation is any method of slowing down the **decay** of food. There are many different kinds of food preservation, such as freezing, canning, drying and smoking. The most modern method is **irradiation**.

Food preservation makes food safe to eat for longer, but some people are worried that it removes essential nutrients from food.

food supply *noun*

Food supply is the production of **food**. It is also the process by which food is passed to consumers. People get their food supply either by growing it themselves, or by buying it from markets or shops. Large amounts of food are grown in the world, but many areas suffer regular shortages of food supply.

The local people became hungry when the food supply ran out.

food web *noun*

A food web is the name given to the complicated network of **food chains** in an **ecosystem**. On a diagram, **ecologists** draw lines between animals which feed on each other. A completed diagram of the food web has a shape like a web.

All the woodland plants were connected in the same food web.

forb *noun*

A forb is a plant that grows on **grassland**. It is any plant that is not **grass**, such as moss campion and smooth fleabane.

After the rains, the grasslands were covered with different kinds of forb.

large bird of prey eats small bird

small bird eats caterpillar

caterpillar eats plant

flower *noun*

A flower is the **reproductive** part of a flowering plant. The main parts of a flower are the stigma, style and ovary, the stamens, and the sepals and petals. Many flowers are brightly coloured to attract insects and other animals for **pollination**. Flowers may produce **nectar** which also attracts animals. Some flowers are **male**, some are **female**. Other flowers are both male and female.
The bright red flower soon opened out in the warm sunshine.

A typical flower has four main parts. The calyx is made up of leaf-like sepals. The corolla consists of the petals. The stamens and the pistil are the flower's reproductive parts.

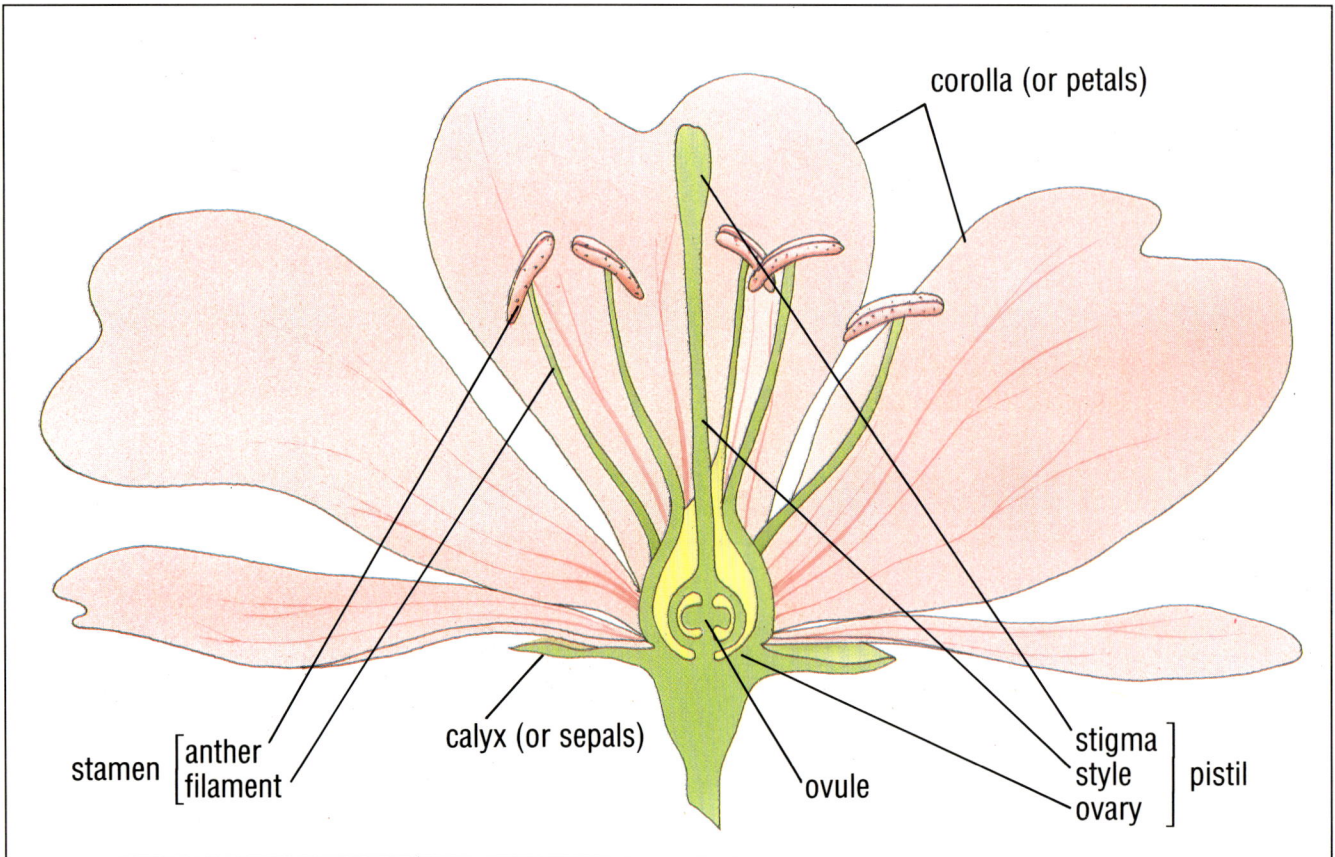

corolla (or petals)

stamen [anther / filament]

calyx (or sepals)

ovule

stigma / style / ovary] pistil

The French marigold is a popular garden annual.

A hybrid tea rose is a perennial shrub grown in gardens.

The East Indian lotus grows in fresh water in the tropics.

The beaver-tail cactus is a plant of desert habitats.

The fire poppy grows on the Californian chaparral.

The smooth fleabane is a flower of the dry plains.

The Rocky Mountain columbine blooms in needleleaf forests of northern North America.

The Arctic lupin is specially adapted to live in the cold tundra.

fruit *noun*

Fruit is the part of a plant that contains the **seeds**. Some fruits are dry and may split open to let go, or release, the seeds. Others may be soft and fleshy. Many soft fruits are eaten by birds and mammals, which then help **disperse** the seeds.

The birds flew long distances to feed on the ripe fruit.

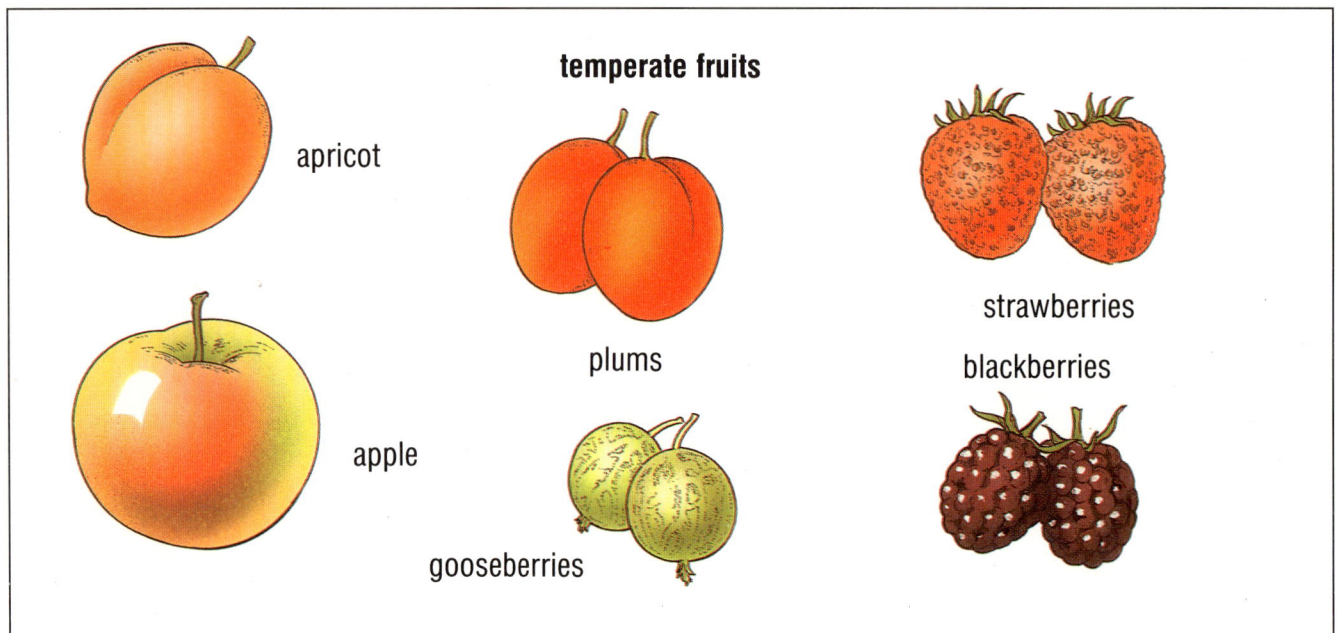

pear

lemon

grapefruit

olives

dates

sub-tropical fruits

bananas

mango

papaya

litchees

tropical fruits

apricot

temperate fruits

plums

strawberries

blackberries

apple

gooseberries

berries

melon

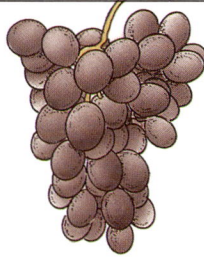
grapes

orange

strawberry

drupes

peach

cherries

plum

pomes

pear

apple

simple fruits

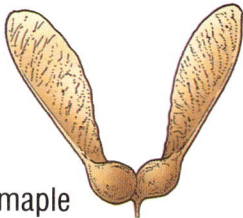
maple

chestnut

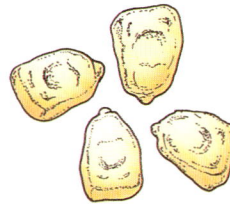
maize

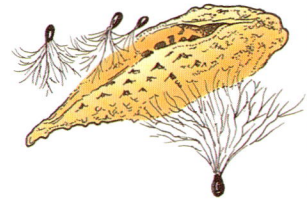
milkweed pod

compound fruits

fig

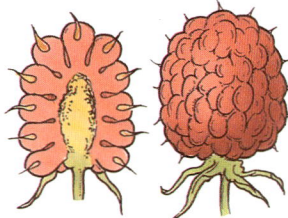
raspberry

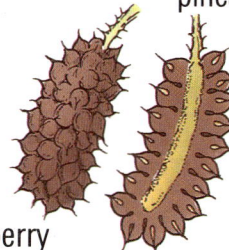
mulberry

pineapple

forest *noun*
A forest is a large area of **woodland**. Some forests are planted and cut at intervals for **timber**. Many forests are **natural**. In northern Europe, Asia and North America, dark **coniferous forests** stretch for many hundreds of miles.
The woodcutter cut down large trees from deep inside the forest.

forest fire *noun*
A forest fire is a fire which burns part of a **forest**. Forest fires are very damaging and difficult to put out. They are especially common in wooded areas which have regular dry periods. Sometimes, forest fires can be halted by chopping down a patch of forest.
The strong wind fanned the flames of the forest fire.

forestry *noun*
Forestry is the planting, growing and harvesting of **forests**. Forestry mostly deals with growing trees as a crop, to produce **timber**. It also involves looking after forests for their wildlife and for people to enjoy.
A person who practises forestry is called a forester.

fossil fuel *noun*
A fossil fuel is fuel which is found **naturally**. Fossil fuels are found under the ground or under the sea. They were formed millions of years ago from the buried remains of plants and animals.
Oil, coal and natural gas are examples of fossil fuels.

fresh water *noun*
Fresh water is a type of **habitat**. It is the water usually found in the ground and in lakes, rivers and ponds. Plants that live in fresh water are called **hydrophytes**. These plants have special features that allow them to live in fresh water.
Water lilies, water milfoil and bladderwort are all plants that live in fresh water.

frond *noun*
A frond is part of a plant. It is a large **leaf**, or leaf-like structure. The leaves of **ferns**, **cycads** and **palms** are called fronds.
The fern fronds covered the flower bed.

fruit ► page 52

fuel *noun*
Fuel is a substance which releases **energy** when it is burned. **Fossil fuels** burn in engines and power stations. Radioactive fuels, such as uranium, produce nuclear energy in nuclear power stations. Animals and plants use **carbohydrates** as **chemical** fuel. Their **cells** burn these chemicals to make the energy needed for life.
He lit the fuel and felt the heat it produced.

fumigate *verb*
Fumigate describes the killing of germs and other **pests** using a smoke. The smoke used to fumigate contains **chemicals** which kill the pests. Fruit farmers sometimes fumigate their crops to kill insect pests which would destroy the developing fruit.
He fumigated the greenhouse to kill the aphids.
fumigation *noun*

fungicide *noun*
A fungicide is a **chemical** used to kill **fungi**. Common fungicides contain sulphur or sulphur compounds. Farmers spray fungicides on their crops to prevent fungus diseases, such as mildew.
They had to use a fungicide to protect the rose bush from disease.

fungus (plural **fungi**) *noun*

A fungus is a plant-like **organism**. Fungi are not plants but belong to their own kingdom. There are over 50,000 species known, but there may be more than 100,000 species in the world. Familiar fungi include **mushrooms** and toadstools. Many fungi are so small they can only be seen with a microscope. Many also live underground, where they grow as long **fibres**. Unlike green plants, fungi have no **chlorophyll** and cannot make their own food.
The fungus grew out from the side of the dead tree branch.

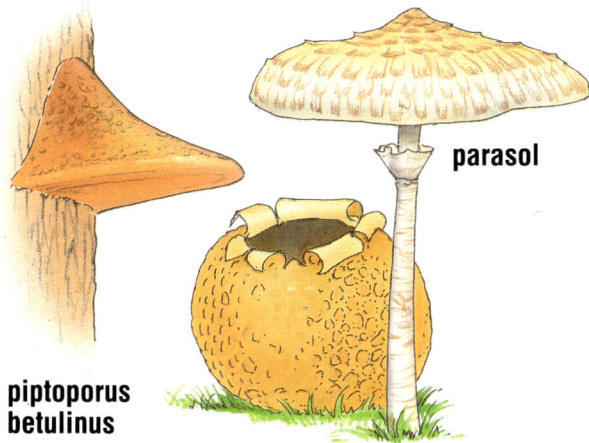

parasol

piptoporus betulinus

scleroderma citrinum

fynbos *noun*

Fynbos is a kind of **vegetation**. It develops in the Mediterranean climate of the southern tip of Africa. Most of the natural fynbos has been destroyed. Fynbos is very rich in species, and it contains many **endemic** plants.
A reserve was set up to protect the remaining fynbos.

Gaia hypothesis *noun*

The Gaia hypothesis is a view of the Earth. In this view, the Earth is seen as behaving rather like a single, living **organism**. It controls itself and its surroundings, or **environment**. The theory was put forward by the British scientist James Lovelock. The hypothesis is not accepted by all scientists. But it has helped people to value the world as a single **ecosystem**, in which all the parts depend upon each other.
The Gaia hypothesis helps us to think about the environment of the world as a whole, rather than separate parts.

gall *noun*

A gall is a growth on a plant. Galls are caused by **parasites** living in the plant cells. These parasites cause the plant cells to grow and form unusual shapes. Galls may be caused by insects, mites, nematode worms, fungi or bacteria. Oakapples and the robin's pincushion are both examples of common galls.
The leaves were covered with a mass of bright red galls.

gamete *noun*

A gamete is a sex **cell**. In plants, the male gametes are contained in the **spores** or in the **pollen**. The female gametes are contained inside the **ovules**. Male and female gametes come together and join during **sexual reproduction**. The cell formed is called a zygote, which then goes on to form the **seed**.
The gametes are produced by the flowers of a plant.

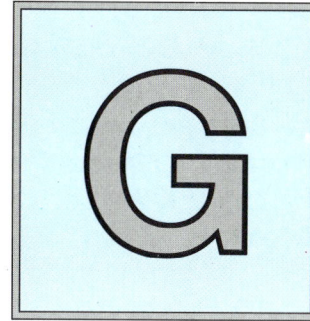

gametophyte   *noun*
The gametophyte is the sexual stage in the **life cycle** of a plant. It is the stage which produces the **gametes**. The other major stage in the life cycle is called the **sporophyte**. In **bryophytes** and **algae**, the gametophyte is the strongest, or **dominant**, form. In flowering plants, the gametophyte is much less important. It is made up only of the pollen tube and embryo sac.
The gametophyte of the moss was very small and hard to spot.

garden flower   *noun*
A garden flower is any flower that is **cultivated**. Some kinds of garden flower are the same as the wild species. Other kinds have been changed in some way by **breeding**. There are three main groups of garden flowers. These are **annuals, biennials** and **perennials**.
Roses are some of the most popular garden flowers.

garrigue   *noun*
Garrigue is a kind of **vegetation**. It is found in Mediterranean climates. Garrigue is made up of low, spiny **shrubs** and scattered **herbs** and **bulbs**. The bulbs die down during the hot, dry season and flower during the cooler, wetter seasons. Garrigue has many scented herbs, such as lavender, thyme and sage.
At the start of the growing season, the flowers of the garrigue were very colourful indeed.

lavender

gas   *noun*
A gas is a substance. A solid or liquid substance becomes a gas when its atoms or molecules are well spread out and very active. Gases spread out to fill their containers and they are very light. All substances become gases when heated to a high enough temperature.
The main gas found in air is nitrogen.

gasohol   *noun*
Gasohol is a liquid fuel. It is a mixture of petrol and alcohol. The alcohol in gasohol is made by fermenting **sugar cane** or **grain**.
In Brazil, many cars use gasohol as a fuel.

gene   *noun*
A gene is part of the centre, or nucleus, of every living **cell**. Genes are found on the **chromosomes** of the nucleus. They are made of the **chemical** DNA. Each gene is an instruction which tells the cell how to make a particular chemical. The full set of genes in each cell contains the instructions for producing the animal or plant.
Genes are passed on from generation to generation during sexual reproduction.

genera ▶ **genus**

generation   *noun*
A generation is the term used for the offspring of the same parent. It also means all individuals produced at about the same period. Generation is also the time covered by the lives of such individuals.
A new generation of poppies grew from that season's seeds.

genetic engineering   *noun*
Genetic engineering is a branch of **genetics**. It usually involves moving **genes** from one **organism** into a tiny micro-organism, such as a **bacterium**. When the bacterium reproduces, it makes many copies of this gene.
Genetic engineering can be used to produce new kinds of garden flower.

genetics *noun*
Genetics is the study of inheritance. It involves studying how features, or characteristics, are passed on from one **generation** of plants or animals to the next. There are many different kinds of genetics, such as medical genetics, plant and animal breeding, and population genetics. **Genetic engineering** is also a kind of genetics.
The scientist developed new kinds of crop by studying their genetics.

gentian *noun*
Gentian is a **family** of flowering plants. There are about 600 species in the gentian family. They grow throughout the world, except in Africa. Gentians have long, pointed leaves and large flowers. The flowers are often blue, but may be white, yellow or red. Each stem of a gentian has one flower.
Many gentians have flowers which never open and they are called bottle gentians.

genus (plural **genera**) *noun*
A genus is a group, or rank, in the **classification** of plants. The genus lies between the **species** and the **family**. Each family contains one or more genera. Species which are sufficiently similar to each other are grouped together in the same genus. In a scientific name, the first name is the genus.
The rose genus is Rosa.

members of the Ranunculaceae genus

geo- *prefix*
Geo- is a prefix used to refer to the Earth.
Geography is the study of the Earth's surface.

geotropism *noun*
Geotropism is a kind of plant growth. It is growth in response to the pull of gravity. In positive geotropism, parts of plants move downwards into the ground. The roots of plants show positive geotropism. In negative geotropism, parts of plants move upwards. Stems show negative geotropism.
If a seed is planted upside-down, geotropism makes sure it grows the right way round.

geranium *noun*
Geranium is a family of flowering plants. It grows in **temperate** regions throughout the world. Many species of geranium are **cultivated** as **garden flowers** or pot plants. Geraniums have round, scented leaves and showy clusters of bright red, pink or white flowers.
A wild geranium called crane's-bill has seed pods that look like cranes' bills.

geranium cultivar

herb robert

germination *noun*
Germination is a kind of growth. It is the growth of a tiny plant from a seed. Germination of ripe seeds is triggered by different factors working together. These include light, warmth and moisture. During germination, the seed uses its stored food and puts out tiny roots and a shoot.
We planted out the seeds and waited for them to germinate.
germinate *verb*

57

gill *noun*
A gill is a part of a **mushroom**. Gills are the fine, thin, leaf-like structures, or divisions, underneath the cap of a mushroom.
The field mushroom has dark brown gills.

ginger *noun*
Ginger is a flowering plant. It has swollen stems which are used to make the **spice** called ginger. When fresh, these are called stem or green ginger. They can also be crystallized, or preserved in syrup. Powdered ginger is a **spice**, which is added to cakes, biscuits and sweets.
The powdered ginger gave the cake a spicy flavour.

ginkgo *noun*
Ginkgo is a special **genus** of **tree**. It is the only surviving species of a family that lived millions of years ago. It makes up its own **order** because it is so unusual. The ginkgo is a tall, deciduous tree with fan-shaped leaves that grow on the ends of shoots. It has fleshy seeds with a hard, nut-like centre. The ginkgo is also called the maidenhair tree.
The botanic garden had a fine pair of ginkgo trees.

glucose *noun*
Glucose is a kind of **sugar**. Plants make glucose from water and **carbon dioxide** by using the energy of the Sun in the process of **photosynthesis**. Many other chemicals, including **starch** and **cellulose**, are then made from glucose by the plant's **cells**.
The nectar of the tropical flower was rich in glucose.

gnetophyte *noun*
A gnetophyte is one of a small group of plants that grow in deserts and tropical forests. Gnetophytes are **gymnosperms** and include **welwitschias**, **lianas** and ephedras, such as the joint pine.
Welwitschias are strange gnetophytes that are found only in the deserts of south-western Africa.

graft *verb*
Graft describes a way of producing, or **propagating**, plants. To graft, a small piece is cut off a plant and inserted into a cut in another plant. Sometimes, the tissues of the two plants grow together. Only closely related **species** can be successfully grafted. **Apples** are often grafted onto the roots of different apple varieties.
The gardener grafted the twig onto a different rootstock.

grain *noun*
A grain is a kind of **fruit**. It is the small, hard fruit found in **grasses** and **cereals**. Grains are like seeds. They have large stores of **carbohydrates**, such as starch. Grains are a good source of **food**. Many grain species, such as **wheat** and **rice**, are used as major crops around the world.
They rubbed the ears of wheat and shook out the ripe grain.

grape vine *noun*
A grape vine is a **climbing plant**. Grape vines are **cultivated** in areas with a Mediterranean climate. These areas include central and southern Europe, California, Chile, South Africa and parts of South Australia and New Zealand. Grape vines produce bunches of **fruits** called grapes. Some varieties are sweet and are eaten raw. Many kinds of grape are used for making wine and vinegar.
They picked grapes from the grape vines.

grass *noun*
A grass is a type of flowering plant. It is a
monocotyledon.There are about 9,000
species of grass, found throughout the world.
Grasses have long, narrow leaves and
rounded, hollow stems. The flowers of
grasses are small and dull. The fruit of a
grass is a **grain**. Most **cereal** crops, such as
wheat, millet and barley, are grasses. **Sugar
cane** is also a kind of grass.
The grass in the meadow grew tall and lush.

grassland *noun*
A grassland is a **habitat** in which the main
kinds of plant are **grasses**. Large grasslands
are found in East Africa and in parts of
central Asia. Grasslands in other parts of the
world have different names, such as the
pampas in South America. Grasslands
develop where there is not enough rain for
trees to grow well. The soil under grassland
is usually very **fertile**.
*The grassland was ploughed up to grow
crops.*

grazing *noun*
Grazing is a form of farming. Grazing
involves growing a pasture of nourishing
grasses. A group of animals, such as cows
and sheep, is then allowed onto the pasture
to graze on the grasses. From time to time,
the animals must be taken away to allow the
grass to recover.
The rich pasture was suitable for grazing.
graze *verb*

green belt *noun*
The green belt is a strip of countryside
surrounding a town or city. Building on a
green belt is limited or prevented altogether.
The green belt stops towns or cities from
growing to cover the nearby countryside.
The houses came to a stop at the green belt.

greenhouse *noun*
A greenhouse is a glass building used for
growing plants. It traps heat from the **Sun**
and so is warmer than the air outside. In a
greenhouse, the temperature and moisture in
the air can be controlled. This prevents frosts
and overheating, and makes the greenhouse
ideal for **cultivating** plants. Many flowers
and fruits are grown in greenhouses,
especially in cooler regions. Another name
for a greenhouse is a glasshouse.
Tomatoes ripen early in the greenhouse.

greenhouse effect *noun*
The greenhouse effect describes the gradual
warming of the Earth's atmosphere. It is
caused by the natural build-up of certain
gases in the atmosphere. These gases are
known as greenhouse gases, and include
carbon dioxide and **methane**. The
greenhouse gases reduce the loss of heat
from the atmosphere and keep the Earth
warm. They trap the Sun's heat in a similar
way to a **greenhouse**.
*Without the greenhouse effect, the average
temperature of the Earth would be about
−18 degrees Celsius.*

greenhouse gas   *noun*
Greenhouse gases are those **gases** which cause the **greenhouse effect**. They are present **naturally** in the lower atmosphere. Greenhouse gases include **carbon dioxide**, **methane**, nitrous oxide and **ozone**. The burning of **fossil fuels** is causing an increase in certain greenhouse gases.
Some scientists think that the build-up of greenhouse gases is causing temperatures on Earth to rise.

groundwater   *noun*
Groundwater is water which is underground. Groundwater usually lies within porous rocks. Where these rocks reach the surface, springs develop. All over the world, supplies of groundwater are being used up. They are also often **polluted** by seeping from waste dumps and by agricultural **chemicals**.
The well pumped up water from the groundwater below.

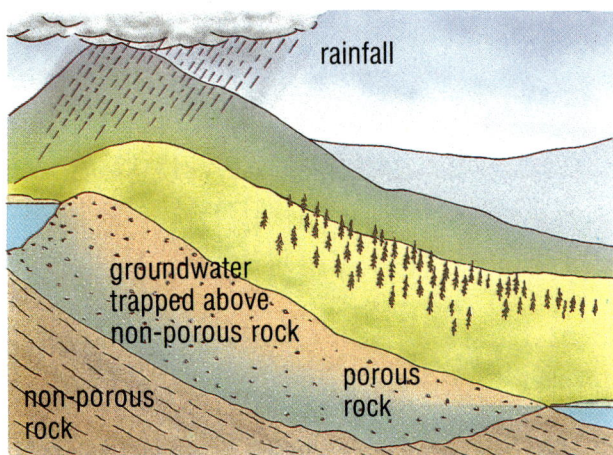

rainfall

groundwater trapped above non-porous rock

porous rock

non-porous rock

grow   *verb*
Grow describes the increase in size and number of **cells** of an **organism**. Plants and animals need **food** to grow. Green plants make their own food by **photosynthesis**. When plants grow, the cells first increase in number by **division**. Then the new cells grow and take on different forms. They become different tissues in the growing body. The way cells grow is decided by the **genes** of the cell.
He watched the plants grow for weeks.
growth   *noun*

growing season   *noun*
The growing season is the time of year when the conditions are right for plants to **grow**. To start growing, plants need warmth, and enough water and light. In **temperate** regions, the growing season begins when the frosts are over and the average daily temperature rises to at least six degrees Celsius. In areas with hot, dry summers, the growing season may be in the mild winter period.
The mild, long summer gave the plants a longer growing season.

gum   *noun*
A gum is any substance which swells in water to form a sticky solution. Many plants produce gums. When a plant is pierced or cut, it may ooze a hard gum which seals the wound. Some **seeds**, such as those of the carob, contain gums. Gums are sometimes used to make glue.
He collected the sticky gum from the bark of the tree.

gutta-percha   *noun*
Gutta-percha is a rubbery substance. It is made from the **latex** that comes from a Malaysian tree called Pelarquium gutta. The milky latex is taken from cuts in bark or from the crushed leaves of the tree. It is then processed to make gutta-percha.
Gutta-percha is used to protect electric wires and in dentistry.

gymnosperm   ▶ page 61

gymnosperm *noun*

Gymnosperms are a type of **vascular plant**. They form the class Gymnospermae, which contains about 700 species. Gymnosperms include the **conifers**, and also smaller groups such as **cycads** and the **ginkgo**. The gymnosperms include the world's largest and oldest trees. These are the redwoods and the bristlecone pine. Unlike **angiosperms**, gymnosperms have naked seeds.
Coal is formed largely from the remains of fossil gymnosperms.

Cycads are found only in warm, tropical regions. They look like palms or ferns and produce large, heavy cones.

scale-like leaves

female big-tree cone

female cedar cone

needle-like leaves

The Californian big-tree grows to a height of 83 metres. It has thick, spongy bark. The leaves are scale-like and pressed against the stems.

The cedar of Lebanon is native to the mountains of Lebanon, Syria and southern Anatolia. It has dark green, pointed leaves on short stems. The female cones are 7 to 10 centimetres long.

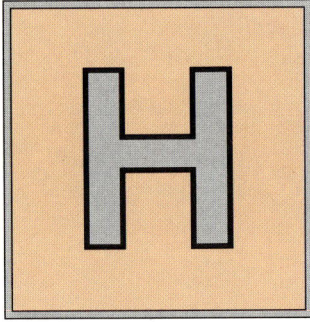

H

habitat *noun*
A habitat is the **natural** home of a plant or animal. Examples of habitats are **salt marsh**, **grassland**, **woodland** and **tundra**. Some habitats, such as **deserts**, are very dry. A **cactus** is a plant of dry, hot habitats. Other habitats, such as **forests**, are cool and damp. Wood anemones, **trees** and **ferns** are found in forest habitats. A **rain forest** is the habitat where the largest number of species of plant and animal is found.
The wild plants grew best in their natural habitat.

hair *noun*
A hair is a thread-like structure that grows from the surface of a plant or animal. Animal hairs are made of the **protein** keratin. Some plant hairs, such as root hairs, take in, or absorb, food materials from the soil. Others give out, or secrete, oils, like those found on lavender plants.
A sundew has sticky hairs on its leaves that trap insects.

halophyte *noun*
A halophyte is a plant that can live in very salty **habitats**, such as on a **seashore** or in a **salt marsh**. Halophytes have special features, or characteristics, that allow them to cope with large amounts of salt in the surrounding water. Some halophytes, such as glasswort, have thick, fleshy leaves in which they store water. Other halophytes, such as samphire, have salt glands in their shoots that give out, or excrete, excess salt.
Sea lavender is a halophyte that lives in salt marshes.

hardwood *noun*
Hardwood is timber from **broadleaf trees**, such as **oak** and **ash**. The trees in **tropical rain forests** are also hardwood trees. They have been widely used by the people for fuel in the countries where they grow. **Mahogany**, **teak** and rosewood are hardwoods which are highly valued for making furniture. Hardwoods are becoming scarce and must be **conserved**.
It is important to let hardwood rain forests grow back when timber is felled.

hardy *adjective*
A hardy plant is a plant which can survive frost damage. All the plants that grow in cold and cool **temperate** regions are hardy.
The garden looked colourful and was easy to manage, because there were lots of hardy perennials in it.

harvest *noun*
A harvest is a **crop** from a plant that is useful to people. A good harvest is gathered when all the conditions have been right during the **growing season**. If the seed or soil is poor or the weather harsh, there may be a poor harvest.
The farmer had a very good harvest that year.

hay *noun*
Hay is **grass** or clover that is cut down and dried. It is stored and used as **fodder** for animals in the winter, when there is no fresh grass or clover for them to eat.
The farmer gathered the hay into stacks.

hazel *noun*
Hazel is a woody **shrub**, or small tree. There are about 10 kinds of hazel, found in Europe, Asia and North America. The male flowers of hazel are **catkins**, which hang down from the twigs. The fruit is an edible **seed** inside a **nut**. Some kinds are good to eat. Hazel wood makes good poles and also firewood.
The squirrels gathered the hazel nuts from under the bushes.

heartwood *noun*
Heartwood is the wood in the centre of a tree **trunk**. It does not contain any living **cells**. It is darker and harder than the wood which is further from the centre, and it is also older. In some trees, the heartwood is full of **resins** and **tannins**.
We could see the heartwood at the centre of the stump.

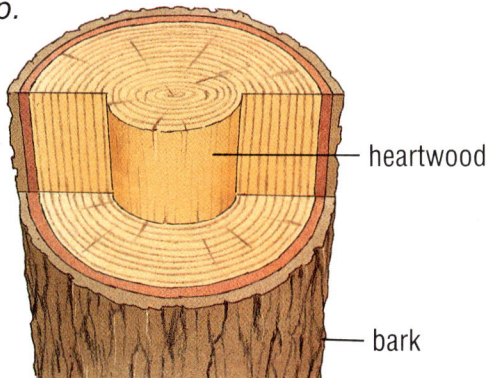

heartwood

bark

heath *noun*
Heath is a kind of **habitat**. Areas of heath can still be found in north-west Europe. Typical heath plants include heathers and gorse. Heath is not **fertile** enough to be suitable for **agriculture**. If it is left alone, heath turns slowly into **woodland**.
Bracken covered a patch of hillside on the heath.
heathy *adjective*

heather *noun*
Heather, or heath, is a family of flowering plants. It is a kind of low, **evergreen** shrub that grows on heath and moors in Europe and Africa. There are more than 600 species of heather. The European heathers have small, bell-shaped flowers, which are pink, purple or occasionally white. Many African heathers also have colourful flowers. In Europe, heather is used to make brooms, brushes and baskets.
Heather makes up a large part of the plant covering of peat bogs.

heathland ► heath

herb *noun*
A herb is a plant which dies down to ground level after one season's growth. Unlike **shrubs**, herbs do not have any woody structures. The word herb is often used to describe plants which are used in medicine and cookery. Some herbs, such as parsley, basil and chives, give flavour to dishes. Other herbs have substances in their leaves, stems or flowers which can be used to make medicines.
He often added herbs to food to increase its flavour.

chives   basil   fennel

herbaceous *adjective*
Herbaceous describes a kind of plant. Herbaceous plants have non-woody, green stems, and they die down completely to ground level in the winter. All **herbs** are herbaceous plants.
The herbaceous border was beautiful all summer but it was a very dull place to look at in the winter.

herbarium (plural **herbaria**) *noun*
A herbarium is a special room used to store plants. In a herbarium, each plant **specimen** that has been collected is stuck to a piece of paper. The paper has the name of the plant written on it. It also has information about where the plant was found. Botanists use herbaria to help them name and **classify** plants.
She compared the plant she had found with a similar one in the herbarium.

63

herbicide *noun*
A herbicide is a **chemical** substance used to kill plants. Most herbicides in use today deal with particular plants that are found as **weeds** in **agricultural** land. Herbicides must be used with care, as they can harm wildlife as well as plants.
The careful use of herbicides makes it possible for more crops to grow on one piece of land.

herbivore *noun*
A herbivore is an animal which eats only plant material. Herbivores have specially **adapted** teeth to grind plants, and their stomachs are adapted to break down, or digest, the plant material called **cellulose**. Elephants and rabbits are examples of wild herbivores. Goats, sheep and cows are examples of domestic herbivores.
Herbivores browse all day to eat enough food for energy and growth.
herbivorous *adjective*

heredity *noun*
Heredity is the way in which offspring come to look like, or resemble, their parents. It is the process of inheritance. Heredity works through **sexual reproduction**. **Genes** from both parents come together and are passed on to the offspring in the next **generation**.
The plant breeder studied the heredity of the new breeds of flower.

hermaphrodite *noun*
A hermaphrodite is a plant that is both male and female. It has male and female reproductive parts and can **fertilize** itself.
Most of the flowering plants called angiosperms are hermaphrodites.

high forest *noun*
High forest is a type of **woodland**. In high forest, the mature trees are well grown and tall. High forest is different from **coppiced** woodland, in which the trees are cut back regularly. High forests give a good idea of how a **natural** woodland would look.
The reserve contained a large area of high forest.

holly *noun*
Holly is an **evergreen tree**. It has shiny, waxy leaves, each with several sharp points, or **prickles**. The flowers of the holly are small and dull, but the fruits are bright red or yellow berries. In many countries, holly is used for Christmas decorations. Holly wood is hard and fine-grained.
When the snow lay on the ground, the birds fed on the berries of the holly tree.

hormone *noun*
A hormone is a kind of **chemical** found in plants and animals. Plant hormones are also called auxins. Hormones are chemical messengers which produce a particular response in the plant or animal. Growth hormones make plants grow.
The shoot tip released hormones which affected its growth.

hornwort *noun*
A hornwort is one of a small group of non-flowering plants. There are more than 300 species of hornwort. They belong to the **bryophite** family, which also contains **mosses** and **liverworts**. Hornworts are found throughout the world, usually on bare, damp, shady soil.
Many hornworts grow beside streams or lakes.

64

horse chestnut *noun*

A horse chestnut is a large, **deciduous** tree. It has **compound leaves**. The European horse chestnut has large, white flowers, arranged in groups. The seeds are large and shiny. They grow inside spiky shells, and ripen in the autumn. The red horse chestnut is often grown in streets and gardens. It has bright red or pink flowers.
The children gathered chestnut seeds under the horse chestnut trees.

horsetail *noun*

A horsetail is a **pteridophyte** plant. There are about 30 species of horsetail. Some grow in moist areas, such as marshes. Others are found in drier places like railway embankments. Horsetails have jointed and ridged stems, with **whorls** of feathery branches and small leaves. Their stems contain large amounts of **silica**. In the past, horsetails were used to clean pans, and are now sometimes used for polishing tools and to make reeds for wind instruments.
The garden had been neglected and was full of horsetails.

horticulture *noun*

Horticulture is the growing of vegetables, fruits, flowers and shrubs to sell in shops and markets. The crops are usually grown in a way that makes most use of the land. They are grown in **greenhouses** in colder climates and with **irrigation** in drier ones.
Modern methods of horticulture are essential to provide enough vegetables for everyone to eat.

host *noun*

A host is an **organism** which provides food and shelter for a **parasite**. The parasite lives on the host, but the host is not usually killed by the parasite. In some cases, the host does not suffer much. In other cases, the host may be weakened, or even killed.
The poplar tree was host to several plants of mistletoe.

house plant *noun*

A house plant is a plant which grows well indoors. Many house plants are from **tropical** countries. They grow well in warm houses. Examples of house plants are grape ivy and weeping fig. **Cacti** and **succulents** also make good house plants.
They chose some house plants to decorate the office.

coleus

begonia

houseleek *noun*

A houseleek is one of a group of **succulent** plants. It grows wild on **alpine** rocks, and is grown in Europe as a cover for house walls and roofs. A houseleek has fleshy leaves arranged in a rosette shape.
Houseleeks have star-shaped flowers.

humus *noun*

Humus is the **organic** material in the **soil**. It is made up of the remains of plants and animals. Humus is a rich source of the **chemicals** needed by growing plants. Fallen leaves turn into humus when they gather on the ground.
The humus made the soil very fertile.

65

hybrid noun

A hybrid is a plant or animal that is produced by **genetically** different parents. The offspring inherits features, or characteristics, from both parents. It often grows stronger, with more resistance to disease than either parent. Some hybrids are **infertile**, which means they cannot produce offspring of their own.

The biologist crossed a yellow marigold with an orange one and grew a hybrid with striped petals.

hydro- prefix

Hydro- is a prefix meaning water. Hydro-electric power stations are less damaging to the environment than coal-fired power stations, which **pollute** the air with the smoke from their chimneys.

Hydro-electric power is electricity made by flowing water.

hydrophyte noun

A hydrophyte is a plant which lives in **fresh water** or very wet **environments**. Hydrophytes have poorly developed root systems, and leaves that float near the surface of the water. Their stems are weak and they rely on the water for support. Hydrophytes cannot stand drought, cold or bright light. Their watery environment means that they never suffer dry, cold or very sunny conditions in **nature**.

One of the most beautiful species of hydrophyte is the water lily, which covers fresh-water ponds in summer.

hydroponics noun

Hydroponics is growing plants without soil. A nutrient liquid is used instead. Water with **mineral salts** dissolved in it is pumped through gravel or peat. In this way, the roots of the plants are bathed in the food material. The method is often used for the cultivation of food crops, such as cucumbers, in a greenhouse.

Hydroponics allows plants to be grown in ideal conditions.

hydrotropism noun

Hydrotropism is a kind of plant growth. It is growth in response to water or moisture. A plant which shows positive hydrotropism bends towards the wetter side of its surroundings, or **environment**.

The light was the same on all sides of the plot, but the plants bent towards the stream, because of hydrotropism.

hyphae plural noun

Hyphae are parts of a **fungus**. They are the thread-like filaments. Each is made up of one or more **cells**. Hyphae grow from their tips. They are the means by which many fungi spread through the earth. Hyphae form the **vegetative** part of the fungus.

The hyphae of the honey fungus spread right through the park, and all the trees were affected by it.

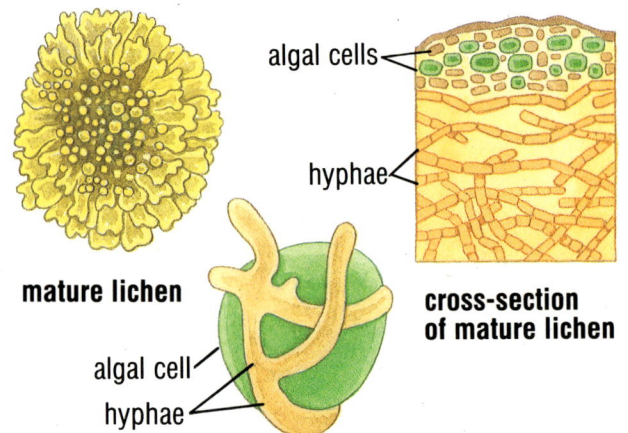

mature lichen

algal cells

hyphae

cross-section of mature lichen

algal cell

hyphae

a lichen forms when hyphae surround an algal cell

I

imbalance *noun*
An imbalance is a lack of balance. Imbalance in a diet, or in certain **nutrients**, may hold back growth in plants or animals. It may also cause deformed growth. In an **environment**, imbalance leads to change in the proportions of different plants and animals.
The imbalance between the water that came into the reservoir and the amount used from it led to drought.

impoverish *verb*
Impoverish describes making something or someone poor. It is easy for a **soil** to become impoverished if too many crops are grown on it and no **fertilizer** is added. The plants take the goodness out of the soil, and it is not replaced. Whole **environments** are impoverished if they are **exploited**.
They grew potatoes on the same plot year after year, and it became impoverished.

indigenous *adjective*
Indigenous describes an **organism** which is **native** to a particular area. The opposite to indigenous is **alien**.
The old oak forest still had most of its indigenous species.

infertile *adjective*
Infertile describes land on which plants do not grow. Land can be infertile because the **rainfall** is not enough. Or it can be infertile because the **soil** does not contain vital **nutrients** needed for growth.
The crops failed because the ground was infertile.
infertility *noun*

infestation *noun*
An infestation describes what happens when a large number of harmful **parasites** gather on the surface of a plant. Sometimes, the infestation can be seen easily, for example when blackfly infest rose bushes or broad bean plants. Sometimes, the parasites are difficult to see, for instance when plants are infested with **rot**.
The infestation of whitefly was so serious that the greenhouse had to be fumigated.
infest *verb*

inflorescence *noun*
An inflorescence is a whole flower head. It includes all the single flowers, or **florets**, on the head.
The geranium had a large, white inflorescence.

innate *adjective*
Innate describes a feature, or characteristic, that comes from within. It describes something that exists **naturally**.
The roots of plants have an innate tendency to grow downwards into the soil.

inorganic *adjective*
Inorganic describes substances which are formed from living things that have never been alive. The rocks of the Earth's crust are inorganic. Coal is not inorganic because it forms from plants.
There were coal seams among the inorganic rocks.

67

insectivorous plants   *noun*

Insectivorous plants are plants which feed partly on animals. They include pitcher plants, sundews, bladderworts and Venus's fly trap. An insectivorous plant catches insects and other small animals. It then absorbs the juices of the animals through its leaves. Some insectivorous plants trap their victims in special, water-filled leaves, others in sticky hairs.

The bog contained many insectivorous plants.

The leaves of Venus's fly trap have hairs that are sensitive to the pressure of an insect landing on them.

The butterwort has a cluster of fleshy leaves. These produce a sticky substance to trap insects.

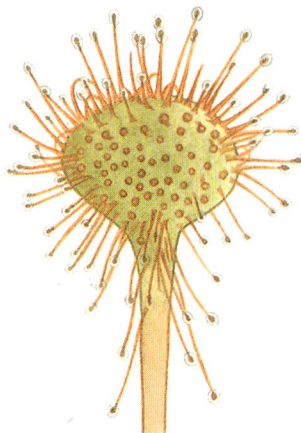

The sundew has sticky hairs on its leaves to catch and hold its insect prey.

The cobra lily is a kind of pitcher plant. It attracts insects with its sweet nectar. Once inside the pitcher, an insect is trapped by downward-pointing hairs on the walls of the pitcher.

insecticide *noun*

An insecticide is a **chemical** used to kill insects. Some insecticides are known as systemic insecticides. They are taken in, or absorbed, by plants, which they do not harm, but they kill insects that feed on them. Other insecticides are sprayed directly onto the insects to kill them. There are many insecticides that are found **naturally**. But most kinds in use today are made from **chemicals**.

Pyrethrum is an insecticide made from the chrysanthemum flower.

insectivorous plant ▶ page 68

intensive agriculture *noun*

Intensive agriculture is a method of farming. In intensive agriculture, money and labour are put into getting the most out of the land. It may depend on the use of large amounts of chemical **fertilizers**, and on **irrigation** in dry areas. Intensive agriculture is usually practised where there are nearby markets to sell the products.

As the population grew, intensive agriculture had to be practised so that everyone could be fed.

iris *noun*

Iris is a family of flowering plants. Irises are **monocotyledons**, found throughout **temperate** parts of the world. Their leaves grow directly from underground stems called **rhizomes**, and are long and sword-shaped. Irises have large, attractive flowers that are many different colours.

Iris flowers are made up of three sets of three petals.

ironweed *noun*

An ironweed is any member of a group of plants in the **composite family**. They have flat-topped dusters of small, tubular flowers. The flowers may be purple, pink or white. Ironweeds grow in North America and Europe.

Ironweeds take their name from their hard, tough stems.

irradiate *verb*

Irradiate describes the way a substance is exposed to **radiation**. Some sources of irradiation are **natural**. Others are the result of human activity, such as nuclear accidents. One new method of **food perservation** is to irradiate it.

The irradiated strawberries were still fresh after several days in the shop.

irradiation *noun*

irrigation ▶ page 70

IUCN ▶ page 72

irrigation *noun*

Irrigation describes putting extra water on the land when there is not enough **rainfall**. Irrigation is done with systems of sprinklers and pipes, or by digging canals and ditches.
By using irrigation, the farmers could grow crops even in the desert.
irrigate *verb*

The four main methods of irrigation

In flood irrigation, water covers a field. Mounds of earth, called dykes, are built to hold the water in. Rice is often grown using this method.

In furrow irrigation, narrow ditches, or furrows, are dug to carry water between rows of crops. The water is brought to the furrows by a pipe. It flows out through openings in the pipe.

In trickle irrigation, tubes with tiny holes in them are laid along furrows between the crops. The water trickles out of the tubes to irrigate the plants.

In sprinkler irrigation, pipes spread a mist of water over a field.

Large areas of desert in the United States of America have been brought into use for farming through irrigation.

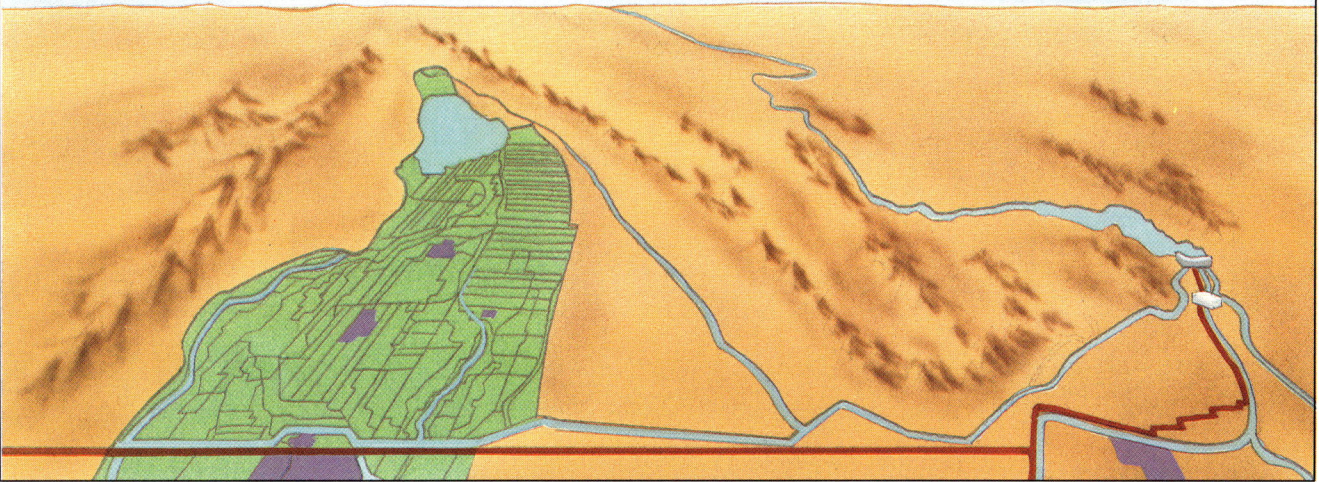

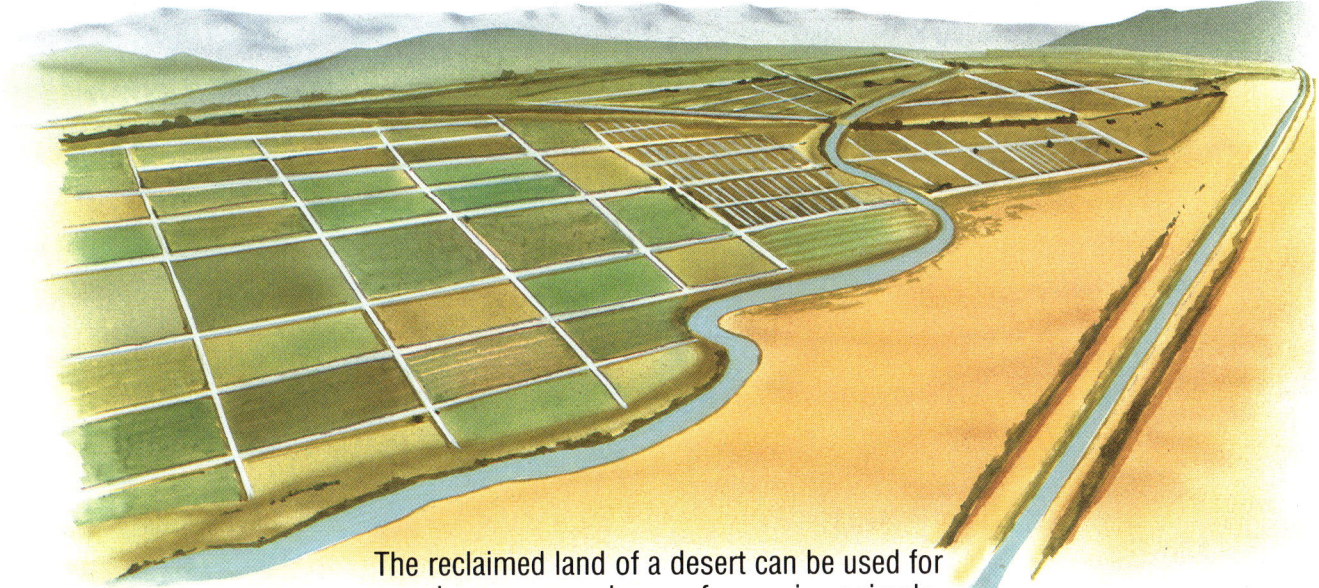

The reclaimed land of a desert can be used for growing crops, and grass for grazing animals.

The shaduf has been used for thousands of years.

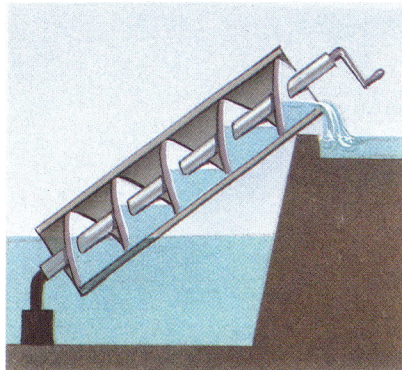

Archimedes' screw is an ancient method of irrigation.

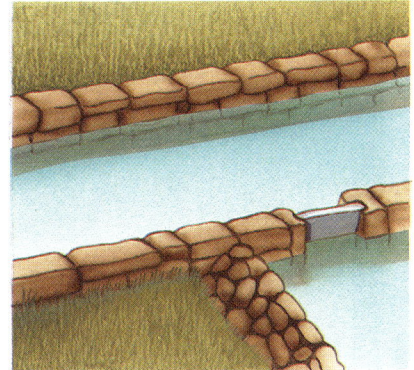

Canals were used in Ancient Assyria.

IUCN *noun*

The IUCN is a **conservation** group. It was founded in 1948. It is an organization made up of governments, non-government agencies, conservation agencies and research bodies. There are over 100 member countries. The aim of the IUCN is to promote conservation throughout the world. IUCN stands for International Union for Conservation of Nature and National Resources.

The IUCN helps to protect the natural world from damage by people.

The Conservation Monitoring Centre is a branch of the IUCN. It provides an information service about such subjects as endangered plants and animals, and the international trade in wildlife species and products. It produces the Red Data Books and Protected Areas Directories.

The work of the IUCN includes monitoring activity in Antarctica.

The IUCN looks after threatened habitats, such as the African savannah.

jungle *noun*

A jungle is a kind of **vegetation**. It is a thick **woodland** which is difficult to walk through because of its dense undergrowth. Jungle commonly develops in **tropical** areas with a damp climate. Many types of **tropical rain forest** are jungles.

They cut their way slowly through the thick vines of the jungle.

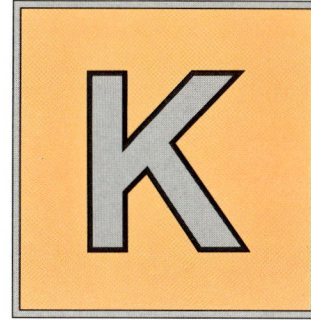

Karroo *noun*

The Karroo is an area of southern Africa where the climate is very dry. The plants of the Karroo are **adapted** to live in dry conditions.

She saw many new kinds of plant on the Karroo.

kernel *noun*

A kernel is the inner part of a seed. It is where the **embryo** is found. The new plant will grow from the embryo. Kernels are very rich in food material, because they provide the **nutrients** for the growing embryo. **Nuts** are the best known kinds of kernel. They are a good source of plant **protein** for humans.

The walnut kernels that had stayed on the ground all winter sprouted into seedlings in the spring.

kieselguhr *noun*

Kieselguhr is a type of rock. It is made up of the shells of tiny plants called **diatoms** that lived in water. Kieselguhr is soft and fine-grained. It has many uses in industry.

Kieselguhr may be used as a filter.

kingdom *noun*

A kingdom is the largest group in the **classification** system of **organisms**. There are five kingdoms: the monera kingdom, the protist kingdom, the fungi kingdom, the plant kingdom and the animal kingdom. Each kingdom is divided into smaller groups. The plant kingdom is divided into division, class, order, family, genus and species.

Mosses, ferns, flowers and trees all belong to the plant kingdom.

kinin *noun*
Kinin is a plant **hormone** that prompts, or stimulates, growth.
Scientists believe that kinin causes plant cells to divide.

L

land exhaustion *noun*
Land exhaustion describes what happens when the land can no longer produce **crops**. The minerals in the soil have all been used up by previous crops and have not been replaced. Land exhaustion is a severe problem in under-developed countries. Here, there are few **natural resources** and the same crops are grown for many years on one piece of land.
Land exhaustion leads to poverty and starvation.

land reclamation *noun*
Land reclamation is the process of bringing land back into use. Waterlogged areas may be drained. Crops that feed the soil may be planted to reclaim land that has become exhausted through over-cropping. Extra **fertilizers** also help with this process. Land reclamation can also be practised in deserts by **irrigation**.
People could reach a higher standard of living because of the success of the land reclamation schemes.

landfill site *noun*
A landfill site is an area where industrial and domestic waste is tipped. The site is dug up. When it is full of waste, it is covered over and the surface **landscaped**. Landfill sites are the cheapest way to get rid of most waste, but care must be taken where dangerous, or hazardous, wastes are involved. Special attention needs to be given to **nuclear waste**. All landfill sites need to be kept clean. This helps to protect the **environment** and prevent any danger to health.
Grass was starting to grow over the landfill site.

Landsat *noun*
A Landsat satellite is a satellite that is placed in orbit round the Earth. It is used to study people's use of the land. Land satellites also study forest, mineral, energy and water **resources**. The first Landsat was launched in 1972. All the information collected is on offer to all nations. But the information is difficult to understand and so is not used as much as it could be.
Landsat satellites have given a lot of information about famine conditions in Africa.

landscape *noun*
A landscape is an area of country. It includes the natural scenery, and also buildings and roads.
The landscape was dotted with trees, with hills in the distance.
landscape *verb*

larch *noun*
A larch is a **tree**. There are nine kinds of larch, found in Asia, Europe and North America. Larches live in cool climates, often with other **conifers**, such as **spruce** and **pine**. Unlike most conifers, larch trees are deciduous, and lose all their leaves at the same time. Larch wood is used for making poles, fences, gates and boats.
The larch needles turned yellow before falling in the autumn.

lateral bud *noun*
A lateral bud is a **bud** on the side of the growing **shoot** of a plant. If the main bud at the tip of a shoot dies for any reason, a lateral bud is likely to develop. It forms the leading shoot. Usually, a lateral bud produces a side shoot and the plant bushes out.
Several lateral buds developed well all the way up the shoot and the plant formed a large bush.

latex *noun*
Latex is the milky juice that comes from the cut surfaces of many plants. The latex is thought to protect and help heal the wound. Dandelions and lettuce produce latex. Latex collected from the **rubber** tree is the source of all natural rubber. **Gutta-percha** is another kind of latex that has many uses in industry.
Rubber latex is a very white, sticky and elastic substance.

layering *noun*
Layering is a method of plant **propagation**. For some plants, stems with buds are pegged down onto the earth. After some months, roots develop and a fresh plant grows. Layering is a method of **vegetative reproduction**.
After the plants had fruited last year, lots of new strawberry plants were produced by layering.
layer *verb*

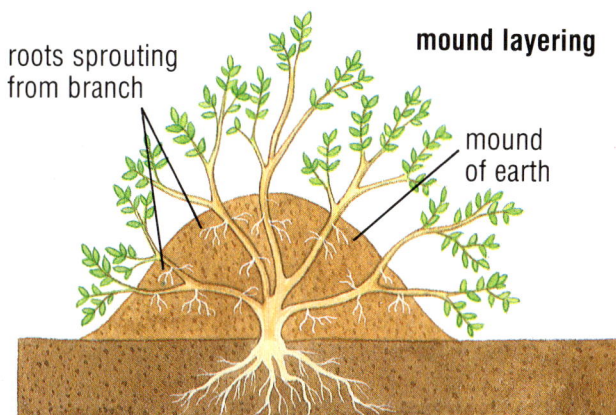

roots sprouting from branch

mound layering

mound of earth

75

leach *verb*
Leach describes the effects of water as it moves down into the **soil**. The water removes **mineral salts** from the upper layers of the soil and carries them further down into the ground. When a soil is leached, the top layers become less **fertile**.
The heavy rains leached the soil.

lead poisoning *noun*
Lead poisoning is the poisoning of plants and animals by lead. It happens when lead in the atmosphere builds up in the bodies of plants and animals. The lead **pollution** comes from industry and from the burning of leaded petrol.
Lead-free paints are used to help prevent lead poisoning.

lead-free *adjective*
Lead-free petrol is petrol that has not had lead added to it. Lead always used to be added to petrol to make cars' engines run better. Today, engines are designed to run well on lead-free petrol.
Their new car ran on lead-free petrol and was kinder to the environment than the old one.

leaf *noun*
A leaf is a growth on the **stem** of a plant. Most leaves are green and are the part of the plant where **photosynthesis** takes place. Water and minerals are carried to the leaves. Sugars are carried from them to be stored and used for **energy** and growth.
The lettuce leaf was crunchy and sweet.

agave   rose   avocado

leaf node *noun*
A leaf node is a part of a plant. It is the point on the **stem** from which a **leaf** grows.
Dark, shiny leaves grew from leaf nodes up the stem of the rubber plant.

leaf scar *noun*
A leaf scar is the mark on the trunk of a **tree** where the leaf stem was attached. In a deciduous tree, the leaves die and fall in the autumn. The bark forms corky wound tissue where the leaves were attached. The pattern of the leaf scar is different for each species of tree.
They recognized the horse chestnut tree because of the horse-shoe shape of the leaf scar.

leaflet *noun*
A leaflet is a part of a **compound leaf**. It is one of the separate blades or divisions that make up the whole leaf.
Each leaf from a black walnut tree has 15 leaflets.

legume *noun*
A legume is a plant of the **pea** family. All legumes have **seeds** in **pods**. When the pods are ripe, they split along their length to release the seeds. In **agriculture**, the word legume is used particularly for **fodder** plants of the pea family, such as clovers. Legumes make very **nutritious** food crops, as they are rich in **proteins**.
Peas, beans and lentils are all legumes.

runner beans   peas

lenticel *noun*
A lenticel is a part of a plant. It is a round or long swelling on the bark of woody **stems** or **roots**. Lenticels act as **pores** to allow gases to pass in or out of the plant.
The rounded marks on horse chestnut stems are lenticels.

lethal *adjective*
Lethal describes anything that can cause death to a living **organism**. Weed-killers are lethal to the weeds they are sprayed on.
Insecticides are lethal to insects.

liana *noun*
Liana is the general name for several **climbing plants** and **vines**. It is used especially for those with woody stems that twine around trees in **tropical rain forests**. Lianas climb against or around the trunks and branches of trees, using them for support.
Lianas have flexible shoots and grow very quickly.

lichen *noun*
A lichen is a plant that is made up of a **fungus** and an **alga** living together as a single unit. Lichens grow as crusty patches on stones and rocks and as pale green growths on trees. They grow in all **environments**, sometimes where other forms of life find it difficult to survive.
Lichens are very sensitive to pollution and are found only where the air is pure.

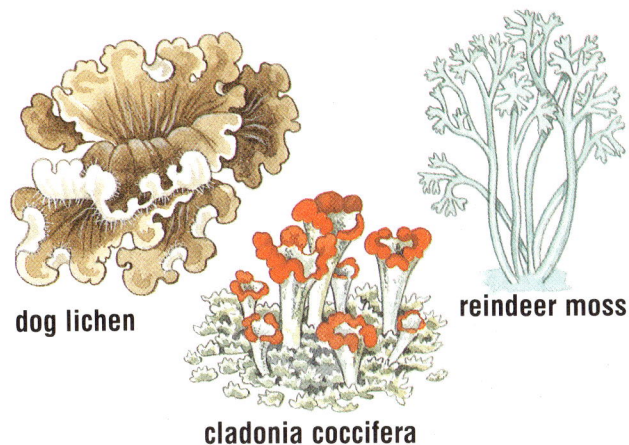

dog lichen

reindeer moss

cladonia coccifera

life cycle ► page 78

lily *noun*
Lily is a **family** of flowering plants. There are about 2,000 species in the lily family. They are **monocotyledons** and grow from scaly **bulbs**. Lily leaves are usually long and pointed and do not have stems. Most lilies have clusters of brightly-coloured flowers on straight stems. The flowers are trumpet-shaped and have six petals. Many are sweet-scented.
Asparagus, hyacinths and leopard lilies are members of the lily family, but water lilies are not.

lime *noun*
Lime is a deciduous **tree**. There are 45 kinds of lime tree, found in Asia, Europe and North America. Limes have sweet-smelling flowers. These attract bees and other insects for **pollination**. Herbal tea can be made from lime flowers. Lime wood is pale and used for carvings.
The bees gathered nectar from the limes.

litter *noun*
Litter is the name of the partly **decomposed** plant remains that collect on the soil in forests. The litter slowly breaks down completely and becomes part of the soil. Litter also means rubbish. It is the remains that humans leave behind when they have finished with anything. This type of litter is often not **biodegradable**.
The forest litter forms a valuable part of the ecosystem.

liverwort *noun*
Liverworts are very simple, small plants. They are found in wet places, such as streams and ditches. Liverworts are made up of a thin plant body, which flattens out into a leaf-like shape. They reproduce by **gametes**. These produce **spores** that grow into new plants.
Liverworts and mosses are the most primitive plants.

life cycle _noun_

A life cycle is all the different stages in the life of an **organism**. The stages in the life cycle of a flowering plant are the seed, the growing plant, the flower and the fruit. The life cycle of a fly includes the egg, the larva, the pupa and the adult.

The plant was able to spread at the seed stage of its life cycle.

life cycle of a fern

spores leave
the sporangium case

a growing
spore

sporangia grow in clusters on the underside of a fern leaf

male cells

female cells

spore grows
into a gametophyte

adult fern

after fertilization, a new fern plant or sporophyte

78

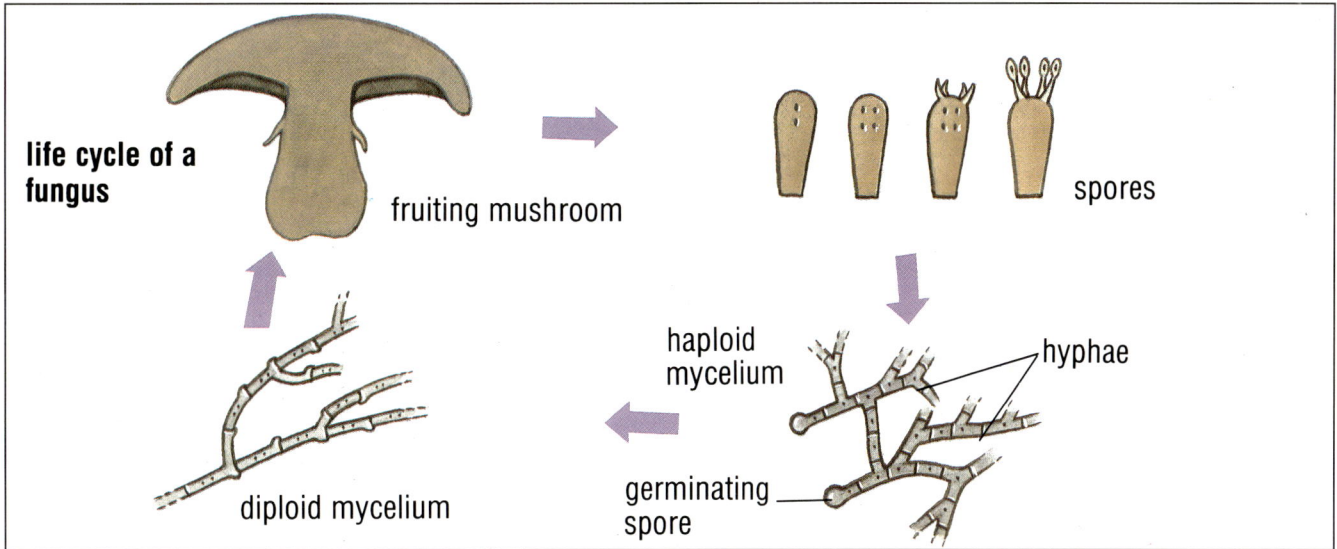

life cycle of a fungus

fruiting mushroom

spores

haploid mycelium

hyphae

diploid mycelium

germinating spore

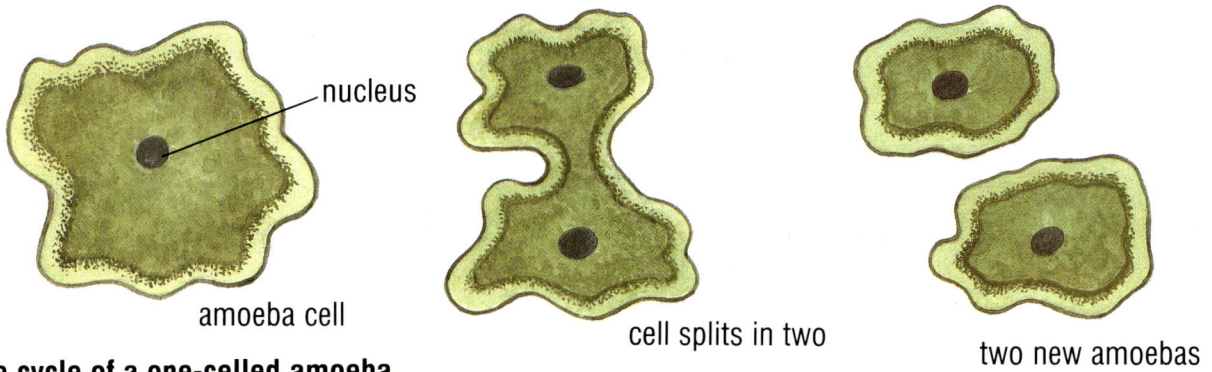

nucleus

amoeba cell

cell splits in two

two new amoebas

life cycle of a one-celled amoeba

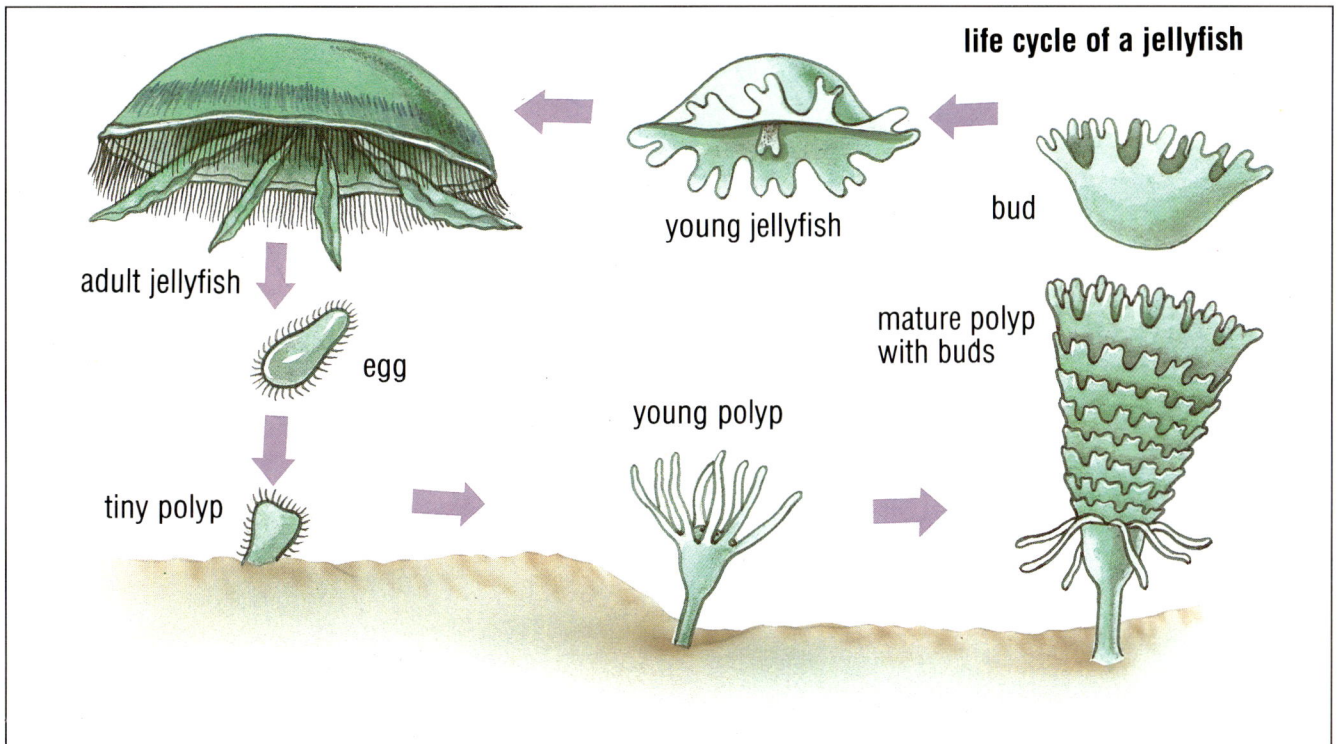

life cycle of a jellyfish

young jellyfish

bud

adult jellyfish

egg

mature polyp with buds

tiny polyp

young polyp

logging noun

Logging is the method of preparing **timber** for use in industry. Forest trees are felled and split into lengths that can be moved, or transported. In some areas, elephants are used to move the logs. In many other areas, the logs are bound into rafts and floated down-river to sawmills.

Trees cut down during logging must be replaced so that forests can grow back.

Where there is a river close by, logs can be floated down to the sawmill.

Tree-felling is commonly done with a chain saw.

At the sawmill, machines slice the logs into sheets of timber.

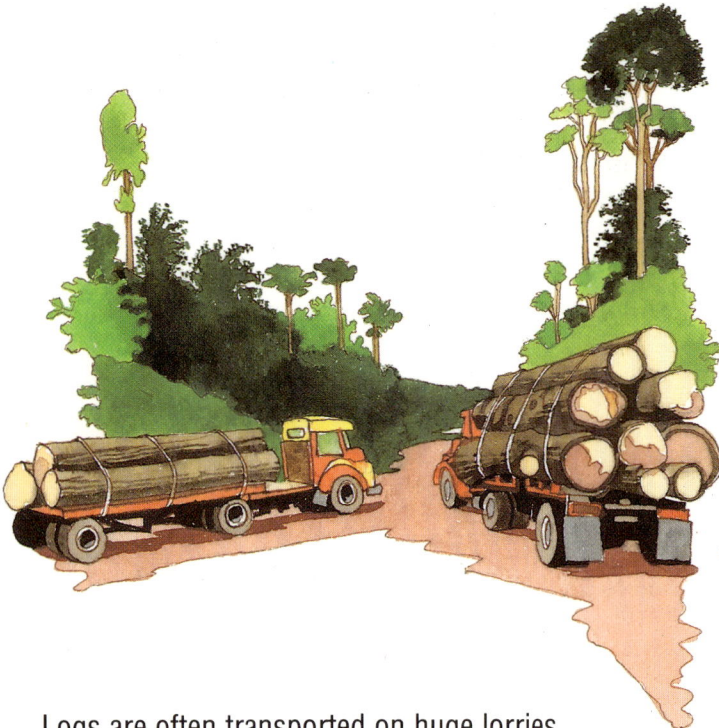

Logs are often transported on huge lorries.

If forest is cut down and not replaced, the soil may become eroded.

loam *noun*
Loam is a kind of **soil**. It is a mixture of **sand** and silt, with small amounts of **clay**.
The farmer grew a fine crop of carrots on the deep loam.

logging ▶ page 80

lumber *noun*
Lumber is the name for sawn logs and timber produced during **logging**. It is a term used mainly in the United States of America and in Canada. The workers who fell the trees and transport them are called lumberjacks.
Lumbering is of major importance in managing the North American hardwood forests.

lycophyte *noun*
A lycophyte is one of a group of non-flowering plants. There are about 970 species of lycophyte, which include **club mosses** and **quillworts**. Lycophytes are **vascular plants**. This makes them different from **mosses**, which do not have a vascular system.
Most lycophytes creep or trail along the ground, but some have upright stems.

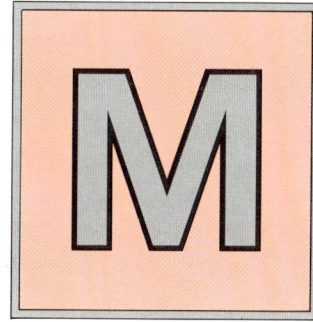

M

mahogany *noun*
A mahogany is a huge, tropical **hardwood tree**. Mahoganies are found in the West Indies, southern Mexico, South America and Africa. They grow in **tropical rain forests**, forming part of the **canopy** of the forests. Mahoganies are cut down, or felled, for their valuable **timber** and are becoming rare in some areas.
Mahogany wood is strong and holds its shape well when used for making furniture.

maize *noun*
Maize is a plant that belongs to the **grass** family. It is the second most important **crop** in the world. Maize has a single, strong stalk with about 15 long, broad leaves growing along it. At the top of the stalk are the male reproductive parts, called the tassel. The female reproductive parts are the **ears**, or cobs, which grow in the middle of the stalk. These cobs are the parts that are used for food. Each cob is covered with bright yellow seeds that are eaten fresh, or dried.
There are several thousand species of maize, which is also called corn.

mallow *noun*
A mallow is one of a large **family** of flowering plants. There are about 1,000 species of herb, shrub and tree in the mallow family. They grow in **tropical** and **temperate** regions of the world. Mallows have flowers with many **stamens** that are joined together to form a tube-like structure. They have tough, fibrous stems and sticky **sap**.
The hibiscus, hollyhock and cotton plant are all members of the mallow family.

mangrove swamp *noun*

A mangrove swamp is a kind of tidal **salt marsh**, found in equatorial regions. Evergreen shrubs and trees with thick, fleshy leaves grow there. Many mangrove plants have **aerial roots**, which help them to survive in the muddy conditions. The roots stick up through the mud and take in oxygen directly from the air.
She saw many birds in the mangrove swamp.

manure *noun*

Manure is a **natural** kind of **fertilizer**. It is made from a mixture of animal dung and straw. Farmyard manure is stored in heaps while it rots. It is rich in **nitrogen**, **potassium** and **phosphorus** compounds. Manure is spread on the soil to fertilize it and to act as a **mulch**.
The organic farmer was concerned about not harming the environment and relied on farmyard manure to improve his plants.

maple *noun*

Maples are deciduous **trees**. There are several **species** of maple, found mainly in Europe, Asia and America. Maple wood is used to make furniture, musical instruments and flooring. The sweet **sap** of the sugar maple is harvested as maple syrup.
The leaves of the maples turned beautiful shades of yellow, orange and red in the autumn.

maquis *noun*

Maquis is a kind of **scrubland**. It is found in some dry areas in the Mediterranean region. These areas have hot, dry summers and warm, wet winters. Many different plant **species** are found in maquis. They include pines, evergreen oaks, olives, and scented herbs such as lavender and thyme. The **vegetation** of the maquis is very dense and becomes very dry in the summer. It is often destroyed by fire.
They became hot and dusty as they walked through the maquis.

marine pollution *noun*

Marine pollution describes what happens when any harmful material is released into seas, oceans or estuaries. The release may be caused accidentally or on purpose. Marine pollution can be caused by sewage, oil or industrial discharge. The direct effects of marine pollution include the killing of fish. It can also have a wide effect on the **ecosystems** of the oceans and along the coasts.
Waste must not be thrown away into rivers, as the waters go down to the sea, causing marine pollution.

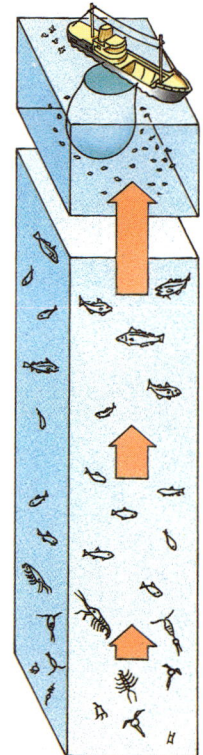

market gardening *noun*

Market gardening is a type of **horticulture**. In market gardening, food and flowers are produced for sale. People practising market gardening usually live near their customers. They often grow their crops in **greenhouses**.
Market gardening is hard work, but the fruit and vegetables fetch good prices.

marram grass *noun*

Marram grass is a kind of **grass** that grows in **saltwater habitats**. It is a **halophyte**, which means it is specially **adapted** to cope with salt water. Marram grass is **perennial**, grows upwards very quickly and increases by **vegetative reproduction**. For these reasons, it is often planted on **seashores** to prevent sand dunes from being blown away.
The marram grass quickly spread over the dunes which protected the fields behind them.

marsh *noun*

A marsh is a **habitat**. It is a piece of low, wet ground. In a marsh, **drainage** is poor and the water often floods over the surface.
Marshes usually have very fertile soils.

mature *adjective*
Mature describes something which is fully grown, or developed. A mature plant or animal is one which is adult. A mature soil has a clear structure because it has formed over many thousands of years. **Crops** grow better on mature soils.
The mature plants were tall and straight, and produced good seeds.

meadow *noun*
A meadow is a **field** that is suitable for **grazing** animals. Some meadows are too wet for growing crops and may be flooded in winter. In the summer, a meadow provides rich **pasture**.
He found many wildflowers in the meadow.

medicinal plant ▶ page 84

melon *noun*
Melons are a kind of **fruit**. They belong to the **cucumber** family. Melons have a soft, sweet, watery flesh. This may be yellow, green or pink. Water melons are larger than melons. They have bright red flesh and green skins.
He chopped up melon for the fruit salad.

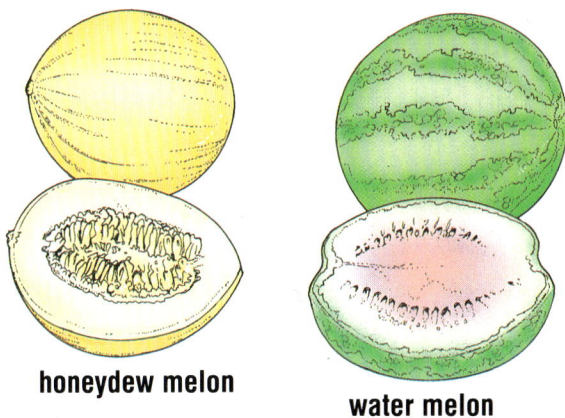

honeydew melon

water melon

membrane *noun*
A membrane is a thin layer of tissue that separates one plant **cell** from another. A membrane is two layers thick. It is made of a substance called lipid, with **protein** embedded in it.
Membranes allow some materials to pass through but prevent others from doing so.

methane *noun*
Methane is a **gas**. It is made of **carbon** and **hydrogen**. Methane is found in **natural gas** and is sometimes called marsh gas. It is formed when **organic** substances break down, or decay.
The methane burned with a clear flame.

microbiology *noun*
Microbiology is the study of tiny organisms called micro-organisms. Micro-organisms are so small that they can only be seen with a microscope. **Bacteria**, **viruses** and **unicellular algae** are all micro-organisms.
Microscopic plants and animals are studied in microbiology.

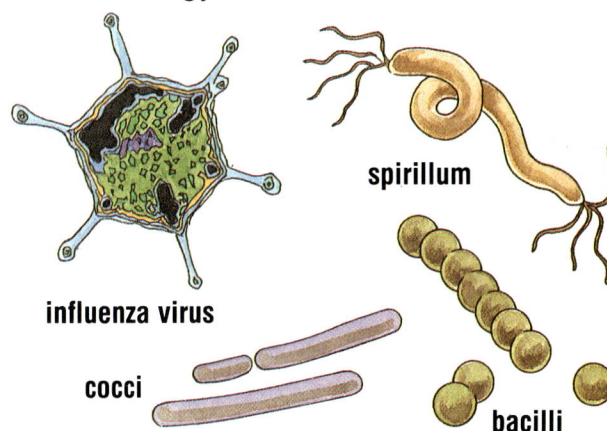

spirillum

influenza virus

cocci

bacilli

microclimate *noun*
A microclimate is a **climate** on a small scale that affects a particular plant or group of plants. It may be different on two sides of a hill. In very cold **habitats**, such as **tundra**, some kinds of plant make their own microclimate. They may trap air with their dense leaves, so it becomes warmer than the surrounding air.
Many alpine plants make a microclimate, so they can survive in freezing temperatures.

millet *noun*
Millet is a plant that belongs to the **grass** family. There are about 10 species of millet, which grow between 30 and 120 centimetres tall. The small, edible **seeds** grow in a cluster at the top of the stem.
Millet is cultivated in Asia and North America.

83

medicinal plants *noun*

Medicinal plants are those plants that contain substances that can be used to make medicines. Some plants contain medicinal substances in their leaves, such as many kinds of **herb**. Other plants produce fruits that contain drugs. Roots, flowers and bark are other parts of plants that can be used to make medicines.

People have been using medicinal plants for thousands of years.

The opium poppy's capsules provide the opium that is used to make several useful medicines, such as codeine.

Belladonna, or deadly nightshade, produces black berries which are very poisonous. Belladonna drugs are made mainly from the roots, but are also contained in the berries and other parts.

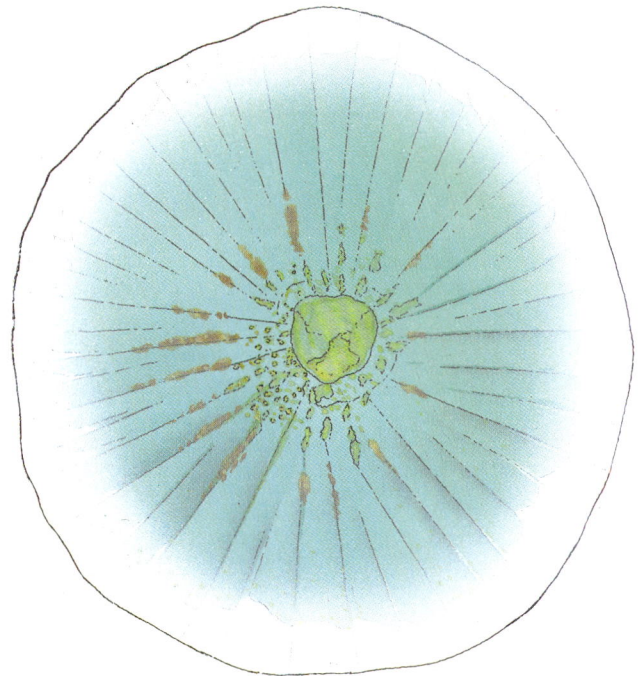

Penicillin is one of the most widely used antibiotic drugs. It is made from a mould, which is grown in huge tanks of broth.

Quinine is made from the bark of a rain forest tree called cinchona.

Ginseng is a Chinese medicine made from the root of the ginseng plant.

The dried leaves of the coca plant are used to make several useful medicines.

A powerful drug called digitalis is made from the leaves of the purple foxglove. It is used to treat certain heart conditions.

mineral salt   *noun*

A mineral salt is a **chemical**. It is formed from a basic mixture of minerals, such as ammonia or sodium hydroxide, and a common, **inorganic acid**, such as hydrochloric acid or nitric acid. Ammonium sulphate and sodium chloride are mineral salts. Mineral salts are essential to life. They are found in **soil** and help plants to grow strong and healthy.
The mineral salts dissolved in the water gave it a salty taste.

mixed farming   *noun*

Mixed farming is a kind of farming when animals and crops are found on the same farm. The crops provide **fodder** for the animals, and the animals provide **manure** for the crops. Mixed farming helps to bring **fertility** to the land. It was the traditional way to farm before artificial **fertilizers** and **herbicides** came into use.
Mixed farming allowed the family to grow all their own food.

moder   *noun*

Moder is a type of **humus**. It is half-way between **mor** and **mull**. Moder is less **acid** and more **decomposed** than mor, but not as decomposed as mull. There are loose mineral particles in moder, especially in the layers that are well below the surface. These particles are formed from the activity of **organisms** in the soil.
The soil was rich in moder and not very fertile, but some crops grew on it.

monera   *plural noun*

Monera are one of the five **kingdoms** of **organisms**. There are about 5,000 known **species** of monera. Monera are very simple, and are usually made up of only a single **cell**. Most kinds of monera live in water. **Bacteria** are now classified as monera, so monera are very widespread. Many monera cause diseases.
Monera form one of the most important classes of life on this planet.

monitoring   *noun*

Monitoring is watching how **organisms**, **environments** and events develop or change. Monitoring is necessary before useful actions can be taken. Monitoring and recording the level of **radioactivity** near a nuclear power station can show that there has been no accidental release of nuclear material.
The conservationists monitored the wild deer population.
monitor   *verb*

monocotyledon ▶ page 87

monoculture   *noun*

Monoculture is a system of farming in which one **crop** is grown on large areas for many years. The crop may be fruit or cereals. If monoculture is practised for too long, it leads to **land exhaustion**. The soil must be **fertilized** to replace the **nutrients** removed by the plants. Pests that attack only that one crop also build up and must be controlled.
Growers can sometimes make high profits by practising monoculture.

moor   *noun*

A moor is an area of open ground, which is higher than the surrounding agricultural land. Moors often have peaty soils, and are found in wet and cool **temperate** regions. Low, **evergreen** shrubs, such as heathers, grow well on moors.
The moor was covered in purple heather in the autumn.

monocotyledon *noun*

Monocotyledons are a group of flowering plants. The other group is the **dicotyledons**. There are about 60 families of monocotyledons. The **embryo** of a monocotyledon has one tiny leaf, or **cotyledon**. Monocotyledons have narrow **leaves** with parallel veins, and simple **flowers**. Many food plants, including cereals, fodder grasses and bananas, are monocotyledons.

Grasses and palms are monocotyledons, and so are familiar flowers such as lilies and daffodils.

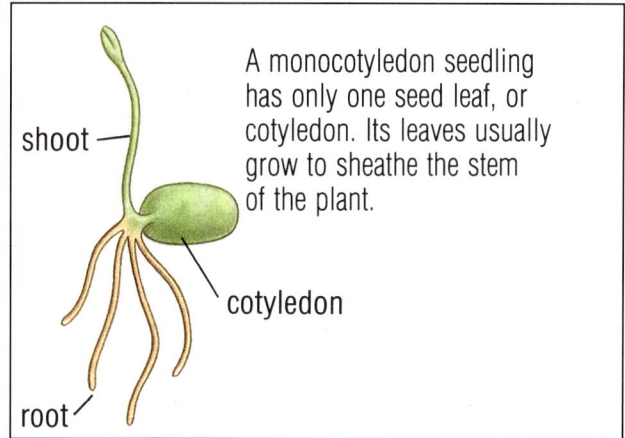

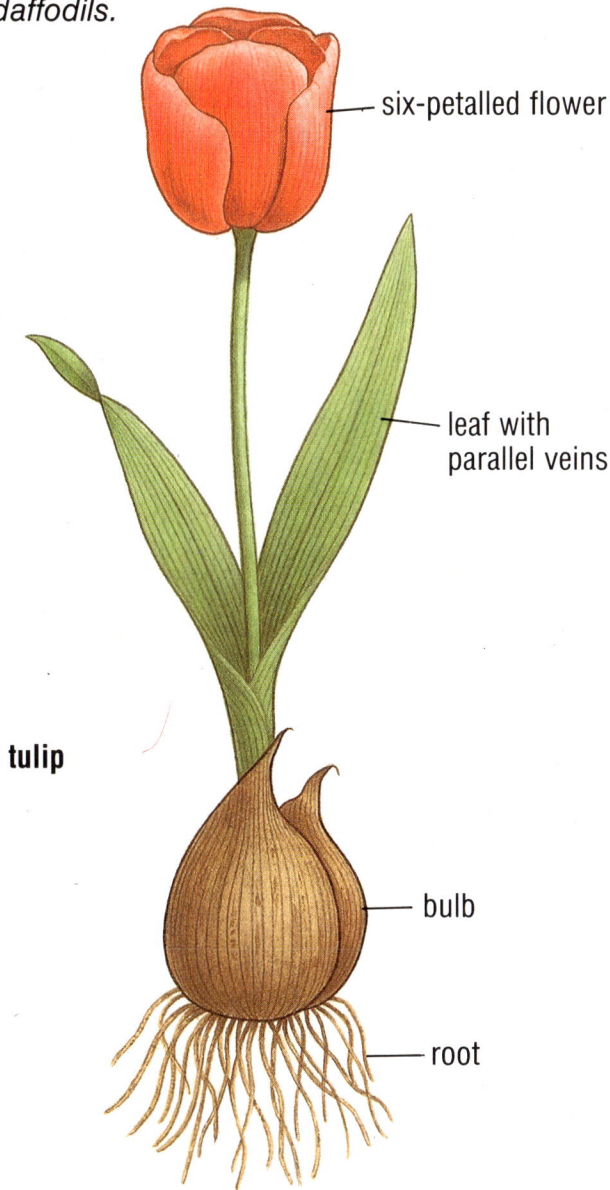

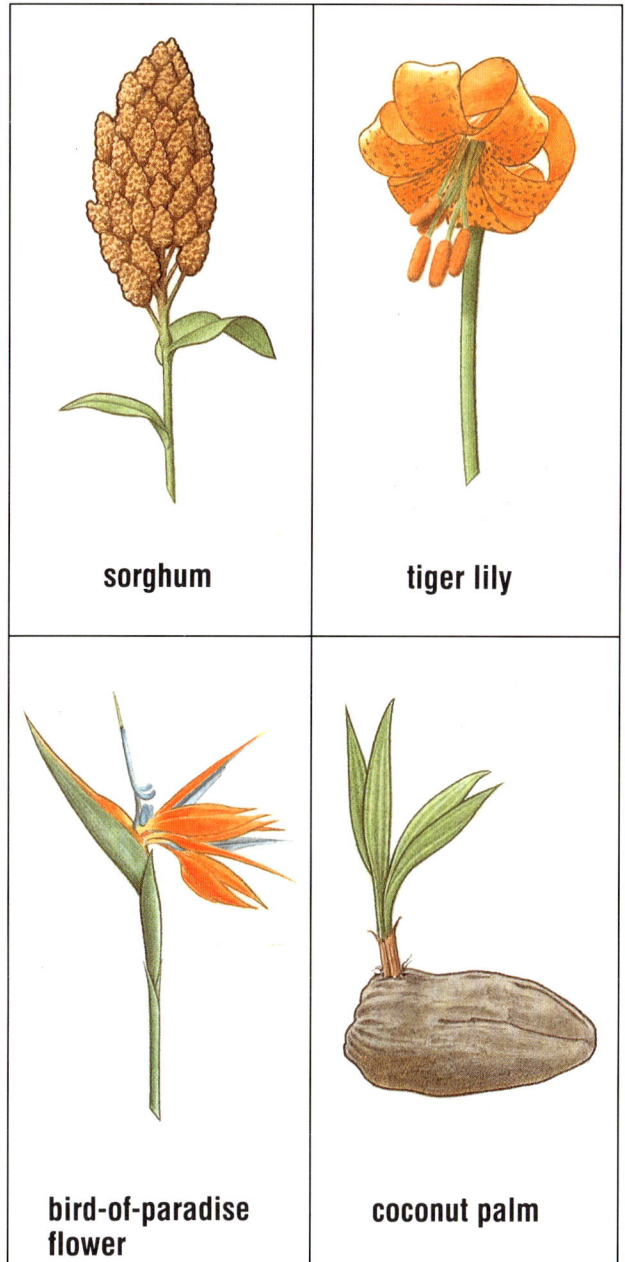

A monocotyledon seedling has only one seed leaf, or cotyledon. Its leaves usually grow to sheathe the stem of the plant.

shoot

cotyledon

root

six-petalled flower

leaf with parallel veins

tulip

bulb

root

sorghum

tiger lily

bird-of-paradise flower

coconut palm

87

mor *noun*

Mor is a type of **humus**. It is the least **fertile** type, found on **acid** soils that are poorly aired, or aerated. Mors are found where there are cold, wet winters and mild, damp summers. They contain few earthworms and a small quantity of other soil animals. The plant **litter** does not become mixed in the soil and does not **decompose** quickly.

Mor is the humus which develops in conifer forests and on moorland.

morning glory *noun*

Morning glory is a **family** of flowering plants. Most morning glories are **climbing plants**. Wild **species** include bindweed, moonflower and sweet potato. Garden morning glories have dark-green, heart-shaped leaves. Their flowers are large and funnel-shaped. They are shades and mixtures of blue, purple, red and white.

The flowers of morning glories open in the morning, but close in the afternoon sunlight.

moss *noun*

A moss is a small, non-flowering plant found throughout the world. There are more than 9,000 **species** of moss. They are in the **bryophyte division**, which also includes **liverworts** and **hornworts**. Most mosses live on land in damp, shady places. Some grow in **fresh water**. Mosses do not have true roots. Their short stems grow from thread-like structures called rhizoids.

Mosses have tiny leaves that grow on the stems in a spiral pattern.

mould *noun*

A mould is a kind of **fungus**. Moulds are often found in damp areas and may be coloured or white, depending on the species of fungus. One type of mould is called mildew. It is a plant **disease** that appears as a powdery covering on grains. Another type of mould is **cultivated** to produce a medicine called penicillin.

The damp wall developed a growth of mould.

mulberry *noun*

A mulberry is one of a family of ornamental **trees** and **shrubs**. It grows in Europe, Asia and North America. A mulberry has oval or heart-shaped **leaves**. Its **flowers** are greenish-white and hang in round clusters from stalks on the branches. Mulberry **fruits** are white, red or purple. The dark red fruits of one species of mulberry are sweet and juicy. They are eaten by people. The fig, breadfruit and **banyan** are also members of the mulberry family.

White mulberries are grown to feed silkworms in the silk industry.

mulch *noun*

Mulch is material that is put on the surface of the soil. It keeps the soil moist, smothers weeds and provides some **nutrients** for the soil. A number of mulches are used in **horticulture**, including grass cuttings, bark shavings, straw and peat. **Manure** may be mixed with straw and used as mulch.

The mulch was put down after a heavy rain shower, to prevent the ground drying out again.

mull *noun*

Mull is a type of **humus**. It is the most **fertile** type, and forms on well-drained and well-aired soils. It comes from the **decomposition** of the leaves of **deciduous** trees. Mull becomes mixed with the underlying soil by the action of earthworms.

The beech seedlings grew well through the mull.

multiple cropping *noun*
Multiple cropping describes the growing of more than one **crop** each year on a piece of land. The crops may be grown one after the other, or two different crops may be grown together. Multiple cropping works only if the soil is rich enough and has enough water to support good crops.
By multiple cropping the villagers were able to grow all their own vegetables.

mushroom *noun*
A mushroom is a type of **fungus**. It is made up of a stalk and a fleshy cap which carries the **spores**. Many mushrooms can be eaten. But care must be taken as some kinds of poisonous **toadstools** look very like edible mushrooms.
They found several species of mushrooms walking in the woods on the damp autumn morning.

mustard *noun*
Mustard is a **family** of flowering plants. It is an **annual** that grows in **temperate** regions. Mustard has large, dark-green leaves and small, yellow flowers. It produces long pods after flowering. These contain seeds which are used to flavour food.
People eat the young leaves of mustard plants as a vegetable.

N

nasturtium *noun*
Nasturtium is the name given to a **family** of **perennial** plants. Many nasturtiums are **cultivated** as **garden plants** in the northern part of the world. They are trailing or climbing plants which can grow to three metres long. Nasturtiums have yellow, orange or red flowers and umbrella-shaped, green leaves.
Nasturtium leaves have a spicy taste.

national park ▶ page 90

native *adjective*
A native species is a **species** that occurs naturally in the **habitat** in which it is found.
Native plants and animals are sometimes threatened by introduced species.

natural *adjective*
Natural describes something that has not been changed by the activities of people. Natural **vegetation** has not been disturbed by farming or other human activity.
There were pockets of natural woodland on the mountainside.

89

national park *noun*

A national park is a protected area of land that has great natural beauty. It is protected for the **conservation** of its flora and fauna. National parks are mostly unchanged by humans. They vary widely in size, and have played a large part in preserving **endangered species** of plants and animals. People are allowed into national parks to enjoy the scenery and wildlife.

The numbers of visitors to national parks is increasing all the time.

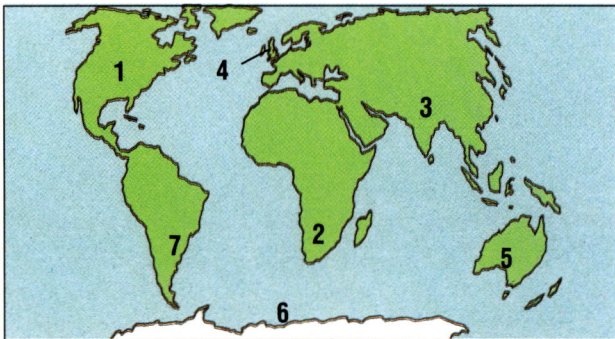

1. Yellowstone National Park lies near Wyoming, in the United States of America. Large herds of elks, or moose, live there.

7. The Amazonian rain forest in Brazil, in South America, is a huge national park. Many plants, such as the bromeliads, live in trees and take in moisture from the air.

6. The whole of Antarctica has been made into a national park. The landscape is bleak and snow-covered, even in summer.

2. In Etosha National Park, in southern Africa, animals such as wildebeest, zebras and gazelles come to drink at the water holes.

3. The colourful Impeyan pheasant is one of 120 species of bird found in the Sagarmatha National Park, Nepal.

5. The red Ayers Rock in Uluru National Park, Australia, is a famous landmark.

4. Trees are scarce on the grassy hills of Snowdonia National Park in the British Isles.

natural fibre *noun*

A natural fibre is a **fibre** made up of **organic** material. Wool is a natural fibre, and can be knitted or woven into cloth. Silk is a natural fibre produced by silkworms.
The cotton plant is the source of the natural fibre cotton.

natural gas *noun*

Natural gas is a mixture of **gases** found underground. Natural gas is very often found with deposits of **petroleum**. It contains **methane** and can be burnt as a fuel.
All the houses in the street have natural gas for heating.

natural resource *noun*

A natural resource is any substance found in **nature** that is of use to people. Minerals, **fossil fuels**, **forests** and the **energy** of the wind, tides and Sun are all types of natural resource. Natural resources may be **renewable**, or **non-renewable**.
The forests nearby provided a splendid natural resource for the timber merchants.

natural selection *noun*

Natural selection is a process that leads to **evolution** of a new **species**. In natural selection, those **organisms** best fitted for survival breed and pass on their features to the next **generation**. After many generations, the improved plant or animal becomes common in the **environment**.
Natural selection leads to the evolution of plants that can survive in cold climates.

naturalist *noun*

A naturalist is someone who studies the wild plants and animals of a region. Naturalists often go on expeditions to look at plants and animals in their natural **habitats**, such as a rain forest or the Arctic tundra.
The naturalist recorded which plants he found in the forest.

nature *noun*

Nature describes the natural state of the Earth, untouched and unchanged by humans.
A huge variety of plants and animals is found in nature.

nature reserve *noun*

A nature reserve is an area where a particular **habitat** is protected from human activity. Nature reserves are managed so that the plants and animals in them can survive. They are usually smaller than **national parks**. Many **endangered species** of plant and animal are protected inside nature reserves.
The children visited the nature reserve to learn about the plants and animals.

nectar *noun*

Nectar is a sugary liquid that is produced by the flowers and leaves of some plants. Nectar is attractive to some insects and birds which come to the plant to feed on it. Insects may follow markings on petals, known as **nectar guides**. As the insect or bird collects the nectar, it also **pollinates** the flower.
The bees gathered the sweet nectar from the flowers.

nectar guide *noun*

A nectar guide is a pattern of spots or lines on a flower's **petals**. The pattern points the way to the flower's **nectar** store. Insects follow the markings to find the flower's nectar.
Many yellow flowers have ultraviolet nectar guides which can be seen by bees but not by the human eye.

needle *noun*
A needle is the name given to some kinds of **leaf**. It has a long, narrow, pointed shape. **Pine** trees have needles which are long, thin and stiff, with sharp ends. The needles of a **spruce** are soft.
The pine needles formed a carpet in the forest, and were uncomfortable to sit on.

needleleaf tree *noun*
A needleleaf tree is a kind of **tree**. The **leaves** of a needleleaf tree are tough **needles**. Most needleleaf trees are **evergreen**. They all have scaly or thick, protective **bark** and **bud scales**.
Pines and firs are typical needleleaf trees.

eastern larch
black spruce

niche *noun*
A niche is the place that a **species** takes up in a **community**. Those species that have a special form occupy a very narrow niche. More **adaptable** species have wider niches. Unrelated species from different parts of the world may have similar niches if they occupy similar **habitats**.
The wood anemone of Europe occupies a similar niche to the dog tooth violet of North America.

nightshade *noun*
Nightshade is the common name given to a **family** of plants which includes the potato, tomato, aubergine and pepper. Some members of the nightshade family contain substances which can be used to make medicines.
Deadly nightshade is a poisonous member of the nightshade family.

nitrate and nitrite *noun*
Nitrates and nitrites are **inorganic oxides** of **nitrogen**. Tiny micro-organisms in the soil form nitrites from ammonia by **oxidation**. By further oxidation, these are changed to nitrates. Nitrates and nitrites are **acidic**, and their presence in the soil makes it acid.
The fertility of the soil depends on nitrites and nitrates.

nitrogen *noun*
Nitrogen is the most common gas in the **air**. It makes up about 78 per cent of the air. Nitrogen is necessary for the growth of plants and animals.
Compounds of nitrogen are used as fertilizers.

nitrogen cycle *noun*
The nitrogen cycle describes how **nitrogen** moves from the **air** and the soil into living things and back again. Nitrogen from the air moves into the soil, where it is used by plants and animals. When **organisms** die, nitrogen is released from their bodies again into the air and soil.
The nitrogen cycle plays a central part in ecology.

nitrogen fixation *noun*
Nitrogen fixation is the changing of **nitrogen** in the air to **organic** nitrogen mixtures, or compounds. It is a very important natural method of turning nitrogen gas into a form in which it can be used for plant growth. Fixation is carried out by **bacteria** and **algae** in the soil, or in the root **nodules** of **legumes**, such as peas and beans.
Nitrogen fixation is an important part of the nitrogen cycle.

nitrogen oxide *noun*
Nitrogen oxides are formed by burning coal and oil. They are a major cause of air **pollution**.
The levels of nitrogen oxides in the atmosphere could be reduced by controlling the use of fossil fuels.

node *noun*

A node is a point on the **stem** of a plant from which a **leaf** grows. The pattern of leaves at the nodes is different in different plants. The nodes may be single, in pairs or in **whorls**. The length of stem between the nodes is called the internode.

node

The plant was propagated by taking a stem cutting at a node and planting it in damp sand.

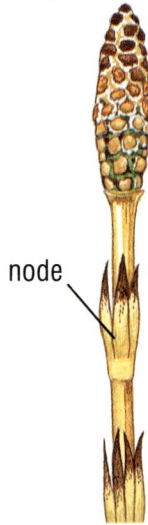

nodule *noun*

A nodule is a knot or lump on the **stem** or **root** of a plant. Nodules are formed on the roots of **legumes** by the action of **bacteria** in the soil. They contain bacteria which take part in the process called **nitrogen fixation**. Root nodules on legumes, such as clover, peas and beans, are valuable in making the soil more **fertile**.

The nodules gave the roots a knobbly appearance.

non-renewable *adjective*

Non-renewable describes **natural resources** which cannot be replaced once they have been used. **Oil** and **coal** are examples of non-renewable energy sources. Wood is **renewable**, if more trees are planted to replace those felled.

People are learning to conserve the Earth's non-renewable resources.

nuclear radiation *noun*

Nuclear radiation is **radiation** given off by the nuclei of atoms. It is given off by radioactive material. Some nuclear radiation is **natural**. Some is produced by people during the splitting and joining of the atom, or nuclear fission and fusion. Alpha particles, beta particles and gamma rays are the main types of nuclear radiation.

Nuclear radiation can be dangerous to living things.

nuclear waste *noun*

Nuclear waste is waste which is **radioactive**. It is produced as a result of nuclear research and the generation of nuclear power. There are three groups of nuclear waste. These are high-level waste, intermediate waste and low-level waste, depending on the level of radioactivity. Each should be dealt with by a different method.

Nuclear waste is a major concern of both the nuclear industry and conservationists.

nursery *noun*

A nursery is a place where young plants are grown. Nursery conditions are generally less harsh than those where the young plants will eventually grow. In particular, care is taken in nurseries to protect plants from drought or cold.

The conifer saplings were taken from the nursery and planted out in the forest in the spring.

nut *noun*

A nut is a kind of **fruit**. It has one seed with a hard, woody shell. Acorns, beechnuts and hazelnuts are examples of nuts. Nuts contain a foodstore for the **seedling**. Many nuts, such as hazelnuts, are nutritious for humans. Some hard-shelled fruits, such as walnuts and Brazil nuts, are called nuts, even though they are not really nuts.

The dormouse collected hazelnuts to feed on during the cold season.

acorn   almond

hazelnut   pecan

nutrient *noun*

A nutrient is a substance needed by an **organism** for healthy growth. Plant nutrients are minerals taken in, or absorbed, by the **roots**. These minerals include **nitrogen**, **phosphorus** and **potassium**.
The soil was poor, so the farmer fertilized the fields to provide sufficient nutrients for good yields.

nutrition *noun*

Nutrition is the use of **nutrients** in all **organisms** to supply energy for growth. Poor nutrition leads to weak growth and a short life.
Current advice about nutrition recommends people to eat more fibre and more fruit and vegetables.

oak *noun*

Oaks are a common kind of **broadleaf tree**. There are more than 600 **species** of oak. They belong to the **beech** family and grow naturally in countries of the northern hemisphere. Oaks can grow to more than 30 metres high. They produce **catkins** in the spring and then fruits called **acorns**. Oak wood is hard and strong and is used to make furniture and barrels.
Most species of oak are known to live for over 200 years.

oakapple ▶ **gall**

oats *plural noun*

Oats are a kind of **grass**. They are part of the same **family** as wheat, barley, rice and maize. Oats are **cultivated** as a food **crop** for people and animals in many **temperate** countries. Each oat plant produces about 100 **seeds** which grow on many small branches at the end of the stem. The seeds are harvested as **grain** and made into food products like oatmeal. Oats have a higher food value than any other kind of cereal.
Meal made from oats is a nourishing food because it is rich in protein.

oil *noun*

Oil is a kind of **fossil fuel**. It is a dark liquid which is made of hydrocarbons. Oil is formed over millions of years from the remains of plants. It is found with **natural gas** and solid hydrocarbons. Oil is produced by refining **petroleum**.
The well pumped the oil up to the surface from deep underground.

95

oasis (plural **oases**)   *noun*

An oasis is a fertile area in a desert. It has a good water supply. An oasis may be a very small area around a spring, or it may cover a whole valley floor. In an oasis, the water allows trees and crops to grow. Animals can drink there, and people may even build houses.

We drove from the dry desert into the lush oasis.

Oases may form where an underground source of water, such as a spring or a stream, comes to the surface.

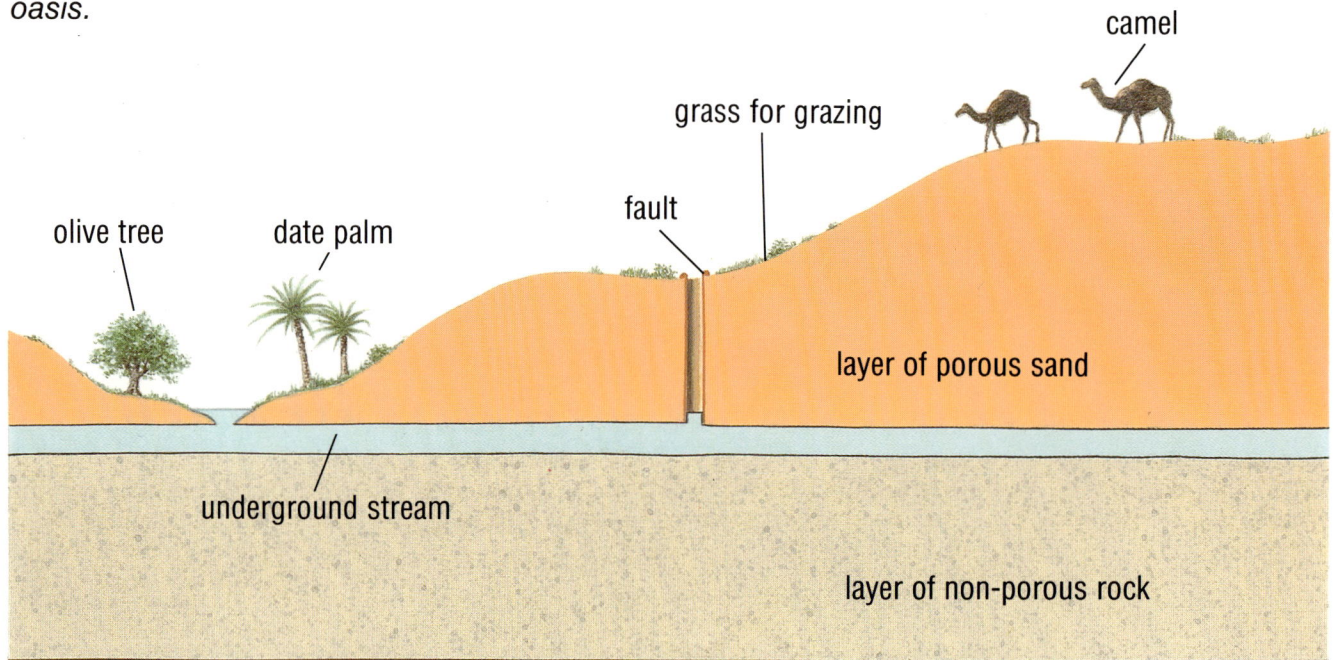

camel

grass for grazing

fault

olive tree

date palm

layer of porous sand

underground stream

layer of non-porous rock

Small oases support a few date palms and provide water for animals to drink.

At a larger oasis, there are date palms and other kinds of tree, such as olives and lemons. A few houses may be built there.

A very large oasis has a plantation with fields of crops and fruit trees. There is a settlement of several houses. The crops are watered by irrigation.

oil slick *noun*
An oil slick describes a leak of **oil** into oceans, estuaries or rivers. The oil may be released naturally, or spilled by humans. If the amount of oil is large and the conditions right, oil slicks can spread over very wide areas. They can cause a lot of damage to marine life.
A large oil slick on the sea showed where the tanker had sunk after the collision.

oligotrophic *adjective*
Oligotrophic describes the conditions in water or soil. Oligotrophic water or soil has few **nutrients**. Oligotrophic soils are found where the rocks that form them are poor. They are also found where the nutrients have been washed, or **leached**, out. Many plants do not grow well in oligotrophic soils.
Waters which are oligotrophic do not have many plants or animals in them.

open-cast mining *noun*
Open-cast mining is a means of mining minerals or coal from the ground. It is done without the use of mine shafts and tunnels. In open-cast mining, the surface soil is stripped to reveal the layer of minerals or coal. These can then be mined. When the useful substances have been removed, the surface soil is replaced. The land can then go back to **nature**.
The coal-field was mined by the open-cast mining system.

orchid *noun*
Orchid is the name given to a large family of **perennial** plants. There are more than 20,000 species of orchid growing throughout the world. Orchids can grow on the trunks and branches of trees, on rocks or on the ground. Most have colourful, long-lasting flowers. These often have a large, central petal with an unusual shape. For example, the central petals of some kinds of orchid make them look like insects.
The flavouring vanilla comes from a vine-like orchid which grows in Mexico.

order *noun*
An order is a group, or rank, in the **classification** of plants. It is the main rank between **class** and **family**. The **conifers** are an order within the **gymnosperms** class.
Cycads are an order of unusual, palm-like shrubs.

organ *noun*
An organ is a part of an **organism** that is specially **adapted** to carry out a particular task. Leaves, roots and stems are examples of plant organs.
Organs are made up from many kinds of cells, which work together.

organic *adjective*
Organic describes substances which always contain atoms of **carbon**. Organic **chemicals** often have many carbon atoms joined together in chains or rings. All living things are made of organic chemicals.
The rich soil contained a large amount of organic matter.

organism *noun*
An organism is any living thing. All plants and animals are organisms, and so are **fungi**. Even the microscopic algae and bacteria are organisms. All organisms have a body made of one or more **cells**. They also feed and reproduce.
Diatoms are tiny organisms found in sea water.

osmosis *noun*

Osmosis is the process by which water passes across a **membrane**. The water moves from a weak solution into a stronger solution across the membrane between. Osmosis is very important in controlling the supply of water to different parts of a plant.
The fruit absorbed water by osmosis.

ovary *noun*

The ovary is a part of a plant. It is the **reproductive organ** that produces the ova, or the female **gametes**. Normally, the female gametes must be fertilized by the male gametes before an **embryo** is formed. The embryos in the ovary grow into the **seeds**, inside the **fruit**.
At the base of the flower, she saw the ovary.

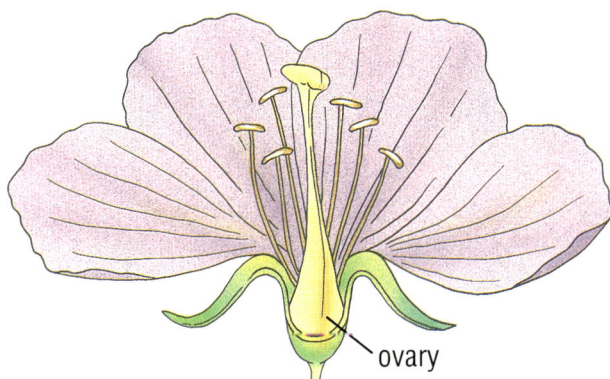
ovary

overgrazing *noun*

Overgrazing describes what happens when too many animals are kept on a piece of land and allowed to eat all the **vegetation**. The land becomes exhausted and cannot feed, or **sustain**, all the animals. They starve unless they are moved to fresh **pastures**.
Overgrazing is a cause of soil erosion.

ovule *noun*

An ovule is a structure found in flowering plants. It is an unfertilized **seed**. An ovule develops into a seed after the egg, inside it has been fertilized. In **gymnosperms**, the ovule is unprotected. In **angiosperms**, ovules are found inside the **carpels**.
After it was fertilized, the ovule developed into a seed.

oxygen *noun*

Oxygen is a **chemical** element. It is a colourless **gas** which is found in the atmosphere. Oxygen is the most common element in the Earth's crust. Nearly all living things need oxygen to survive.
The waterweed was covered in bubbles of oxygen.

ozone-friendly *adjective*

A material is said to be ozone-friendly when it does not produce **chemicals** which might destroy the **ozone layer** in the atmosphere. The harmful chemicals are called chlorofluorocarbons. Many countries are now replacing chlorofluorocarbons used in industry with ozone-friendly materials. This is helping to remove one of the major causes of **depletion** of the ozone layer.
The spray-can contained ozone-friendly propellants.

ozone layer *noun*

The ozone layer is a part of the Earth's atmosphere. It lies about 22 kilometres above the surface of the Earth. The ozone layer protects the Earth from harmful **radiation** from the Sun. Certain **chemicals**, called chlorofluorocarbons, may damage the ozone layer.
Scientists have found that the ozone layer becomes thinner over Antarctica each spring since the 1970s.

P

paddy *noun*
A paddy, or paddy field, is a small, flooded area where **rice** is grown. Rice grows under water for three-quarters of its **growing season**, so paddies must not dry out. The water level is kept up by having soil that holds water. The fields have high sides, and irrigation is used as necessary.
The tourists passed large areas of paddy fields on their trip through China.

palm *noun*
A palm is a woody **monocotyledon**. The palm family has about 2,800 species. Palms have feathery branches called **fronds**. They are found in **tropical** areas, particularly on islands in the oceans. Palm trunks are covered in structures called leaf-sheaths, or scars where the leaf-sheaths once grew. At the top of the trunk is a crown of leaves. Some species of palm provide fruits, such as **dates** and **coconuts**. Palms also provide **timber**, **sugars** and **waxes**.
The monkeys jumped from one palm tree to another.

palynology *noun*
Palynology is the study of **pollen grains**. The pollen grains studied can be from living or fossil plants. Pollen from a particular plant has its own structure. In this way, even very old pollen grains can be identified. The history of the vegetation of an area can be worked out by studying pollen in the earth.
The botanists used palynology to build up the history of the area.

pampas *noun*
Pampas is a kind of **grassland**. The pampas is found in South America, mainly in Uruguay and Argentina. Trees are scarce on the pampas. Tall **grasses** are the main, or **dominant**, plants.
The farmer led his cattle out onto the pampas.

paper *noun*
Paper is a thin material for writing on or for wrapping. Paper is usually made of wood **pulp**, but it can also be made from other plant **fibres** or from rags. It is possible to recycle old paper to make more paper.
The gift was wrapped in coloured paper.

papyrus *noun*
Papyrus is a **water plant** which grows in Egypt. It has reed-like stems which grow to three metres high. Ancient Egyptian people made paper from papyrus by crushing layers of the stems into flat sheets.
The sheets of papyrus had turned brown with age.

paramo *noun*
Paramo, or puna, is the **vegetation** of high, tropical mountains in South America. High **grasslands**, with shrub plants and tree-like rosette plants make up the paramo. The paramo suffers frequent severe frosts, in spite of being placed in the tropics. The reason for this is the high altitude of the paramo.
The botanists climbed high into the Andes to study the paramo.

parasite *noun*
A parasite is an **organism** that lives in or on another organism which is called the **host**. The parasite lives off the host during all or part of its life and causes it some harm. An example of a parasitic plant is the dodder plant. The stems of this plant wrap themselves around a host plant. Special **suckers** on the stems become attached and share the host's food supply. Some parasites eventually kill their host.
Mistletoe is a parasite that lives on trees.

parent *noun*
A parent is an **organism** that has produced offspring. The offspring may be produced by **sexual reproduction**, when there is a male and a female parent, or by **asexual reproduction**.
The parent tree was surrounded by its young seedlings.

parsley *noun*
Parsley is a **family** of flowering plants. Most varieties of parsley are garden vegetables. They have clusters of crumpled, green leaves. The leaves are often used as a flavouring for food such as salads. Parsley is rich in vitamins and minerals.
The cook added some chopped parsley to the finished soup.

pasture *noun*
Pasture is an area of **grassland** used for raising farm animals. It is **grazed** by animals and is not cut for **fodder**. **Natural** pastures include the **prairies** in North America and the **steppes** in Asia.
The cattle grew fat on the lush pasture.

pea *noun*
The pea is one of a large family of **climbing plants** which produce **pods**. Pea pods contain round seeds, also called peas, which are a popular food when cooked. The pea is an **annual** plant which is often **cultivated** as a garden vegetable in northern countries.
Garden peas have a sweet taste.

peanut *noun*
The peanut plant is a flowering plant in the **pea** family. It bears many seeds, also called peanuts. The seeds are in brown **pods**. The pods grow from stems which push downwards into the soil, so that the seeds develop underground. The peanut is a valuable source of **protein**, so it is **cultivated** as a food crop. Peanuts are removed from the pods and roasted or crushed to produce oil.
Peanuts are often called groundnuts because of the way the pods grow underground.

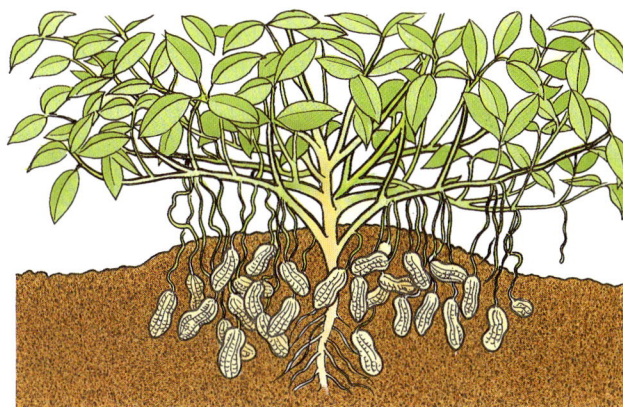

peat *noun*
Peat is a kind of **soil**. It is made from the decaying remains of plants, mainly certain kinds of **moss**. Peat is dark brown in colour. It develops under wet conditions in **bogs** or peatlands over long periods of time. Peat is a very good source of **humus**. It can also be burned as a fuel when dry.
The plants had their roots in a thick layer of peat.

pectin *noun*
Pectin is a substance which is found between the **cell walls** of fruits. Some fruits, including apples and plums, are higher in pectin than others, such as strawberries and apricots. Pectin thickens fruit juices when the fruit is cooked. This makes it a useful substance when cooking foods such as jam, which need to be solid.
She added powdered pectin to the strawberry jam to make it set.

perennial *noun*

A perennial is a plant which lives for several years. One group of perennials dies down above ground each year. The plants survive because they have underground parts, such as **bulbs**, **corms** and **rhizomes**. The second group of perennials has strong, woody tissue above ground, which lasts through bad weather. Crocuses, tulips, irises and delphiniums are all examples of perennial plants.
The gardens were planted with perennials, which did not have to be renewed each year.

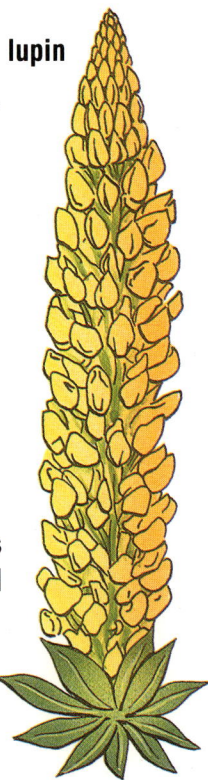

lupin

perfume *noun*

A perfume is a scent or odour. Perfumes are special to the **organisms** that produce them. The perfumes from some **flowers** attract insects to the plants for **pollination**. Perfumes may be taken out, or extracted, from some flowers with the help of alcohols. Some perfumes are made from the oil that comes from flowers. This oil is called essential oil. It is often extracted from flowers such as jasmine and lavender.
The perfume from the flowers of the lime trees scented the whole area.

permafrost *noun*

Permafrost describes ground which is permanently frozen. It occurs in about a fifth of the world's land. Permafrost is found in regions which are very cold, such as in the **Arctic**. The ground may be frozen to a depth of 900 metres. When the surface of the soil melts in the Arctic summer, it becomes very wet. The reason for this is that the permafrost below stops the water draining away.
We could not dig very deep because of the permafrost.

pest *noun*

A pest is an **organism** which damages **crops**. Most pests are insects, but many other animals can be pests, including mammals, birds and tiny micro-organisms. Some pests are very specific, which means they attack only one organism or group of organisms.
The gardener sprayed the flowers to destroy the pests.

locusts

pest control *noun*

Pest control is the control of **pests**. Many methods are known, including the use of natural predators which live on the pest. This is called **biological control**. More often, **chemicals** are used to control pests and to increase crop **yields**.
The college of agriculture had a lecture course on methods of pest control.

pesticide *noun*

A pesticide is a **chemical** which kills a **pest**. Some pesticides are natural, like pyrethrum which comes from chrysanthemum flowers. Other pesticides are artificial, like **DDT**. These stay in the environment and may harm wildlife. Types of pesticide include **insecticides** which control insects, **herbicides** which control weeds and **fungicides** which control disease-spreading fungi.
He used a pesticide spray to kill the blackfly on the crops.

102

petal *noun*
A petal is part of the **flower** of a plant. Petals are leaf-like structures, set in a ring around the flower. The petals together are known as the **corolla**. Petals are often brightly coloured, but they may be pale or white. Some plants do not have petals.
The bright red tulip petals made a very colourful show.

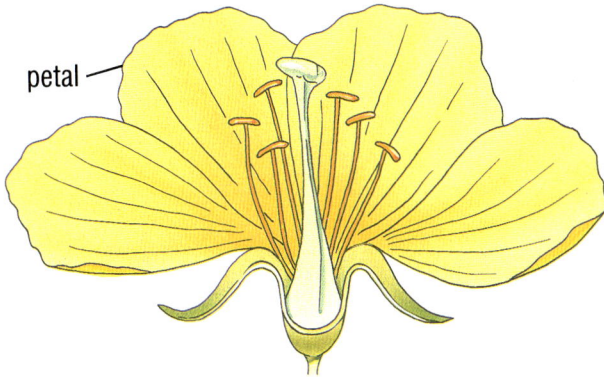

petal

petiole *noun*
The petiole is the stalk of a **leaf**. Veins run through the petiole and carry water to the leaf. Food material made in the leaf is carried through the petiole to other parts of the plant where it is used or stored. When leaves fall off **trees**, the **leaf scar** marks the position where the petiole was attached to the trunk.
The aspen leaf quivered on its long petiole.

petroleum *noun*
Petroleum is a dark, oily liquid which is found beneath the Earth's surface. Some deposits of petroleum lie under the sea-bed. Petroleum is sometimes called crude oil and is a mixture of hydrocarbons. Petroleum is refined to make fuels, such as **oil**.
Engineers drill deep into the ground to search for petroleum.

petunia *noun*
A petunia is a flowering plant in the nightshade family. It grows wild in Argentina and Brazil. Petunias are widely cultivated as garden flowers. They have large, funnel-shaped flowers in white or shades of red.
The petunia plant is covered in tiny hairs.

phloem *noun*
Phloem is a kind of tissue in the **stem** of a plant. The phloem is a set of tubes through which food material, or **nutrients**, made in the leaves is carried to other parts of the plant. Phloem is made up of long sieve tubes that have **pores** between them. These make it easy for the nutrients to pass up and down the plant.
She could see the phloem in the cross-section of the plant stem.

phlox *noun*
Phlox is a **family** of flowering plants. There are several species of phlox, some of which are **cultivated** as garden plants in northern countries. Wild phlox is native to the United States of America. Phlox plants have clusters of brightly coloured flowers growing at the top of the stems. The name 'phlox' comes from the Greek for 'flame'.
Sweet william is a wild variety of phlox which has blue or lilac flowers.

phosphate *noun*
A phosphate is a kind of **chemical**. Farmers add phosphates to the soil to help crops grow well. Phosphates are also added to cleaners, such as soap powder and detergents, to make them more powerful. These phosphates sometimes cause **pollution** if they are washed into rivers.
Rain washed the phosphate from the field into the stream.

phosphorus *noun*
Phosphorus is an element. It is found in many different types of rock and mineral, mainly as a mixture, or compound, with calcium. Phosphorus is used to make matches, and in fertilizers. All living things need phosphorus. Plants absorb phosphorous from the soil. They use it in **photosynthesis**.
The crops were unhealthy because there was not enough phosphorus in the soil.

photosynthesis ▶ page 104

103

photosynthesis *noun*

Photosynthesis is the process by which plants make food from water and sunlight. Photosynthesis takes place in the green parts of plants, where the pigment **chlorophyll** absorbs **energy** from light. Photosynthesis is the only way in which sunlight is used, or harnessed, for energy by plants.

All plant life is based on photosynthesis.

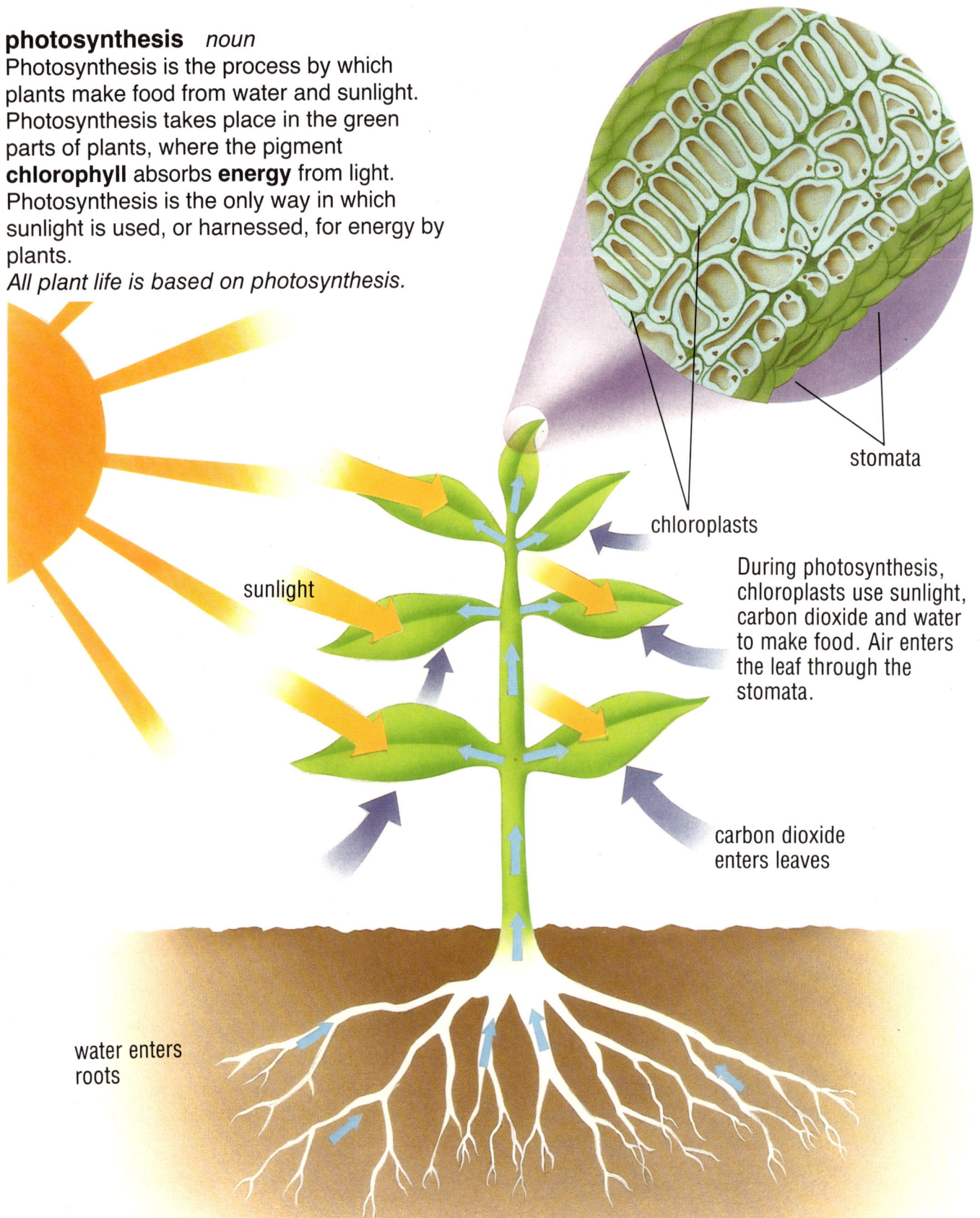

stomata

chloroplasts

During photosynthesis, chloroplasts use sunlight, carbon dioxide and water to make food. Air enters the leaf through the stomata.

sunlight

carbon dioxide enters leaves

water enters roots

When a potato tuber is left in a
dark place, the leaves and stems
are very pale. They have very little
chlorophyll, which gives plants
their green colour.

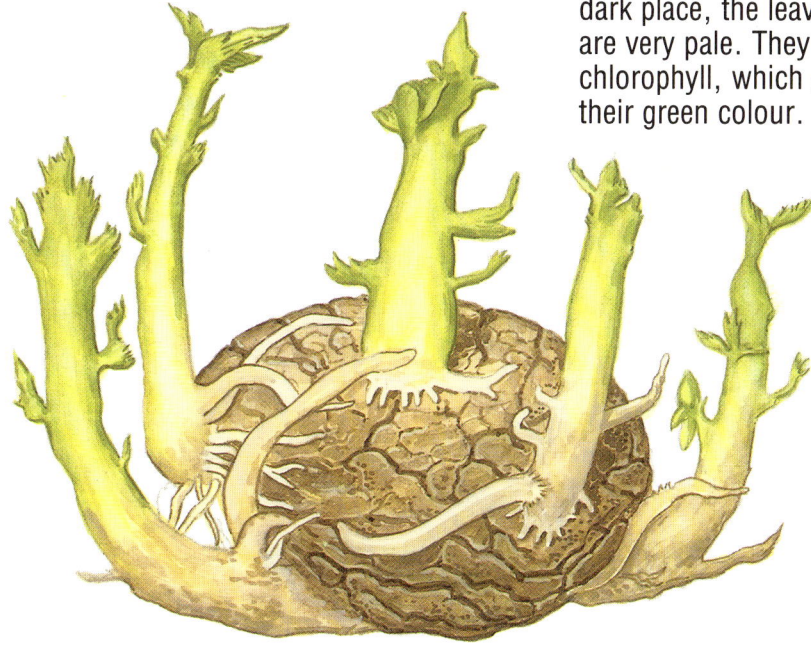

When the same tuber is placed
in the light, it starts to grow
very quickly. The leaves and
stems are now very green, due
to chlorophyll produced during
photosynthesis.

phototropism *noun*
Phototropism is a kind of plant growth. It is growth in response to light. In positive phototropism, plant stems bend towards the light. In negative phototropism, some leaves turn from the light, when it is strong.
The plants leaned towards the window because of phototropism.

phytoplankton *noun*
Phytoplankton are very tiny plants that are found in sea water and in fresh water. Most phytoplankton are so small they can only be seen with a microscope. They drift with the main mass of water near the surface. Here there is plenty of light for growth. Plankton form the basis of all **food chains** in the sea.
Many marine animals eat phytoplankton.

pigment *noun*
A pigment is a coloured **chemical** which is found in the bodies of plants and animals. Flowers, fur, feathers, skin and other tissues are all coloured by pigments. The pigment in the petals of a flower gives it a bright colour. Green plants contain the green pigment **chlorophyll** in their stems and leaves.
The autumn leaves were full of rusty coloured pigments.

pigweed *noun*
Pigweed is a common annual **weed**. Pigweeds have large leaves and small, green-coloured flowers.
Another name for pigweed is goosefoot.

pine *noun*
Pine is a family of **conifer** trees. There are about 100 species of pine found throughout the world. Most pines grow quickly and have straight, tall trunks. Pine trees have evergreen, pointed leaves called **needles**. Pines produce both male and female flowers. The female flowers take two years to ripen, when they become hard, brown **cones** containing **seeds**.
Pine wood is a popular timber because it is hard-wearing.

pioneer community *noun*
A pioneer community is the first set of plants to, start growing well, or become established, on a bare surface. A typical pioneer community includes **lichens**, **mosses** and **grasses**. These are all species that can grow in harsh conditions. When the pioneer community has provided some shelter and **nutrients**, other species colonize the site and outgrow the pioneer plants.
It was some years after the volcano had erupted before a pioneer community became established on the bare mountain slopes.

pistil *noun*
The pistil is the reproductive part of a female flower. It is made up of the **ovules** in the **carpel** or carpels, with the **stigma** and **style**. The pistil is found in the centre of the flower.
The botanist opened up the flower to look at the pistil.

pistil

pith *noun*
Pith is the central part of the **stems** and **roots** of green plants. It is a spongy tissue, found inside the cylinder of **xylem** and **phloem** cells. Pith is also the name for the white, fibrous lining of the skins of **citrus** fruit.
The orange was peeled, but the pith was left covering the fruit.

plain *noun*
A plain is a flat area of lowland. Many plains stretch for hundreds of kilometres. Plains are often well populated because the rich soils found there are good for farming. The plains of East Africa are covered with scattered trees and **grassland**. The Great Plains of North America are important for growing grain crops.
The grassland stretched away across the open plain.

plankton *noun*
Plankton is the name for plants and animals which float about hanging in the water, or in the air. Marine plankton crowd, or teem, in the upper layers of the sea. They form food for other animals, including fish. Many plankton can only be seen with a microscope. Aerial plankton include tiny insects and spiders which are swept up in air currents.
The shoal of fish followed the plankton in the sea.

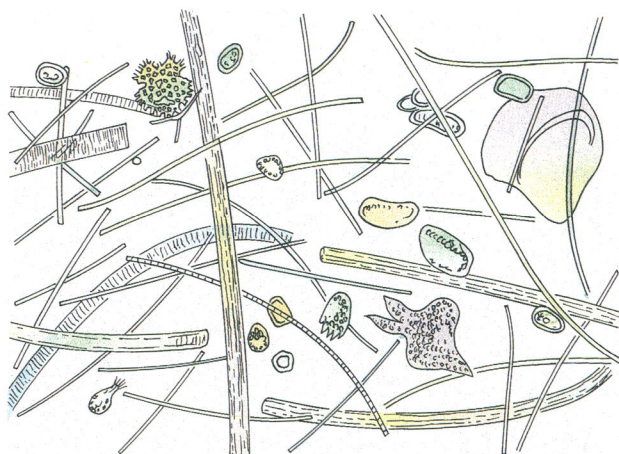

plant *noun*
A plant is a living **organism** that makes its food from **inorganic** matter. Plant **cells** have **cellulose** in their walls. Plants do not move from place to place, but remain fixed in one spot. Most plants have some green parts, because they contain **chlorophyll**.
There was a wide variety of plants in the Botanic Gardens.

plantation *noun*
1. A plantation is a large area of land where a single **crop** is usually grown.
Crops grown on a plantation include coffee, tea, bananas and sugar cane.
2. A plantation is a large area of trees, grown specially to be harvested. Most plantations in temperate regions are of coniferous trees, such as **pine** and **spruce**.
The trees in the plantation are felled every few years to make timber.

plantlet *noun*
A plantlet is a small or young plant. Plantlets are usually formed by buds or runners from the parent plant. Some species of plant form plantlets more readily than others. They are then a good way to **propagate** the plant.
He watered the plantlets regularly and they soon grew into large, healthy plants.

plumule *noun*
A plumule is a kind of **shoot**. It is the tiny shoot produced by a developing plant **embryo**. The plumule produces the stem and leaves of a plant, once it breaks above the ground. In a **dicotyledon**, the plumule grows up between the two **cotyledons**. In some seeds, the plumule is protected by the cotyledons until it reaches the soil's surface.
The plumule of the germinating seed soon became visible.

plumule—
runner
bean seed

roots

107

pod *noun*

A pod is the fruit of a plant of the **pea** family. Pods are divided lengthwise into two halves, and contain a row of seeds. When they are ripe, pods dry out and split. Some pods open with a small explosion, flinging the seeds some distance away. Sometimes, the whole pod with the seeds inside is eaten as a vegetable. String beans are examples of these. Sometimes, just the seeds of a pod are eaten.
The children each took a pea pod and counted the peas to see who had most.

cacao pod

cacao beans

poison *noun*

A poison is a substance that is harmful to an **organism**. Some poisons are **natural** substances, and may be produced by an organism to protect it from being eaten. Other poisons are made by people, to use against **pests**. Poisons are commonly used to kill household pests, such as rats, mice and cockroaches.
Deadly nightshade berries contain a strong poison to stop them being eaten by animals.

poisonous plant *noun*

Poisonous plants are plants that produce poisons which can be dangerous to humans or animals. These plants can injure or kill if they are touched or eaten. The poison can be found in the whole plant, or in specific parts of the plant, such as the **berries**. Some families of plants, such as the **buttercup** and **nightshade** families, contain many poisonous species.
She touched the poison ivy plant and developed a severe skin rash.

polar *adjective*

Polar describes something found close to, or coming from, the North or South pole. Polar air is cold air moving from the polar regions. Polar plants and animals are specially **adapted** to withstand the cold conditions at the poles.
The explorers set out to cross the polar ice.

polder *noun*

A polder is a piece of land which was once covered with water but has now been drained. To make a polder, mounds called dikes are built around the area to be drained. The water is then pumped away.
Polders can be found in the Netherlands.

policy *noun*

A policy is a plan made by people to carry out an action. People concerned with the **environment** try to put together policies which look after the natural environment and yet allow people to live comfortably.
The policy of providing recycling centres resulted in more trees being saved.

pollen *noun*

Pollen is the fine powder produced by the male part of a plant. It is made up of **pollen grains** which are the male sex cells, or **gametes**, of the plant. Pollen is scattered by a number of methods depending on the species of plant. Bees and other insects carry pollen from plant to plant as they take **nectar**. In trees with **catkins**, the wind blows pollen from tree to tree.
The pollen made the boy sneeze.

pollen grain *noun*

A pollen grain is a tiny particle of **pollen** produced by the **anther** of a plant. Each pollen grain can develop into a male sex cell, or **gamete**, which may join with a female gamete from the same or another plant. This forms a **seed**. Each species of plant produces pollen grains of a different type.
He looked at the pollen grains under the microscope.

108

pollination ► page 110

pollution *noun*
Pollution is the release, of impurities or unwanted substances into the **environment**. Untreated sewage sometimes causes pollution of streams and rivers. Smoke and waste chemicals from factories cause pollution of the air and water.
Acid rain is a kind of pollution.

pome *noun*
Pome is the name given to one of the four types of **simple fruits**. Pomes have a fleshy outer layer and a core which contains more than one seed. The other types of simple fruit are berries, drupes and dry fruits.
Apples and pears are pomes.

pond *noun*
A pond is a small area of water that is surrounded by land. It is usually shallow enough for sunlight to reach the bottom. Ponds often contain a variety of plant and animal life. The **species** found in a particular pond depend on where the pond is found and the quality of its water and soil.
The water in the pond had been polluted.

pondweed *noun*
Pondweed is a plant that is found growing mainly in calm water. It often has two kinds of leaves. One kind floats on the water and one kind is found beneath the water.
The pondweed flower is small and green.

poplar *noun*
Poplars are deciduous **trees** belonging to the **willow** family. There are 35 kinds of poplar, found in northern **temperate** countries. Poplars grow in damp soils, often alongside rivers. They grow quickly, and have light wood which is used as timber and also to make matches. The flowers of the poplar are dangling **catkins**.
In just a few years, the poplars had grown to form a small wood.

poppy *noun*
Poppy is a **family** of flowering plants. There are about 50 **species** of poppy. They have large flowers with four or six petals on top of a single stem. The flowers can be white, pink, red or purple. The opium poppy is the most important species of poppy. The drug opium comes from a milky substance found in the poppy's young seed **capsules**. The seeds of the opium poppy can be used as a flavouring or pressed to provide oil.
Many important medicines are made from the capsules of the opium poppy.

population *noun*
A population is a group of single plants or a **species** living in one area. The **population density** can be measured at any time. If a population falls too low, the species may eventually die out, or become **extinct**, in that area. Population **biology** is the study of populations of plants and animals.
The population of wood anemones that year was much larger than the previous year.

pollination *noun*

Pollination is the movement of pollen from the male part of a **flower** to the female part. The pollen joins with the **ovule** during **fertilization**, to form the **seed**. Pollination can be between the two parts of the same flower, or from the **anther** of one to the **ovary** of another. In some plants, such as many **trees**, pollination is carried out by the wind. Plants with bright flowers may use insects or birds in pollination.

They carried out pollination of the tomato plants by brushing pollen onto the stigmas.

pollinate *verb*

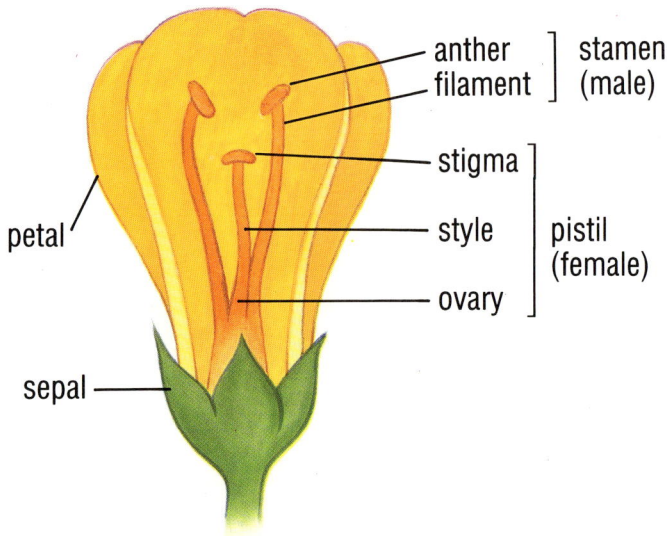

anther ⎤ stamen
filament ⎦ (male)

stigma ⎤
style ⎥ pistil
        ⎥ (female)
ovary ⎦

petal

sepal

In self-pollination, pollen produced by the male stamen of one flower falls onto the female stigma of another flower of the same plant.

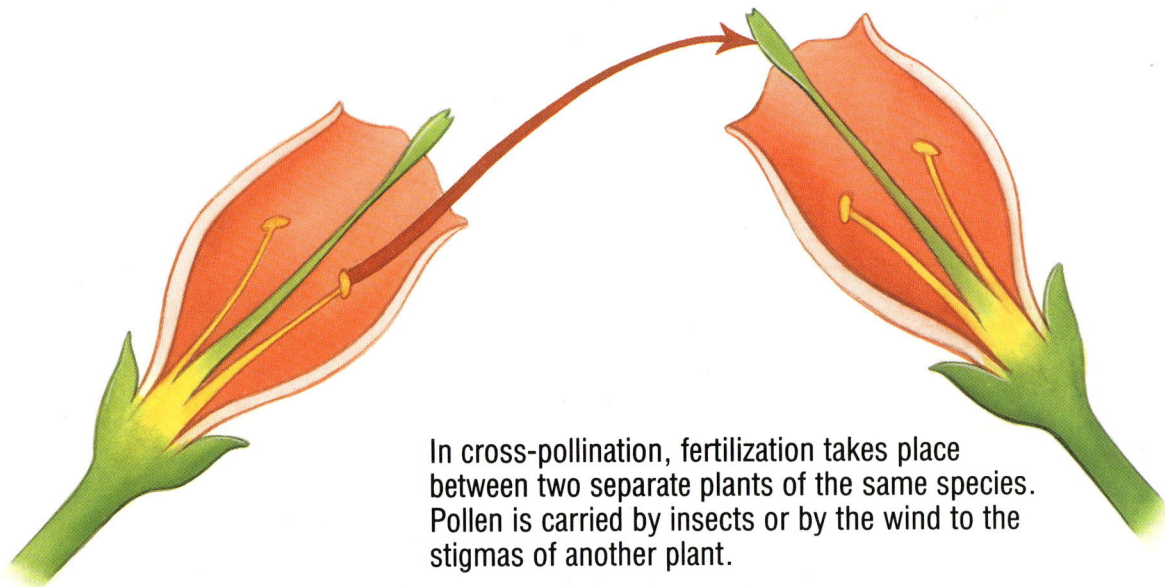

In cross-pollination, fertilization takes place between two separate plants of the same species. Pollen is carried by insects or by the wind to the stigmas of another plant.

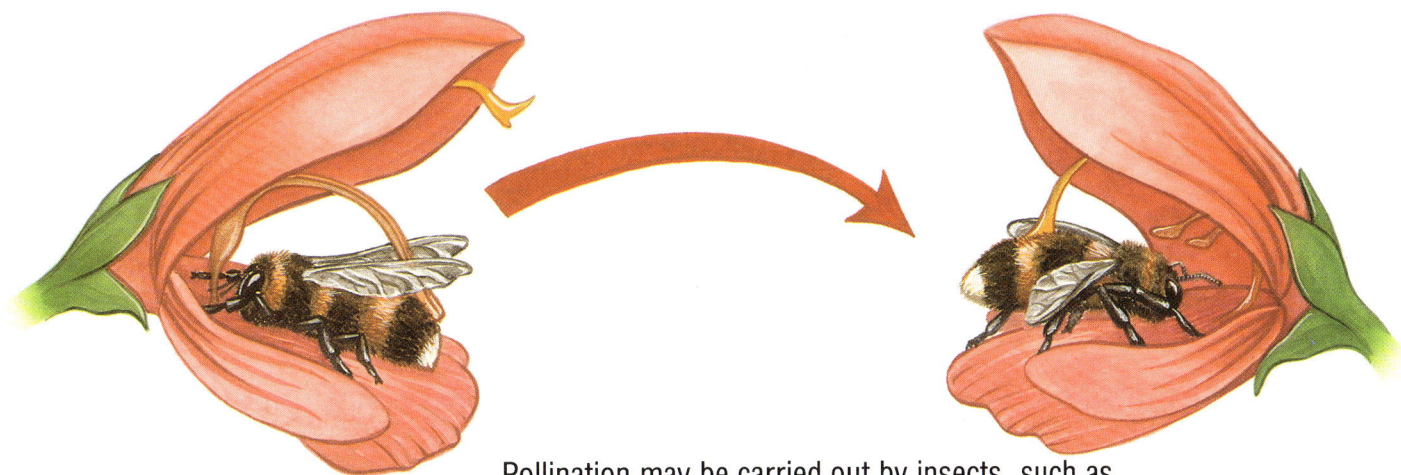

Pollination may be carried out by insects, such as bees, which visit flowers to gather nectar. Pollen brushes off onto the bee's furry body and is transferred to the next flower the bee visits.

Some plants rely on the wind to carry pollen from one flower to another.

Small birds, such as hummingbirds, may pollinate flowers in a similar way to bees.

population cycle *noun*
A population cycle is the regular rise and fall of a **population**. The sizes of all populations change with time, and some rise and others fall continuously.
A population cycle happens only when conditions, such as climate, are stable.

population density *noun*
The population density is the number of members of one **species** in an area. The density may increase because of movement from another area, or increased health of the **population**. It may decrease if the rate of **reproduction** falls, or if the climate becomes harsh. The population density varies in different parts of any country.
The conservationists monitored the population density of the orchids.

potash *noun*
Potash is a mixture, or compound, of **potassium** carbonate and other potassium salts. Potash is found with other salts, such as common salt, in salt lakes. It is also found in ash. Potash is used as a **fertilizer** for plants.
She put potash on the garden soil.

potassium *noun*
Potassium is an element and a metal. It is found in many minerals, and also in sea water. Potassium is essential for all life.
The plants grew badly since there was no potassium in the soil.

potato *noun*
The potato plant is a member of the **nightshade** family. There are about 150 species of potato. It is the world's most widely grown **vegetable** and an important food crop. Potatoes are leafy, **annual** plants. They have fleshy **tubers**, also called potatoes, which grow from underground stems. These are the edible part of the plant, and there can be up to 20 on each plant.
Potatoes are delicious baked, boiled, fried or mashed.

prairie *noun*
The prairie is the treeless, grassy plain in the centre of the North American continent. In the prairie, the rain falls mostly in the summer, when it is also hot. In winter, it is dry and cold. **Wheat** and **maize** grow well on the prairie.
The cowboys rode on horseback over the open prairie.

precipitation *noun*
Precipitation is the water which falls from the atmosphere onto the Earth's surface. It includes snow, sleet, hail and dew, as well as rain.
The ground was wet from the precipitation.

prehistoric plant *noun*
Prehistoric plants are plants that existed during prehistory, or the period before humans learned to write 5,500 years ago. The first land plants probably appeared on Earth about 430 million years ago and were different from any plants known today. The first flowering plants appeared about 240 million years ago. By the time the first people lived on Earth about 5 million years ago, forest and grasslands covered the tropical and temperate regions.
Magnolia trees were among the first flowering prehistoric plants.

prickle *noun*
A prickle is a sharp point formed at the surface of a stem or leaf. Prickles help to prevent the plants being eaten by animals with soft mouths.
The holly leaf had rows of prickles.

primary forest *noun*
Primary forest is original forest which has not been changed by people. True primary forest is now rare, and many primary forests are protected in **reserves**. Forest which has re-grown after felling is **secondary forest**.
The most interesting plants and animals lived deep in the primary forest.

primary producer *noun*
A primary producer is a plant at the start of a **food chain**. The primary producer changes the **energy** of the Sun into food material. This is eaten by plant-eating animals, the **primary consumers**.
Primary producers on land are crops, and in water they are phytoplankton.

primary root *noun*
A primary root is the first **root** of a plant to develop from a seed. The primary root produces many branches called **secondary roots**. In a **taproot** root system, the primary root remains larger than any of the secondary roots and grows straight down. In a **fibrous** root system, the secondary roots may be longer than the primary root.
A carrot is a fleshy primary root or taproot.

primrose *noun*
Primrose is a **family** of flowering plants which has more than 500 **species**. Primroses are popular garden plants in many northern countries. These plants have been developed from the common primrose. This grows wild in woodlands and meadows in Europe and has pale yellow flowers.
Primroses usually flower in early spring.

prop root *noun*
A prop root is a type of **root**. It holds up, or supports, a plant by growing downwards into the soil from above the ground. Mangroves and maize are kinds of plant that are supported by prop roots. Screwpines and banyans are examples of trees with prop roots.
The thick prop roots of the banyan looked like many small trees crowded together.

propagation *noun*
Propagation is the process by which gardeners increase the number of plants. There are three main methods of propagation. Some plants are propagated by **layering**. Others are propagated by **grafting**. The third method of propagation is by **cutting**.
The young plant produced by propagation is exactly the same as the parent.
propagate *verb*

protected species *noun*
A protected species is a **species** of plant or animal which must be **conserved** to make sure that it does not become **extinct**. Most countries have laws to control the way rare species are treated, and to protect them. It is often against the law to dig up roots of protected plants, or to pick the flowers. This would prevent seeds developing.
The walkers were given a list of protected species, so they would recognize any they saw.

protein *noun*
A protein is a kind of organic **chemical**. Proteins are made by living **cells** and form a large part of plant and animal bodies. Some kinds of protein are called **enzymes**. Muscles, blood, eggs, skin, bones and seeds all contain proteins.
Everyone needs to eat proteins to stay healthy.

protist *noun*
Protists are tiny **organisms**. They form a **kingdom** of their own, the Kingdom Protista. About 120,000 **species** have been named, about half of which are fossil kinds. Most protists are too small to be seen without a microscope. They are found in land and water all over the world. Protists usually have a **flagellum**, with which they move. Biologists think that all animals, plants and fungi developed, or **evolved**, from protists.
The pond water was full of many different kinds of protist.

113

prune *verb*
Prune describes the cutting back of plant growth. Most cultivated **perennials** are pruned so that they grow well and produce better flowers and fruit. It is usual to prune plants after they have flowered. Shrubs that flower in the winter are pruned in the spring. Shrubs that flower in the summer are pruned in the autumn.
The gardener picked the apples and pruned the trees before winter set in.

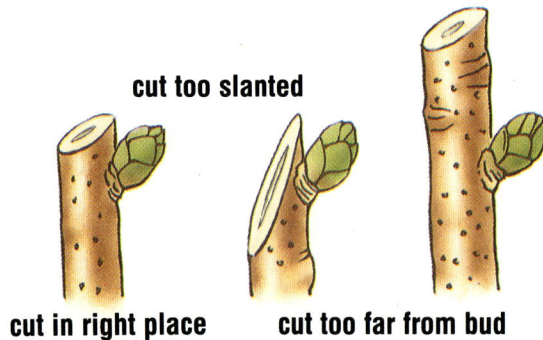

cut too slanted

cut in right place   **cut too far from bud**

pteridophyte ▶ page 115

puffball *noun*
Puffball is the name of a **fungus**. It is ball-shaped and contains **spores**. As the puffball grows older, it becomes full of powdery spores. These can come out in clouds, like a puff of smoke, if the puffball is touched.
Puffballs are also called devil's snuffbox.

pulp *noun*
Pulp is a soft, fibrous material. It is formed by processing rags, straw, wood and old paper, to make new paper. **Conifer** forests in the **temperate** regions of the world produce the **softwood** which is used for pulp.
They visited the paper mill and saw the wood turned to pulp.

pulse *noun*
A pulse is the **seed** of a **legume**. Peas, beans and lentils are all pulses.
The village shop sold many kinds of pulse.

pumpkin *noun*
A pumpkin is a **fruit** belonging to the **cucumber** family. Pumpkins are large and rounded in shape. The biggest pumpkins can weigh around 90 kilograms and are the world's largest fruits. The flesh of pumpkins can be eaten when cooked. It can be made into pie or soup.
The huge pumpkin won first prize at the vegetable show.

puna ▶ **paramo**

114

pteridophyte *noun*

Pteridophyte is the name of the groups of plants that include **ferns**, **club mosses** and **horsetails**. There are many examples of fossil pteridophytes, as they were very common **prehistoric plants**. Pteridophytes reproduce by producing **spores**, unlike the other major group of plants, the **angiosperms**.

Pteridophytes were very common in the Carboniferous period, when some formed large tree ferns.

Many fossils have been found of ferns that lived millions of years ago.

Stag's horn club moss has needle-like leaves and two fertile cones at the end of each stem.

The great horsetail grows in damp woods and on banks beneath hedges. Its leaves grow in whorls.

Tree ferns can grow to a height of 20 metres. They are found in tropical forests in mountain areas of Asia and Australasia.

Q

quarantine *noun*
Quarantine is a way of isolating an animal or plant that may be carrying an infection. When something is in quarantine, it is kept isolated in a special place for a certain length of time. This is to make sure that no infectious diseases have been brought into a country with the animal or plant.
The imported dog had to stay in quarantine for six months before they could take it home.

quota *noun*
A quota is a limited quantity of animals, plants or products. Quotas are established by law to protect species which are in danger through over-collection or over-harvesting.
The fishermen were not allowed to exceed their quota for the season.

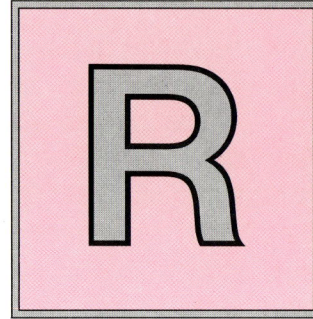

R

raceme *noun*
A raceme is a kind of flower cluster. Plants with racemes have a central stem called a peduncle. This produces a number of flowers on individual stalks called pedicels.
Racemes can be seen on lily-of-the-valley plants.

radiation *noun*
Radiation describes how energy particles move very quickly through space. Light, **ultraviolet** rays, X-rays, and **radioactive** atoms all travel by radiation. Every living thing on Earth depends on radiation from the Sun. Green plants use sunlight to make their own food by **photosynthesis**.
Radiation is essential to life, but too much can be harmful.
radiate *verb*

radicle *noun*
The radicle is the part of a **seed** which develops into the first root, or **primary root**, of a plant. When the seed **germinates**, the radicle then grows downwards into the soil.
The radicle takes in water and nutrients from the soil.

radioactive *adjective*
Radioactive describes some substances which give off high-energy **radiation**. Some elements, such as uranium and radium, are naturally radioactive. The raw materials and the products of nuclear power stations are radioactive.
The scientist found that some of the rocks were radioactive.
radioactivity *noun*

radioactive waste *noun*
Radioactive waste is a by-product of nuclear power stations. Three kinds of radioactive waste are formed, low-, intermediate- and high-level. All radioactive waste is dangerous and remains dangerous for thousands of years. Low- and intermediate-level waste is usually stored in underground pits. High-level waste is kept in liquid form in solid steel or glass containers and buried deep underground.
The scientists tried to find the best place to store the radioactive waste.

rain forest ▶ page 118

rainfall *noun*
Rainfall is the total amount of water falling on a particular area or country. Areas close to the sea, with onshore winds, usually have a high rainfall. Where there is low rainfall, **deserts** may develop. Rainfall is normally measured in millimetres per year.
The rain gauge measured the amount of rainfall.

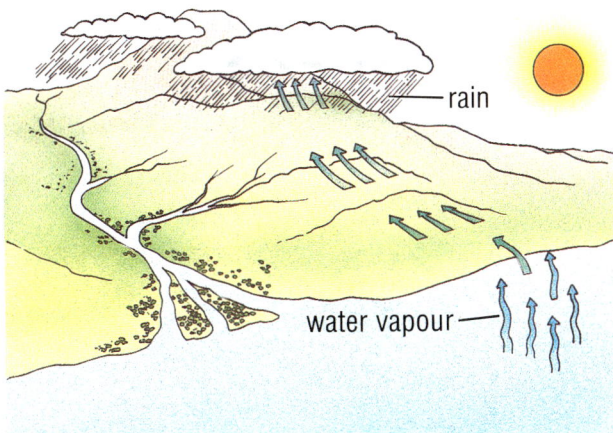

rain

water vapour

rare *adjective*
Rare describes an animal or plant **species** which has a low **population**. Rare species often need special protection if they are to **survive**. **Nature reserves** are sometimes set up to protect rare species and their **habitats**.
The island was well known for its rare species.

raw material *noun*
Raw materials are natural substances which are used to make other things. The oil industry uses crude oil as a raw material, to make petrol and other products. **Sugar cane** and **sugar beet** are the main raw materials used for making sugar.
The factory relied on a continuous supply of raw materials.

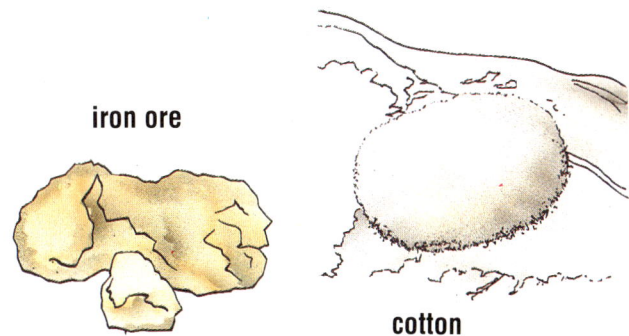

iron ore

cotton

ray floret *noun*
Ray floret is the name for the petal-shaped flowers which make up the flower head in some plants. Ray florets can be seen in members of the **composite** family of flowers, such as the daisy and dandelion.
Up to 100 ray florets make up a dandelion head.

reafforestation *noun*
Reafforestation is the planting of trees on land where forest once grew. Now that so much natural forest has been removed, reafforestation is becoming more important.
By reafforestation, they were able to return the hillsides to their former wooded state.

receptacle *noun*
The receptacle is the swollen end of a **flower** stalk. It forms at the base of the flower and contains the female parts of the flower, the **ovaries** and **ovules**. After fertilization has taken place, the receptacle begins to swell as the seeds develop.
The seeds were dispersed from the receptacle.

rain forest *noun*

Rain forests are found in tropical regions with a high rainfall. The trees in rain forests grow very tall, and there are many climbing plants in the **canopy** and **understorey** of the forest. South America, Africa and South-east Asia have many rain forests. Rain forests are the world's richest **ecosystems**.

They saw monkeys and parrots in the rain forest.

After an area of rain forest has been cut down, it may quickly flood. The soil is washed away and the area becomes barren.

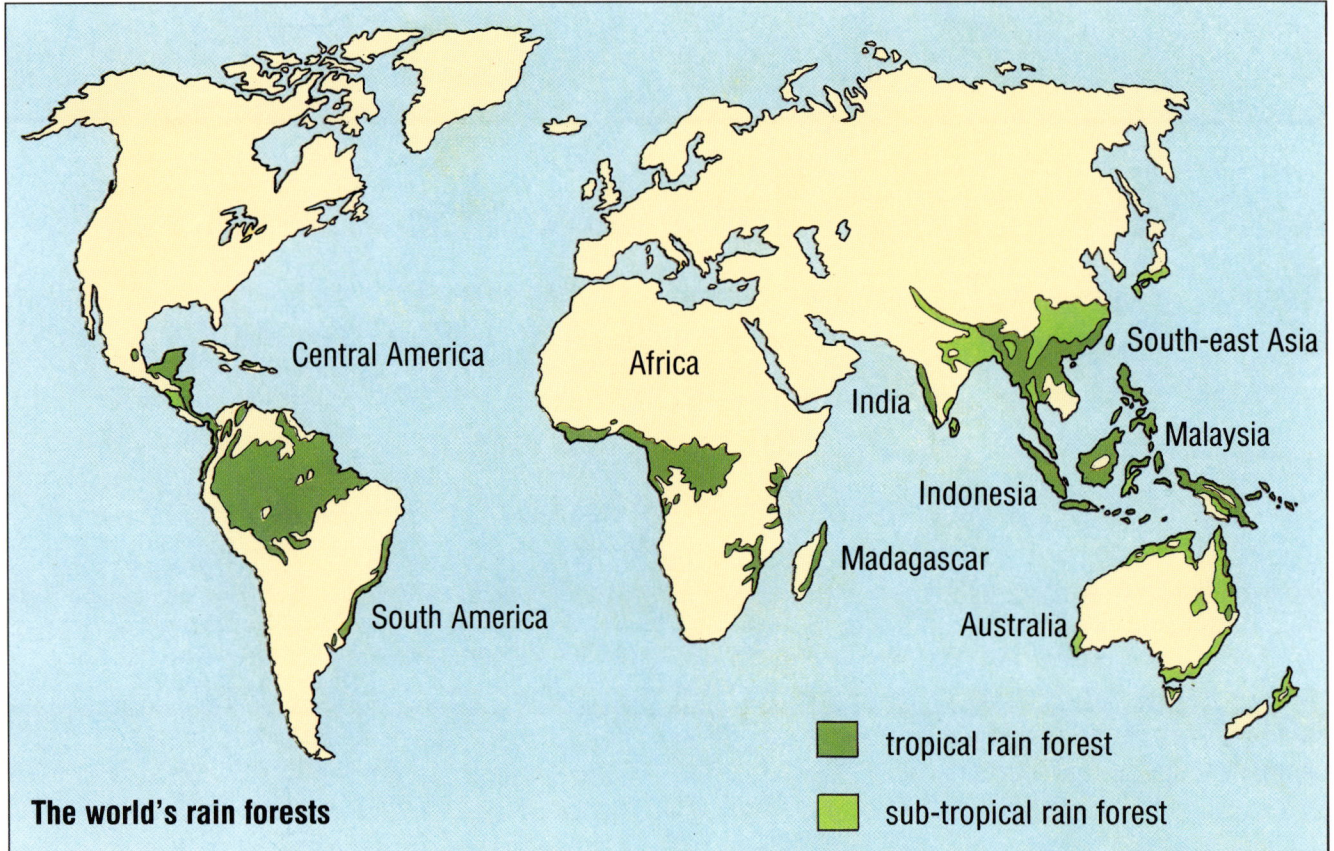

Central America

Africa

India

South-east Asia

Malaysia

Indonesia

Madagascar

Australia

South America

tropical rain forest

sub-tropical rain forest

The world's rain forests

A rain forest is made up of three layers of vegetation. At the top is the canopy, where the crowns of the tallest trees form a dense cover of leaves. In the middle is the understorey, where smaller trees and many climbing plants and animals live. At the bottom is the field layer, where plants such as mosses and ferns grow.

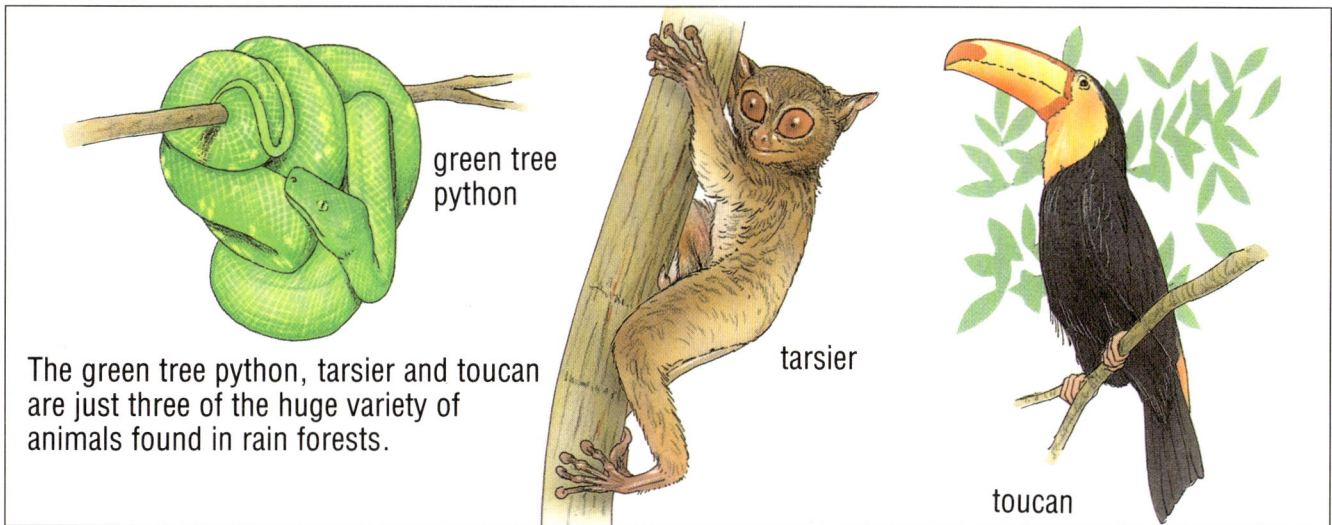

emergent tree

liana

canopy

understorey of smaller or younger trees

field or herb layer

smooth trunk with no branches

green tree python

tarsier

toucan

The green tree python, tarsier and toucan are just three of the huge variety of animals found in rain forests.

reclaim *verb*

To reclaim is to improve land that was not useable so that it can be used. Flooded land can be reclaimed from the sea or from a lake. Open-cast mines can be filled, and wasteland can be cleared.
Desert land can be reclaimed through irrigation.

Red Data Books *noun*

Red Data Books record **rare** plants and animals. This series of books gives data on different groups of plants and animals, for different countries and continents, and shows how rare they are. The Red Data Books recognize three levels of rarity, rare, vulnerable and endangered.
Many of the rare plants were listed in the Red Data Books.

reed *noun*

A reed is a type of **wetland** plant. Reeds are a kind of **grass** with tall stems and feathery flowers. They grow in waterlogged soils, around fens and marshes. They can also be found in shallow lakes and ponds. Reeds are sometimes harvested to provide thatch for houses. Reed pulp is used to make paper and cardboard. Rare marshland birds and flowers live amongst reeds.
The reserve had a large area of reed surrounding the lake.

branched burr-reed

great reedmace

refuge site *noun*

A refuge site is a kind of natural **habitat**. Refuge sites provide a home for many plants and animals which used to be found over a larger area. In the refuge site, the conditions have remained suitable for the species, which may have declined elsewhere through habitat loss or other changes.
The mountain forest was a refuge site for many rare species.

regeneration *noun*

Regeneration is the ability of a plant or animal to grow a new part to its body when part of it is injured or removed. Most plants can regenerate when **pruned** or injured. Many invertebrate animals can regenerate and, to a lesser extent, some vertebrates.
The tree soon began to regenerate new branches after it had been cut back.

crab loses claw in fight with predator

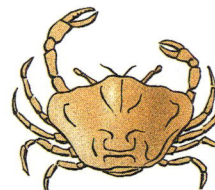

claw regenerates

regulation *noun*

Regulation describes a way of limiting the numbers or extent of something. In nature, the numbers of most **species** are regulated by predators, and by climate. Competition with other plants and animals also regulates numbers.
The pests caused a regulation in the number of weeds in the field.

remote sensing ► page 121

renewable resource *noun*

A renewable resource is a **resource** which replaces itself. The trees in a forest and the fish in the sea are two examples of renewable resources. Other kinds include solar energy, water and wind power. When biological resources are used too quickly, they do not have the time they need to renew themselves.
Everyone needs to use more renewable resources so as not to upset the balance of the planet.

remote sensing *noun*

Remote sensing is a method of collecting scientific data about the surface of the Earth and the atmosphere. Aerial photography from planes is one kind of remote sensing. Another kind uses satellites in orbit around the Earth. These satellites can record changes in the weather, and on the surface of the Earth.

The scientists recorded the loss of rain forest by remote sensing.

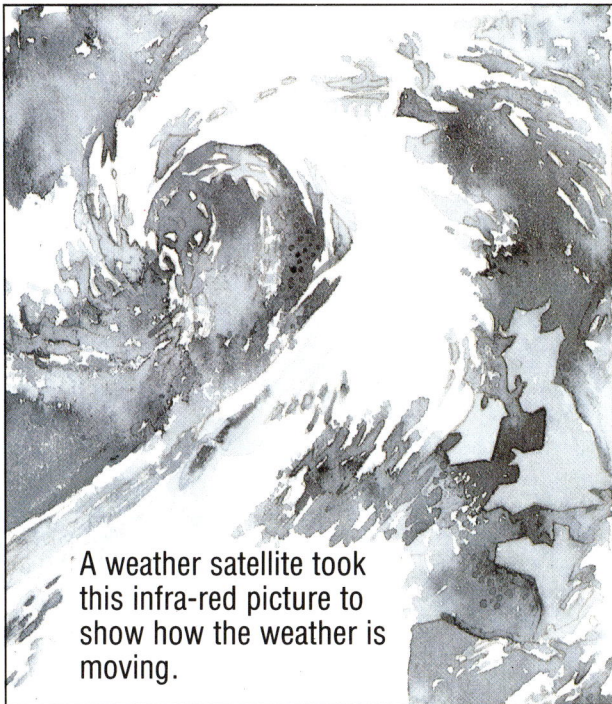

A weather satellite took this infra-red picture to show how the weather is moving.

High-altitude photographs, such as this one of San Franciscos, are taken on special film. They give very clear and detailed information.

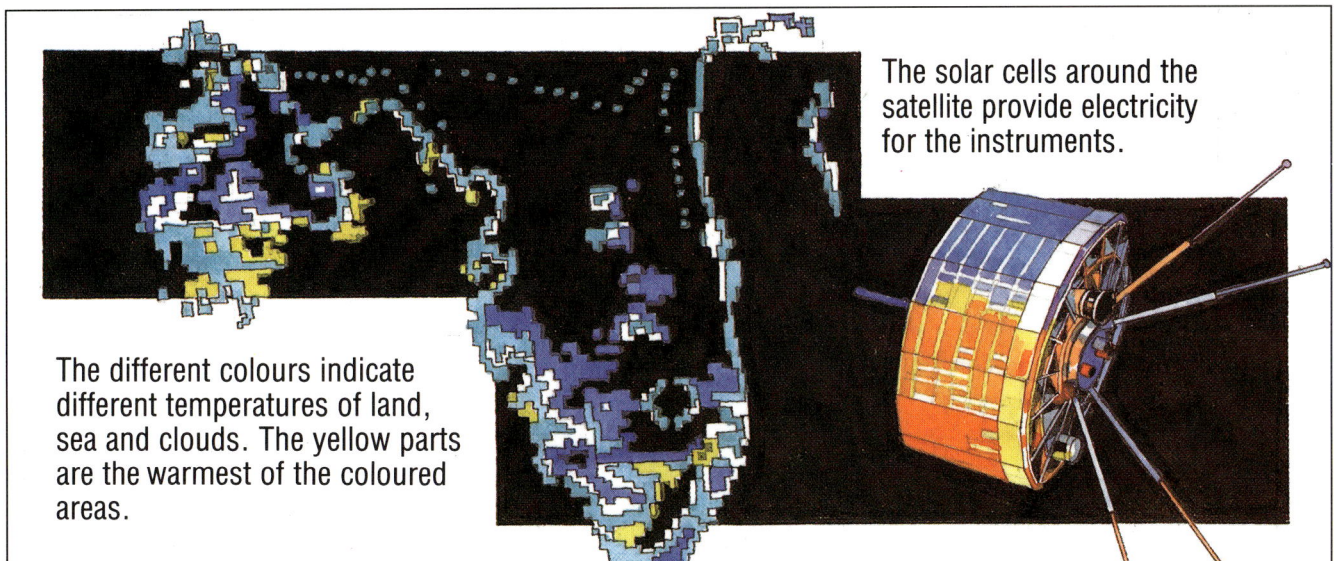

The different colours indicate different temperatures of land, sea and clouds. The yellow parts are the warmest of the coloured areas.

The solar cells around the satellite provide electricity for the instruments.

replant *verb*

To replant is to set up, or establish, new **habitats**, **plantations** or **crops**. When a forest is cut down, it is sometimes replanted with a mixture of suitable trees. Many areas of tropical rain forest that have been cut down, are now being replanted. Farmers replant their fields after harvesting a crop.

After the fire, they replanted the trees to grow a new wood.

reproduction *noun*

Reproduction is the process whereby living **organisms** make more organisms like themselves. Reproduction makes sure the **species** continues to **survive**. The two main kinds of reproduction are sexual and **asexual reproduction**. In **sexual reproduction**, the offspring are different from the parents because they take some **genes** from each parent. In asexual reproduction, the offspring are identical to the parents.

The weeds had a very rapid rate of reproduction.

research *noun*

Research is the work scientists do to make new discoveries. During scientific research, scientists test out ideas by doing carefully planned experiments and by analysing data. All major scientific advances depend upon thorough research.

The agricultural scientists directed their research into breeding new varieties of crops.

reserve *noun*

A reserve is an area of land set aside for **conservation**. Reserves vary in size from just a few square metres to thousands of square kilometres. They may be set up to protect particular **rare** plants or animals, or to conserve entire **habitats**. Some reserves include areas which can be visited by tourists, or which can be used by local people.

The estuary was such an unusual habitat that it was turned into a reserve.

reservoir *noun*

A reservoir is a large, artificial lake. Reservoirs are used for storing water, for supplying public drinking water or for irrigation. Most reservoirs are made by stopping a river at a dam.

He saw many interesting birds on the reservoir.

resin *noun*

A resin is a kind of chemical compound. Many trees and other plants produce natural resins, some of which smell sweet. Resins are brittle when solid and sticky when liquid. Artificial resins are used to make plastics and powerful adhesives.

The resin oozed slowly from the trunk of the tree.

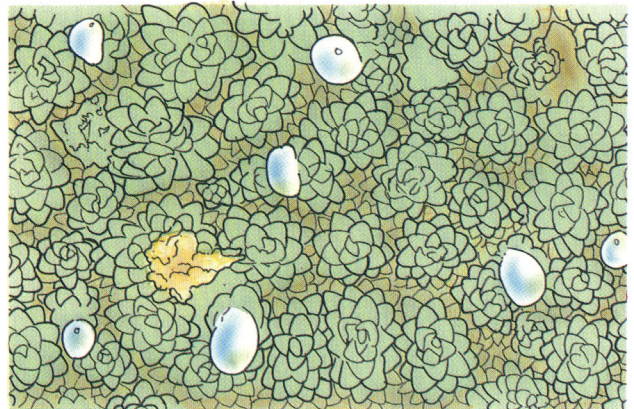

resource *noun*

1. A resource is any substance that living **organisms** need for their survival. Water, **oxygen**, **carbon dioxide**, minerals and **nutrients** are resources needed by animals and plants.

The plants died when the soil became depleted of its resources.

2. A resource is any substance of economic importance. Minerals, **fossil fuels**, **forests** and the energy of the wind, tides and Sun are all types of **natural resource**. Resources may be **renewable**, such as forests, or **non-renewable**, such as fossil fuels.

The factory used the oil from the nearby wells as its resource.

respiration *noun*

Respiration is the process by which living things make energy. During respiration in plants, **carbon dioxide** is taken in and used in the process of **photosynthesis**. Oxygen is given off.
The growing seeds began to use up carbon dioxide in respiration.

rhizome *noun*

A rhizome is part of a plant. It is a **stem** which grows under the ground, like a root. However, unlike roots, rhizomes grow horizontally. They branch and sprout upwards to form new stems above the surface. Some plants reproduce by sending out rhizomes that grow upwards and form new plants.
The bamboo spread quickly by sending out rhizomes.

stems

rhizome

roots

rice *noun*

Rice is a **cereal grain** produced by the rice plant, which belongs to the **grass** family. It is grown as a food crop in many tropical countries. Each plant produces several stems which grow heads called panicles.
A panicle can hold up to 150 grains of rice.

ripe *adjective*

Ripe describes a **fruit** which is fully grown and ready to **disperse** its **seeds**. In a ripe, edible fruit, the flesh is ready to eat and may be very sweet, juicy and full of flavour.
The cherries changed to a dark red colour when they were ripe.

river *noun*

A river is a large stream of flowing water. Rivers flow along in a channel. Rivers start at their source, which is often high up in the hills or mountains. They flow down towards the sea and are joined by smaller steams called tributaries as they go. The longest rivers are thousands of kilometres long. The Nile river in Africa is the longest river, flowing 6,671 kilometres.
Near the coast, the river was slow and very wide.

root *noun*

A root is part of a plant. Roots grow down into the soil and anchor the plant in the ground. They also absorb water and minerals from the soil and carry these to the rest of the plant. Some roots, such as beets and cassava, become swollen with stores of food. Some plants, such as **epiphytes**, have **aerial roots**.
When the tree blew down, he could see its roots.

root crop *noun*

A root crop is a **crop** that develops mainly under the ground. Examples of root crops are potatoes, turnips, yams and sugar beet. Potatoes are actually swollen, underground stems, but they are still called root crops. Many root crops have to be harvested by hand.
The fields nearby were planted with root crops.

carrots

beetroot

rosin *noun*

Rosin is a **resin** found in some varieties of North American and European **pine** trees. The three main types of rosin are gum rosin, wood rosin and sulphate rosin. They are used to make a large number of products, including paints, soaps, adhesives and varnishes.
Rosin is sometimes used on stage floors to help prevent people from slipping over.

rot *verb*

Rot describes how natural materials **decay**. When animals and plants die, their bodies rot in the soil. **Decomposers** in the soil break down the tissues and feed on them, turning them into smaller and smaller pieces. Eventually, the fully rotted **humus** mixes into the soil.
The dead leaves on the forest floor soon began to rot.

rubber *noun*

Rubber is a tropical tree. It is also a very important **natural resource** that is obtained from the milky **latex** of the rubber tree. The latex oozes from cuts made in the trunk of the trees. The rubber tree is native to Brazil, but Malaysia is now the largest rubber producer. Rubber can also be made synthetically from chemicals.
Rubber is water-resistant, it absorbs shock, and it springs back into shape if stretched.

runner *noun*

A runner is a kind of plant **stem** that creeps along the ground. Runners often form new plants at intervals along their length.
The strawberry plants spread by runners.

rural *adjective*

Rural describes something to do with the country. The rural landscape is made up of trees, woods and fields. Rural depopulation is the movement of people out of the country and into towns and cities.
Farming has an enormous effect on most rural landscapes.

rush *noun*

Rush is the name for a **family** of grass-like, flowering plants which grow in marshes and at the edge of ponds and streams. Rushes have round stems and straight leaves, and their flowers are green or brown. Stalks from rush plants are widely used in basketwork. The **pith** can be used as a wick for candles called rushlights.
The basket was made from rushes.

rye *noun*

Rye is a **cereal grain** and a major, worldwide food crop. It belongs to the **grass** family, and is grown in Northern Europe, Asia and North America. The plants grow to between one and two metres in height. Rye plants are similar to wheat, with stalks which end in two or more spikes or ears of grain that are covered with stiff hairs. The seed grains grow in pairs. Most of the world's rye is used to make flour for bread.
Rye bread is also called black bread because it is dark in colour.

S

Sahel ▶ page 126

salt marsh *noun*
A salt marsh is an area of wet ground near the coast which is occasionally flooded by the sea. Only specially adapted plants can grow on a salt marsh. These plants are called **halophytes**.
The salt marsh attracted many interesting birds.

salt water *noun*
Salt water is water which contains a high level of dissolved salts. It tastes salty, and only certain kinds of plants and animals can live in it. The oceans and seas, and some inland lakes contain salt water.
The children knew they were near to the sea because the river contained salt water.

sand *noun*
Sand is a loose collection of tiny grains of rock, such as quartz. Sand is often found at the coast, where the waves bring it up onto the shore to form a beach.
Sand can be added to heavy garden soil to improve drainage.

sap *noun*
Sap is the liquid that moves through plants. Sap contains a solution of **mineral salts** and sugars that are used by the plant. Some saps contain substances useful to people. For example, **maple** syrup is prepared from the sap of the sugar maple and **latex** comes from the rubber tree.
In the spring, the sap rose through the trees and their leaves came out.

sapling *noun*
A sapling is a young tree. When an area is planted as part of an **afforestation** scheme, saplings grow up quite close together. They are thinned to allow room for them to grow as they mature. Saplings may need to be supported by stakes to stop the wind from blowing them over.
The pine saplings grew straight and tall and were cut for timber.

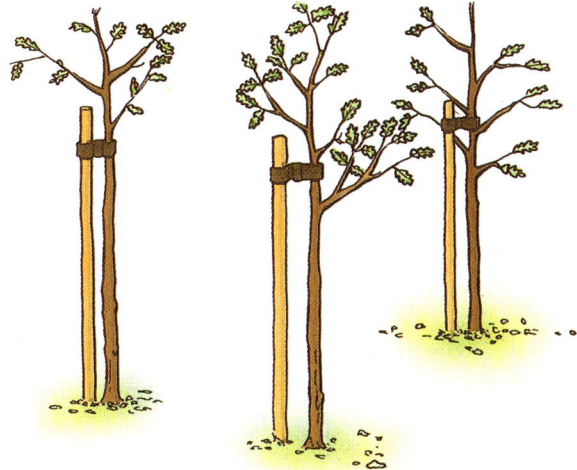

saprophyte *noun*
A saprophyte is a plant or other **organism** which gets its food from dead or decaying **organic** matter. Saprophytes live by breaking down the cells of their **hosts** to obtain energy for growth and reproduction. Some plants, fungi and bacteria are saprophytes.
Saprophytes play a very important part in the carbon and nitrogen cycles of nature.

sapwood *noun*
Sapwood is the wood that grows just under the bark of trees. It is the wood that grows nearest to the **cambium**. Sapwood contains living cells which transport water and sap up and down the tree. Sapwood is paler and softer than **heartwood** and decays more easily.
After the trees were felled, the timber was left until the sapwood had properly dried out.

Sahel *noun*

The Sahel is an area of dry country in North Africa. It lies around the southern edge of the Sahara. In the Sahel, the **vegetation** is between desert and **savanna**. The rainfall is irregular, with long periods of **drought**. People living in the Sahel find it difficult to grow crops, and famines are common there. *The travellers drove right across the Sahel from the Red Sea to Senegal.*

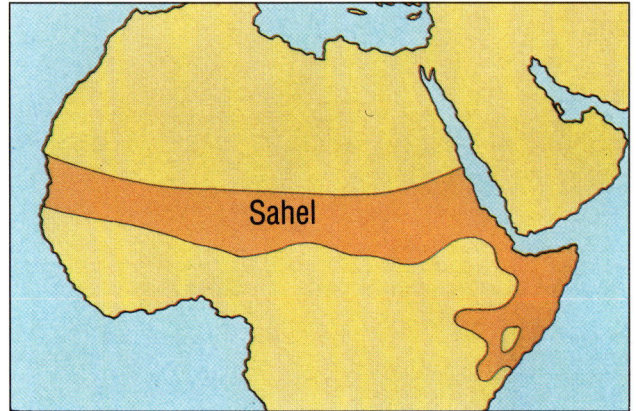
Sahel

Parts of the Sahel can support a small number of people and their animals.

But when the population increases, the land may be over-grazed and over-cultivated.

Winds from the Sahara blow away the dry soil and cover the land with sand.

A swarm of locusts can strip a crop with incredible speed, leaving the soil exposed to erosion.

If rain falls on a very dry area of desert, it may wash away what remains of the soil.

savanna *noun*
Savanna is a kind of dry, lowland plain. A savanna has patches of **grassland**, with scattered bushes and trees. Large savannas are found in the tropics and lie between **deserts** and **rain forests**. They are found in regions that have rainy seasons and dry seasons. Savannas cover more than two-fifths of Africa, and large areas of India, South America and Australia.
Grass on the driest savannas only grows a few centimetres high.

saxifrage *noun*
Saxifrage is a **family** of flowering plants. Scientists know of about 30 **genera**, which grow in cold and temperate regions of the northern hemisphere. Some saxifrages grow to almost one metre in height, but others creep along the ground. They have thick leaves and long flower stalks. The flowers usually grow in clusters, and vary in colour from white and yellow to pink and purple.
The gooseberry is a member of the saxifrage family.

scent ▶ **perfume**

sclerophyllous *adjective*
Sclerophyllous describes a plant that has tough, waterproof **leaves**. These help the plant to resist drought, as little water is lost through them. Sclerophyllous plants grow in hot, dry areas. They are usually **evergreens**, and the leaves have a thick, waxy coating, made up of thick-walled cells with few air spaces between them.
All the plants in the desert region were sclerophyllous.

scrubland *noun*
Scrubland is the name for a habitat with many small bushes. Sometimes, scrub grows up after forests have been removed. Other types of scrub grow where there is not enough rainfall to support tree growth.
They travelled through miles of scrubland to reach the river.

sea water *noun*
Sea water is the water found in oceans and seas. It covers more than 70 per cent of the Earth's surface. Sea water plays an important part in the Earth's climate, because it provides the moisture for rainfall. Sea water is a solution of dissolved salts, traces of other natural elements and dissolved gases.
Sea water makes up about 97 per cent of the Earth's water.

seashore *noun*
The seashore is the area where sea meets land. The three main types of seashore are rocky shores, muddy shores and sandy shores. Many animals and plants thrive on the seashore. Different species **adapt** to living on different parts of the seashore, depending on how long the area remains submerged under a high tide.
Some varieties of lichen and algae thrive on the seashore.

season ▶ page 128

seaweed *noun*
Seaweed is an **alga** that grows in water. There are about 7,000 species of seaweed. All seaweeds need light for **photosynthesis**, so they do not grow where the light cannot reach them. Seaweeds do not have stems, leaves, flowers or true roots. They are anchored to rocks or other objects by a root-like part.
Many seaweeds are rich in vitamins and minerals and are used as food.

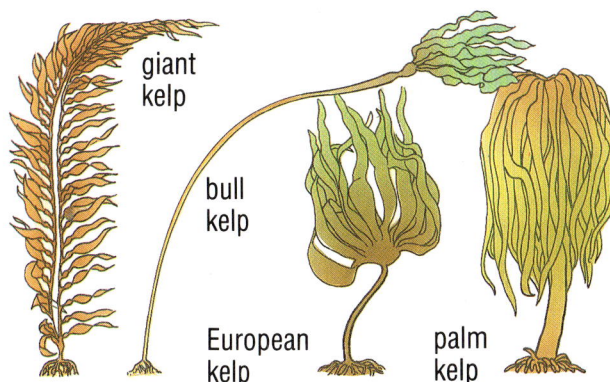

giant kelp

bull kelp

European kelp

palm kelp

season *noun*

A season is a part of the year that has a particular **climate**. In **temperate** regions, there are four seasons. These are spring, summer, autumn and winter. The four seasons vary in temperature and **rainfall**. In **tropical** regions, there are usually two seasons. These are the hot, dry season and the hot, rainy season.

In temperate regions, spring and summer are the growing seasons.

The Earth turns on its axis once every 24 hours. It takes one year to go round, or orbit, the Sun.

In December, the South Pole is tilted towards the Sun. Regions in the southern hemisphere have more than 12 hours of daylight.

For a few days around June 21, the Arctic Circle has continuous sunlight, known as the Midnight Sun. When the Earth turns, the rest of the Earth has dark nights as usual, but the Arctic Circle stays in sunlight.

In September, the Earth is sideways on to the Sun. The days and nights are the same length.

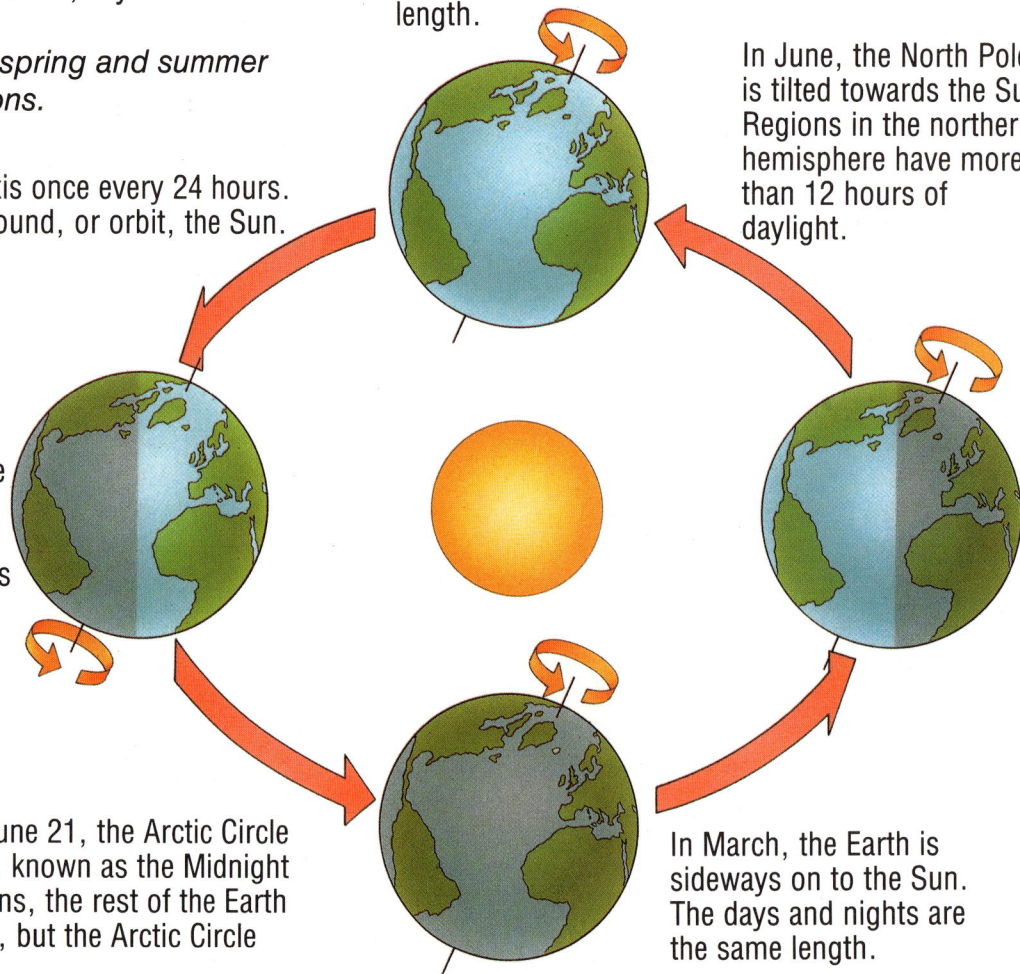

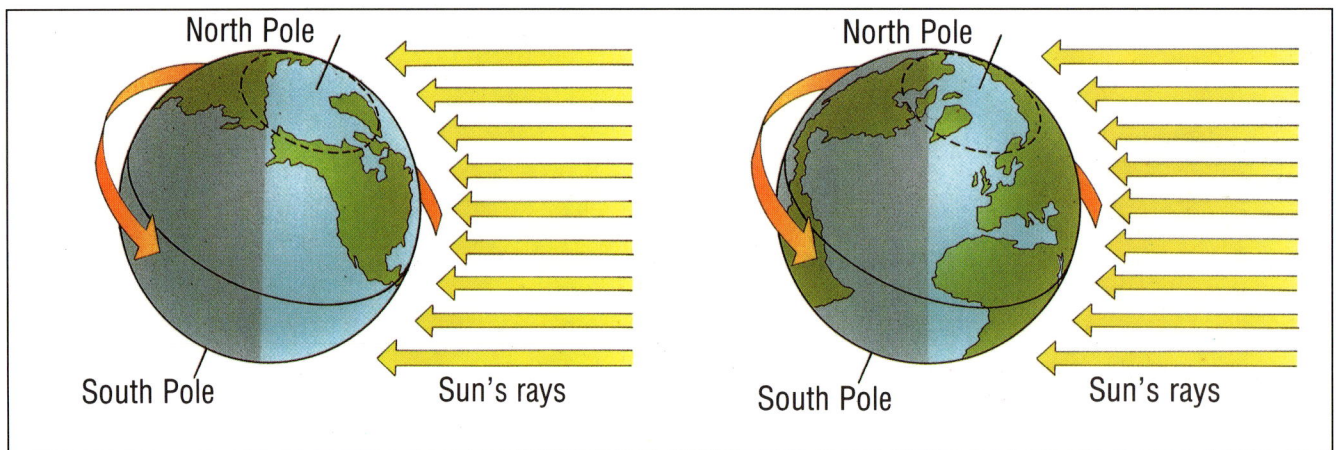

In June, the North Pole is tilted towards the Sun. Regions in the northern hemisphere have more than 12 hours of daylight.

In March, the Earth is sideways on to the Sun. The days and nights are the same length.

North Pole

South Pole

Sun's rays

North Pole

South Pole

Sun's rays

secondary forest　*noun*

Secondary forest is forest that replaces **primary forest** after primary forest is cleared. If the disturbance has been relatively small, the species in the secondary forest gradually give way to primary forest species.

After the land became exhausted, the farmers moved on, and secondary forest soon grew up.

secondary root　*noun*

Secondary roots are roots which grow out of the main, **primary root** of a plant. Secondary roots branch out over a wide area and take in water.

When the gardener dug up the shrubs, he was careful to include all the secondary roots.

sedge　*noun*

Sedge is a family of grass-like plants. Sedges grow throughout the world in wet regions. Sedges look like **grasses**, but are different in some important respects. Their **stems** are solid and usually triangular or round. The sheath at the base of sedge leaves is closed around the stem, while the sheath round a grass leaf is split and overlaps. Sedges bear small flowers that do not have petals.

The sedge called papyrus was used by the Ancient Egyptians to make paper.

seed　▶ page 130

seed dispersal　▶ dispersal

seed pod　▶ pod

seedling　*noun*

A seedling is a small plant which grows from a **seed**. When gardeners grow plants from seed, they often sow a lot of seeds together and choose the healthiest seedlings to carry on growing.

We planted out the tomato seedlings once there was no more danger of frosts.

self-pollination　*noun*

Self-pollination of a plant happens when the **pollen** from the **anther** is transferred to the **stigma** of another **flower** on the same plant.

In self-pollination, only one plant is needed to produce seed.

sensitive　*adjective*

Sensitive describes an organism which reacts to something. All plants and animals are sensitive to their **environments**. Some plants are sensitive to touch, and their leaves close when they are touched. They are often called sensitive plants.

The Venus's fly trap closed up when the fly touched its sensitive hairs.

sepal　*noun*

A sepal is a kind of **leaf**. Sepals grow just outside the **petals** of a **flower**. They are usually green. Sepals form the **calyx**, the outer ring of the flower. They protect the flower bud. Sometimes sepals are the same colour and look the same as the petals.

The rose sepals opened in the warm weather.

sexual reproduction　*noun*

Sexual reproduction is the process where a male and a female cell join together to produce an offspring. Organisms produced by sexual reproduction are not identical with either parent, but share some of the characteristics of both.

The plants produced seeds by sexual reproduction.

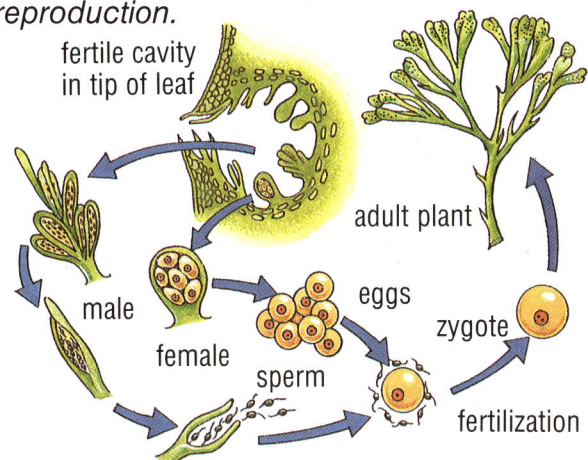

fertile cavity in tip of leaf

adult plant

male

female

eggs

sperm

zygote

fertilization

seed *noun*
A seed is a structure which plants produce when they **reproduce**. The seed contains the fertilized **ovule**, which grows into the **embryo** of a new plant. With enough warmth and moisture, the seed **germinates** and begins to sprout. Each seed has a store of food, to feed the **seedling** as it grows. Some seeds are light and blow about. Some may have wings to twirl in the wind. Other seeds are found inside fleshy fruits.
The seed soon began to sprout in the damp soil.

A sunflower seed falls onto fertile soil. When the conditions are right and it has warmth, light and moisture, the seed will start to germinate.

seed

After fertilization, new seeds develop at the centre of the flower. These are scattered by the wind when they are ripe, and the process begins again.

130

The first part of a seed to start growing is the root, or radicle. It always grows downwards into the soil.

The next part to grow is the plumule. It pushes up towards the light. Wrapped tight around the tip of the plumule can be seen two tiny leaves.

The stem of the seedling lengthens, and two pairs of leaves unfold as it grows. The root system is becoming longer and stronger.

A bright yellow flower grows at the top of a tall stem. At the flower's centre is a mass of velvety stamens.

sharecropping noun

Sharecropping is a kind of farming. In sharecropping, the farmer working a piece of land gives the owner of that land part of what he produces, as rent. The owner usually provides the equipment and the tenant provides the labour.
Sharecropping is a common form of farming in the poorer countries of the world.

shelter belt noun

A shelter belt is a row of trees planted as a **windbreak**. Shelter belts reduce soil **erosion** and protect crops. The effectiveness of a shelter belt depends on the height, thickness and shape of the group of trees. Poplars grow quickly and make good shelter belts.
The farmer noticed that his crops were better once the shelter belt had grown up.

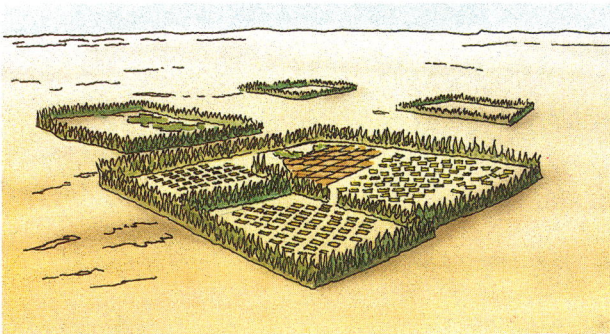

shifting cultivation ▶ page 133

shoot noun

A shoot is the first part of a plant to appear above the ground. It develops from the **seed** and grows upwards towards the light. Fresh growth from the buds of a tree or shrub are also called shoots.
The first sign of spring was the appearance of shoots in the forest.

shrub noun

A shrub is a kind of plant. Shrubs have woody stems, but they are smaller than trees. Unlike trees, most shrubs do not have a single main trunk. Shrubs grow underneath the tree-layer in a wood.
Shrubs make popular garden plants.

silage noun

Silage is green **fodder** which is used to feed cattle. Silage is made from plants such as legumes, grasses, kale and rape. The plants are compressed in special pits or silos to squeeze out the air. The plants ferment and turn into silage.
Silage is very nutritious and it can be stored for many months.

silica noun

Silica is a chemical element contained in the **cell wall** of **diatoms** and **horsetail** stems.
The silica in the wall of a diatom is transparent.

silviculture noun

Silviculture is a kind of **forestry**. In silviculture, trees are grown and harvested to provide a continuous crop. Foresters plant different species of tree to suit the climate and soil conditions in the area.
Silviculture is a modern development in forestry.

simple fruit noun

A simple fruit is a **fruit** belonging to one of the two main groups of fruit. The other group is **compound fruit**. A simple fruit is one that develops from a single **carpel**, or two or more carpels of the same flower. Simple fruits may be fleshy, such as peaches and grapes, or dry, such as nuts and grains.
Nearly all the members of the grass family bear dry simple fruits.

simple leaf noun

A simple leaf is a leaf which is not divided or lobed. Divided leaves are known as **compound leaves**. Beech is an example of a tree with simple leaves. In many simple leaves, the midrib is a continuation of the leaf stalk, or **petiole**. Simple and compound leaves are sometimes found on the same branch of a plant, though some species of plants only bear simple leaves.
The children drew privet leaves as examples of simple leaves.

shifting cultivation *noun*

Shifting cultivation is a kind of farming in which a piece of land is worked for crops and then left **fallow**. The fallow period is longer than the cultivated one. After it, the land can be worked again. Shifting cultivation allows the nutrients in the soil to build up again. The site is often first cleared by felling the trees and burning the wood.

The forest people practised shifting cultivation by clearing small areas of forest each year.

Crops fail if the land has become exhausted through over-use.

Many people slash-and-burn areas of forest so that they can use the land for cultivation.

A four-year crop rotation makes sure that the land stays fertile.

slash-and-burn cultivation *noun*
Slash-and-burn cultivation is a kind of farming. It involves first cutting and burning the natural **vegetation**. The ash from the wood adds **nutrients** to the soil. Crops are then planted in the fertile soil. When the soil becomes less fertile, the farmers move on and slash and burn a new area.
Slash-and-burn cultivation is most common in tropical countries, especially in tropical forests.

snow-line *noun*
The snow-line is the level on a hill or mountain above which there is always snow lying on the ground. The height of the snow-line varies with latitude and climate. It also depends upon the direction of the wind.
Mosses and lichen grow close to the snow-line.

society *noun*
A society is a **community** of **organisms**. The members of animal societies live in co-operation with each other. In some insect societies, the members of the community have different functions within the society. A plant society is a community of plants, with many **species** mixed together.
The study of plant and animal societies is part of the study of ecology.

softwood *noun*
Softwood is the wood of **conifers**. Conifers grown for their wood include pines and cedars. Softwood is particularly suitable for making paper and for carpentry. Wooden houses are often clad on the outside with the softwood from the American red cedar tree.
He used softwood to make the frame for the cupboard.

soil *noun*
Soil is the loose layers of earth which lie over the solid rock on the Earth's surface. Soil is a mixture of small pieces of rocks, minerals and **humus**.
Most plants need soil in order to grow.

sow *verb*
To sow is to plant small seeds. It is usual to sow seeds in straight lines to make the best use of the available space when a crop is grown. Seeds can also be sown by walking across a field and scattering them by hand.
The farmer sowed his barley in the spring.

soya bean *noun*
The soya bean is a **legume** that is grown mostly in the United States of America, Brazil and China. The mature soya bean plant is from 60 to 120 centimetres high. Close to the stem it bears a number of **pods**, each of which contains two or three beans. These soya beans are an excellent source of **protein** and form a staple part of the diet of many people and animals all over the world.
Soya beans can be processed into oil, flour, sauce and many other products.

species (plural **species**) *noun*
A species is a group of living things. Members of the same species can breed together and produce fertile offspring. The species is the basic unit in the scientific classification system. Each species is given a double Latin name. The first part of the name is the **genus**, and both names together indicate the species.
The Norway spruce and the Sitka spruce are two different species in the same genus.

specimen *noun*
A specimen is an example of something. A botanist may collect specimens of plants.
The boy collected a specimen of leaves from the wood.

134

sperm *noun*
Sperm are the sex cells of a male plant or animal. When animals reproduce, the male's sperm meet eggs of the female. A sperm joins with an egg cell in the process of fertilization. A new baby plant or animal may then develop from the fertilized egg.
The fish released its sperm into the water.

sphenophyte *noun*
A sphenophyte is a kind of primitive plant. Most sphenophytes are extinct. The only existing members of the **class** are the **horsetails**.
Fossil sphenophytes have been found dating from about 395 million years ago.

spice *noun*
A spice is food flavouring that is made from plants. Many spices are strong tasting, such as pepper and ginger. Often, the hard parts of the plant, such as the seeds or the fruit, are used as spices, but some flower buds, roots and stems may also be used as spices. Cardamom and nutmeg are both examples of spices.
The cook added spices to the cake to make it taste better.

spiderwort *noun*
Spiderworts are a family of flowering plants. They grow mostly in **tropical** regions. Many spiderworts have grass-like leaves, which may be striped. Their flowers are blue, white or purple. The flowers are very fragile and may turn into watery jelly. Some kinds of spiderwort grow upright and some creep along the ground. Spiderworts are **perennial**.
The wandering jew is an example of a creeping spiderwort.

spike *noun*
A spike is a kind of **flower**. In a spike, there are many small flowers growing together on a single main stalk. Grasses such as wheat carry their flowers in spikes.
The spikes of barley grew tall in the field.

spine *noun*
A spine is a sharp, pointed structure on the stems of some plants. Spines are modified leaves or stems, and they are usually hard and woody. Roses, brambles, thistles and cacti are all plants with spines.
Spines help to protect a plant from being eaten by grazing animals.

spines

sporangia (singular **sporangium**) *noun*
Sporangia are the structures in which **spores** are produced in some plants. They are found in **fungi** and **algae**, and in **mosses** and ferns.
The sporangia of the ripe toadstool opened.

spore *noun*
A spore is a small reproductive body that can grow into a new organism. Spores are produced by some plants, including **fungi**, **algae**, **mosses** and **ferns**, as well as by **bacteria** and **protozoa**. They are often produced in very great numbers and spread long distances by wind, water or animals. Some spores have thick walls which enable them to survive cold or harsh conditions.
They identified the spores in the soil sample.

sporophyte *noun*
The sporophyte is a stage in the lifestyle of some plants. Plants reproduce in two stages, the asexual and the sexual stage. During the sexual stage, a fertilized egg develops into a sporophyte. The sporophyte produces **spores**, which then develop into **gametophytes**. These produce egg and sperm cells ready for fertilization.
The botanist explained that the fern was the sporophyte part of the life cycle.

sprout *verb*

To sprout is to begin to grow. A plant sprouts when it puts out new leaves in the spring, or when a bud appears above the ground.
The buds sprouted as the days grew warmer, and produced large, green leaves.

spruce *noun*

A spruce is a pyramid-shaped tree that belongs to the **pine** family. There are about 50 species of spruce. They grow widely in the cooler areas of the northern hemisphere. Spruce trees are **evergreen conifers**. The egg-shaped spruce **cones** hang down from the branches. The scales remain on the cones, without falling off as the cone ripens.
Some of the best pulp for paper-making is obtained from spruce trees.

stalk *noun*

The stalk is the stem of a plant. Stalks support the leaves and the flowers. Food and water are carried to all parts of the plant through the stalks.
The long, thin stalks of the grasses bent in the wind.

stamen *noun*

The stamen is the male reproductive part of the flower. A stamen has two main parts, the stalk or **filament**, and the **anther**. The stamens carry the **pollen**. Pollen is taken from the stamens to the female reproductive part of the same or another flower, to produce seed.
The lilies had bright orange stamens which showed up against the white petals.

starch *noun*

Starch is a chemical stored by plants. It is a **carbohydrate** which is found in granules in plant cells. Starch is made from carbon dioxide and water in sunlight. It breaks down to give sugars which are used for growth and energy. Some plants store starch in their leaves, and others in stems or roots.
Potatoes are an example of a good source of starch.

statistics *noun*

Statistics are collections of data. Biologists collect statistics about the numbers of animals or plants. They then use these statistics to learn about animals and plants. Statistics may be the numbers of certain species, or information relating to any aspects of the organisms.
We collected statistics about the numbers of trees in the wood.

stem *noun*

The stem is the main support of a plant. The stem carries leaves and buds, and flowers, often on short stalks. Food and water is carried through the stems of plants. Some stems run underground, and are called **rhizomes**.
The arum lily grew such a large flower that the stem bent under the weight.

steppe *noun*

A steppe is a dry, grassy plain without trees. Steppes are found in climates which are too dry for trees to grow, such as in southern Russia. Steppe soils are deep and fertile. Steppes are called **prairies** in North America.
The grassland stretched for miles across the steppe.

sterile *adjective*

A sterile organism is one which cannot reproduce. Environments are also said to be sterile when there are no living organisms in them.
The sterile plant was propagated by a vegetative method.

stigma noun
The stigma is part of a **flower**. It is part of the female reproductive system of the flower. The sticky stigma catches and traps **pollen** from the **anthers** of another flower.
The bee touched the stigma and placed pollen on it as it drank the nectar.

stipule noun
A stipule is a small, leaf-like structure. Stipules are found on either side of the leaf-stalk in many plants. Their function is to protect the bud.
Although it was a frosty night, the buds were protected from damage by the stipules.

stock noun
The stock is the main part of a plant onto which a part of another plant can be grafted. A stock is usually the roots and a section of stem growing from it. Many fruit trees are grown on stocks.
The vines were grown on old root stocks.

stoma (plural **stomata**) noun
A stoma is a small hole in the epidermis of a leaf. Every leaf has many stomata. The stomata close in dry conditions to prevent the plant from drying out. They open again when it is damp, to allow gas exchange between the plant and the atmosphere.
She saw the stomata on the undersides of the leaves.

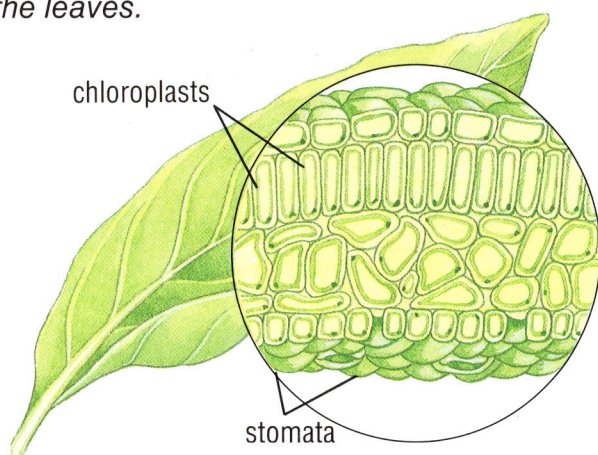

chloroplasts

stomata

strange plants ▶ page 138

style noun
The style is part of the female reproductive system of a **flower**. The style is a stalk which connects the **stigma** to the **ovary**. The style may help in **seed dispersal**.
At the centre of the flower we could see the long style.

subsistence farming noun
Subsistence farming is the ability to produce just enough food. Subsistence farmers can mostly support themselves, but do not have enough produce to sell. Subsistence farming is most common in the developing countries.
The local people relied upon subsistence farming.

sub-tropical adjective
Sub-tropical describes a region just to the north or south of the tropics which are near the equator. In the sub-tropical region, the climate is less hot than in the tropics, but warmer than in the **temperate** regions.
There was no danger from frost in the sub-tropical climate.

succession ▶ page 140

succulent noun
Succulent describes a plant that has thick, fleshy cells that store water. Some succulents, such as **cacti**, store water in their stem. Others store it in their large leaves. Many succulents have deep or broad root systems.
Succulents grow in deserts and places with little rainfall.
succulent *adjective*

strange plants *noun*

Strange plants are plants with special features that make them unusual in some way. Plants vary greatly in size and appearance. The largest living thing in the world is a plant. It is the giant sequoia tree of California in the United States of America. It can reach a height of 88 metres. The oldest plants on Earth are also found in the USA. They are the bristlecone pines, some of which are more than 5,000 years old.
The smallest flowering plant in the world is the duckweed.

The traveller's-tree of Madagascar got its name because it has a store of water at the base of each leaf stalk. Travellers could quench their thirst from the water stores.

The curious, dangling fruits of the sausage tree may weigh up to seven kilograms. They are used in Central Africa in medicine and magic.

The baobab tree of Africa has a huge, swollen trunk. People hollow out the trunk to live in or to store water in. They eat the baobab's fruit, seeds, roots and leaves.

Mistletoe is a plant parasite that grows on trees and feeds off them.

The night-blooming cereus is a climbing cactus. Its white flowers open only at night.

The fly orchid of Europe has central petals that look exactly like a fly settled on the flower.

The rafflesia is the largest flower in the world. It has a smell like rotting meat to attract insects.

Chlamydomonas is a tiny plant that lives in water. It can swim, using its whip-like tails, or flagella.

As its name suggests, the strangler fig eventually kills the tree it grows on.

succession *noun*

A succession is a sequence of vegetation. In a succession, the species change gradually. An example of a succession is the gradual change from grassland, through scrub to woodland. Each succession ends with a stable **community**, called a **climax community**. On rich, lowland soils, the end of the succession is often woodland of some kind.

As the forest regenerated after the timber was felled, the botanists studied the succession.

1. A shallow lake may turn into a bog in the process of succession.

2. The first plants to grow are mosses, which gradually cover the water with a spongy blanket. Peat forms below the blanket when the mosses die.

3. Other plants start to grow in the bog, such as sedges and insectivorous plants. A few trees, such as the black spruce and white pine, may also grow there.

1. After a forest fire, the land will become forested again by succession. First, small birch saplings push up through the burnt soil.

2. The deciduous birch trees are the first trees to thrive in the new forest.

3. After about 60 years, the birch trees give way to pines.

4. In another 150 years or so, spruce trees gradually take over from the pines.

sucker noun
A sucker is a branch or stem which grows under or along the ground from a plant, and then forms a new plant. The sucker develops its own leaves and roots to allow it to live on its own. Many plants spread **vegetatively** by suckers.
The strawberry plants produced lots of suckers.

sucrose noun
Sucrose is a chemical compound. It is a kind of **sugar**. Sucrose is made by plants and stored in their cells. Some kinds of plant, such as **sugar cane** and **sugar beet**, produce large amounts of sucrose.
They harvested the sugar cane to extract the sucrose.

sugar noun
Sugar is a simple **carbohydrate**. It is formed in plants from carbon dioxide and water in the light, by **photosynthesis**.
All green plants produce sugar, though it does not always taste sweet.

sugar beet noun
Sugar beet is a plant that grows in temperate regions. Above ground, it has a cluster of dark green leaves. Below ground is a swollen **root** that contains a high level of **sugar**. Sugar beet is widely **cultivated** for the production of sugar.
Sugar beet used to be fed to animals before efficient sugar processing was developed.

sugar cane noun
Sugar cane is a tall plant that belongs to the **grass** family. It grows in tropical and semi-tropical areas of the world where the rainfall is high. The woody stem grows from two to five metres high. It contains a large amount of sugary **sap**. The stems are harvested to obtain the sugar.
He chewed a section of sugar cane.

sulphur dioxide noun
Sulphur dioxide is a poisonous gas. It is made when chemicals containing sulphur are burned. Smoke from chimneys often contains sulphur dioxide. It is one of the causes of **acid rain**.
The trees were badly damaged by the sulphur dioxide emissions from the factory.

sunlight noun
Sunlight is the light which reaches the Earth from the Sun. All life on Earth depends upon sunlight. Plants need sunlight to make their food by **photosynthesis**. The animals which feed on the plants also depend on sunlight.
The green plants needed the sunlight to survive.

survive verb
To survive is to continue living. It is important that a range of **species** continues to survive on the Earth. But it is sometimes difficult to ensure the survival of **endangered species** which may be threatened by human activity.
The birds could not survive the long winter.
survival noun

sustainable adjective
Sustainable describes something which can continue to be produced, without using up the supply. An example of a sustainable, or **renewable, resource** is **timber** from forests which are replanted. **Fossil fuels** are not sustainable because they are being used up and not replaced. Conservation involves the sustainable use of natural products.
The foresters made sure of a sustainable supply of wood by planting new trees.

swamp *noun*

A swamp is a kind of **wetland**. In a swamp, the water level is high, so that the plants growing in it are always waterlogged.
They got very wet as they trudged through the swamp.

sycamore *noun*

Sycamore is a deciduous **tree**. It is a kind of **maple**. In North America, some plane trees are called sycamores. Sycamore wood is useful for making furniture, musical instruments, and also for kitchen utensils. The fruits of the sycamore tree are winged. They twirl in the wind as they drop to the ground.
The children ran to catch the sycamore fruits.

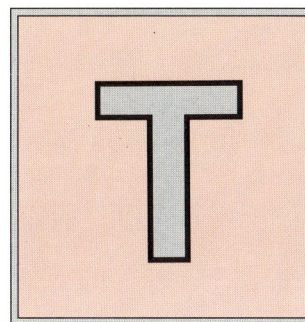

T

taiga ▶ **boreal forest**

tap root *noun*

A tap root is part of a plant. It is the name for the main root. The tap root is the largest root, and it often grows a long way down into the soil. Many **biennial** plants have swollen tap roots which contain stores of food, such as starch and sugars.
He tugged at the carrot and pulled up the large tap root.

tea *noun*

Tea is a **family** of plants. It is also the name of one **species** of plant from which the drink tea is obtained. The tea plant is an **evergreen shrub** grown mainly in India and China. The wild tea plant can reach a height of nine metres. Under **cultivation**, tea is kept to about one metre high. It has fragrant, white flowers with a yellow centre. The leaves of the tea plant are picked and dried. The drink is made by pouring boiling water on the leaves.
The tea plant grows quickly where the air is warm, and more slowly where the air is cool.

teak *noun*

A teak is a **hardwood** tree that grows in the tropical forests of South-east Asia. During the dry season, the tree loses its leaves. New leaves grow when the rainy season starts. The timber has a pleasant smell. It is very durable, and water-resistant. Teak wood is valued for ship-building and making fine furniture.
Mature teak trees grow to a height of about 45 metres.

143

temperate *adjective*
Temperate describes a region or climate which is neither very hot nor very cold. The temperate zones lie between the tropics and the polar regions.
Broadleaf trees grow well in temperate climates.

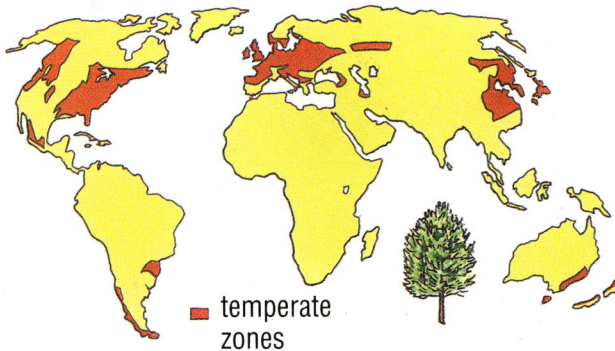
temperate zones

tendril *noun*
A tendril is part of a plant. It is a specialized kind of stem, leaf or flower which twists as it grows. **Climbing plants** use tendrils to help them get a grip as they grow.
Plants with tendrils include the grape vine and the Virginia creeper.

terminal bud *noun*
A terminal bud is a bud at the end of a stem or twig.
Each branch grew from the terminal bud.

terrace farming *noun*
Terrace farming is a method of using the land on a hillside. The slope is divided into narrow strips, or terraces, of flat land.
Terrace farming makes the land easier to work.

terrain *noun*
Terrain is the surface of a landscape or area of country. In a flat terrain, the surface is level, but in hilly terrain it is steep.
They crossed the rocky terrain.

terrarium (plural **terraria**) *noun*
A terrarium is a tank for keeping plants and small animals. It consists of a glass tank with a small layer of soil in the bottom and perhaps some rocks and plants as well. Some terraria also have an area of water.
He kept the snakes in a terrarium.

thermal pollution *noun*
Thermal pollution is the release of heat into the **environment**. Nuclear power stations affect nearby sea water with thermal pollution. Houses and factories also heat up the environment, so that most cities are warmer than the surrounding countryside. Warm water entering a river or lake can cause changes to the animals and plants which live there.
The vegetation of the lake changed because of the thermal pollution.

thorn *noun*
A thorn is a sharp **spine** on a plant. Thorns are usually found on the stems and twigs of some bushes and trees. They are woody and hard and sometimes quite dangerous. Examples of plants with thorns are roses, hawthorn, blackthorn and acacias.
Thorns help protect the plant from grazing by animals.

thorns

threat *noun*
A threat is any kind of danger. Threats to habitats and rare animals and plants include **pollution**, land use change and hunting. There are also threats to the global **environment**, such as the increasing **greenhouse effect** and the destruction of the **ozone layer**.
Pollution from the new factory posed a serious threat to the nearby estuary.

tiller *noun*
A tiller is a kind of **shoot**. Tillers are shoots which grow after a plant has been cut or injured. Tillers grow from the base of a stem. Some plants, such as some grasses, produce tillers naturally.
The shrub sent out tillers after it had been pruned.

timber *noun*
Timber is the wood harvested from trees. **Coniferous** trees such as pine and spruce produce **softwood** timber. This is used for building houses and frames. **Hardwood** timber comes from broadleaf trees like oak, ash and walnut. This kind of timber is used to make furniture.
The plantation was cut regularly to supply timber.

tissue *noun*
Tissue is a collection of animal or plant cells. Examples of plant tissues are the meristem, the xylem and the phloem. Each group of cells in tissue is specialized to do a particular job.
Under the microscope, the xylem tissue was stained red.

tobacco *noun*
Tobacco is a plant grown as a **crop**. The leaves of the tobacco plant are dried and used to make cigarettes and pipe tobacco. Some kinds of tobacco plant are also grown in gardens for their pretty, scented flowers.
The southern states of the USA grow a lot of tobacco.

topsoil *noun*
Topsoil is the uppermost layer of the **soil**. The topsoil is the richest part of the soil, as it contains the most **humus**. It is a very important **natural resource** and can take hundreds of years to develop. The soil below the topsoil is called the subsoil.
The gardener dug over the topsoil before planting the seeds.

toxic *adjective*
Toxic describes something which is poisonous. Many chemicals are toxic to animals and plants. Pollution from chemical factories sometimes releases toxic chemicals into the environment.
The birds failed to breed because they had eaten toxic chemicals.
toxin *noun*

transpiration *noun*
Transpiration is the loss of water vapour from the **leaves** of a plant. Transpiration takes place largely through tiny holes in the leaves called **stomata**. Most leaves have stomata, especially on their undersides.
The plants began to wilt as they lost water through transpiration.
transpire *verb*

transplant *verb*
To transplant is to move a plant from one place to another. Gardeners often transplant **seedlings** to a new site when they have grown larger.
They transplanted the trees to make way for the new road.
transplantation *noun*

treaty *noun*
A treaty is an agreement. A treaty is signed by governments which then try and follow its advice. Treaties have been drawn up to limit the development of nuclear power. Other treaties try to prevent over-fishing or the production of too many **greenhouse gases**.
The treaty was written and signed by all the countries.

tree ► page 148

tree fern *noun*
A tree fern is one of a group of tropical **ferns**. Tree ferns have a tall, woody stem. The typical fern **fronds** grow from the top of this stem. Tree ferns look like **cycads**, but their leaves are more fern-like.
We found many tree ferns in the moist forest.

tree-line *noun*
The tree-line is the upper limit of tree growth on a mountain. It is also the limit of tree-growth towards the poles.
Beyond the tree-line, it is too cold for trees to survive.

tropical *adjective*
Tropical describes something found in the tropics. A tropical climate is a warm climate found in areas around the equator.
In a tropical climate, there are no warm and cold seasons.

tropical rain forest *noun*
Tropical rain forests are found in warm tropical regions, with a high rainfall. The trees in tropical rain forests grow very tall, and there are many climbing plants in the undergrowth. South America, Africa and South-east Asia have the most tropical rain forests. They are the world's richest **ecosystems**.
There are more species of plants in the tropical rain forests than anywhere else.

tropism *noun*
Tropism is growth in response to a stimulus. There are different kinds of tropisms. **Phototropism** is growth towards or away from the light, **geotropism** is growth towards or away from the ground. The shoots of most plants show a tropism towards the light. In roots the tropism is towards the ground.
The seedlings showed a positive tropism towards the light.

trunk *noun*
A trunk is part of a woody plant, usually a **tree**. It is the thick, main stem above the ground. Trunks are strengthened by layers of bark and they provide the main support for trees and large shrubs.
The trunk of the conifer towered above us.

tuber *noun*
A tuber is a kind of swollen **stem** or **root**. Tubers grow underground and are used by the plant to store food. **Potatoes** are in fact stem tubers formed by the potato plant.
We dug in the ground to gather the tubers.

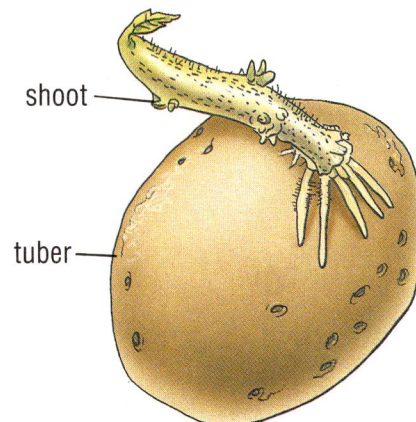

shoot

tuber

tundra *noun*
The tundra is a kind of treeless **habitat** found in the Arctic region. The tundra replaces the **taiga** in the far north of North America, Europe and Asia. The plants growing in the tundra are mainly low shrubs, grasses, mosses and lichens.
In the spring, the birds flew north to breed on the tundra.

146

tussock *noun*
A tussock is a raised clump of grass. Tussock grasses such as tussock sedge often grow in damp ground. When the ground floods, the tussocks stick out above the water.
The grass in the centre of the tussock was protected from damage.

twig *noun*
A twig is part of a tree or shrub. The twigs are the thinnest part of the woody branches. Leaves grow from buds in the twigs. Many birds use twigs to construct their nests.
In the autumn, the leaves fell from the twigs.

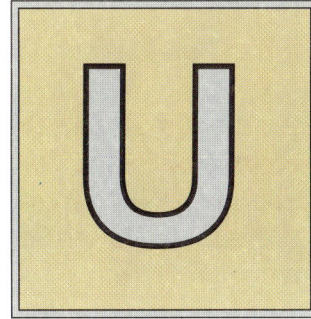

U

umbellifer *noun*
An umbellifer is a plant in the **parsley** family. There are about 250 **genera** of umbellifers. Their name comes from the flat-topped cluster of flowers, called the umbel, that they bear.
Many familiar food plants are umbellifers, such as carrots, cumin, celery and coriander.

understorey *noun*
Understorey describes one of the layers in a forest. It lies between the **canopy** and the **field layer**. Little sunlight reaches the understorey, and the plants that grow there usually reach a height of no more than 10 metres. Plants in the understorey often rely on insects to carry out **pollination**.
Some plants in the understorey grow large, colourful or scented flowers to attract insects.

unicellular *adjective*
Unicellular describes something that has one cell. Some **algae** are unicellular.
Some unicellular organisms live together in colonies.

unleaded *adjective*
Unleaded describes a kind of petrol that is **lead-free**. Some petrol still contains lead. This always used to be added to improve the smooth running of the car's engine. However, lead is poisonous in the air. All new cars are now made to run smoothly on unleaded petrol.
The engineers converted the car so that it could use unleaded petrol.

tree *noun*

A tree is a large, woody plant with a tall stem, or **trunk**. Some trees are **evergreen**, and carry their leaves all year round. Other trees are **deciduous**, losing their leaves for part of each season. The largest trees live for many hundreds of years and may reach heights of over 100 metres.
The forester used a power saw to fell the tall tree.

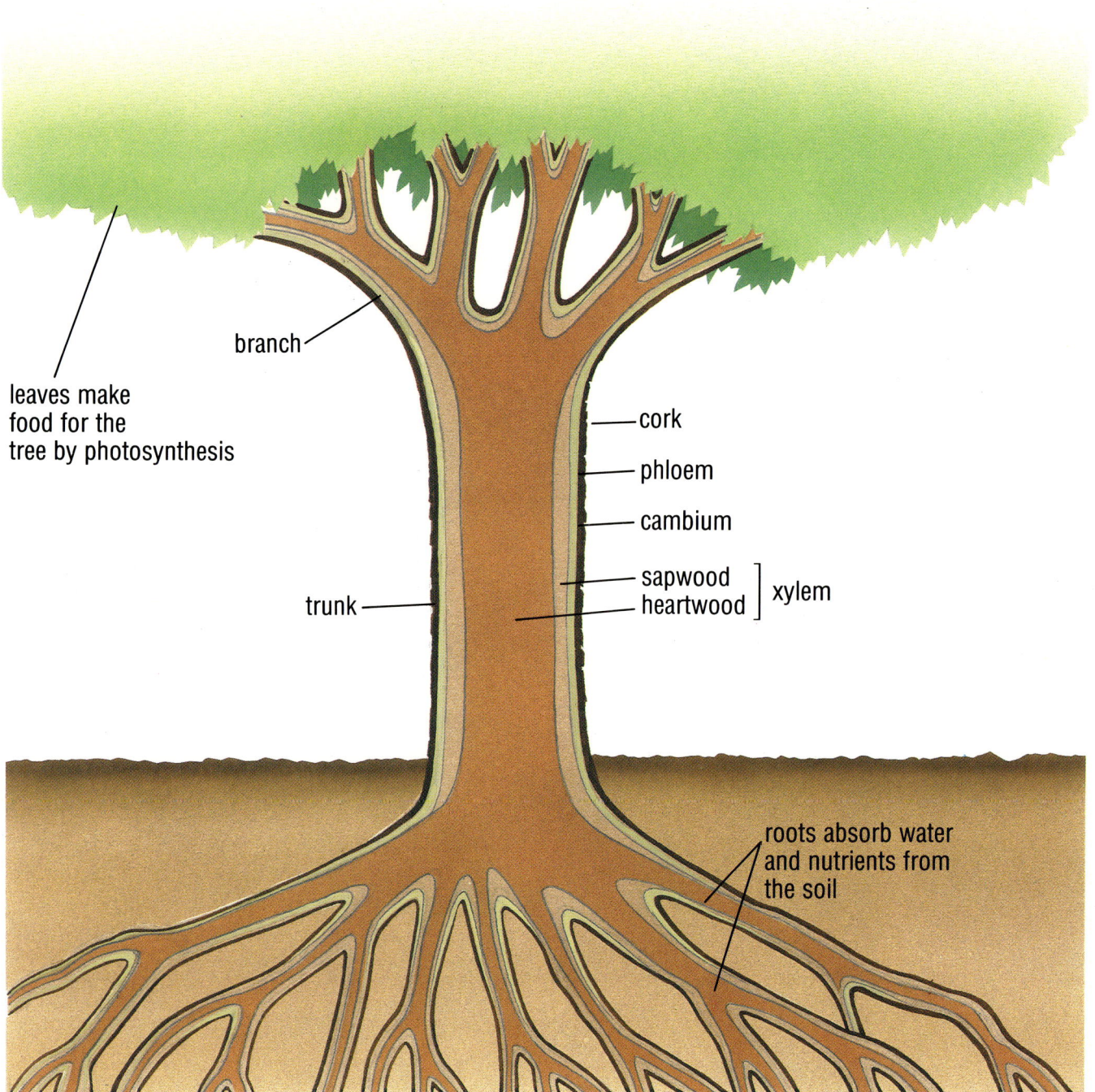

branch

leaves make
food for the
tree by photosynthesis

cork

phloem

cambium

sapwood
heartwood } xylem

trunk

roots absorb water
and nutrients from
the soil

fruit, or key

leaf

maple

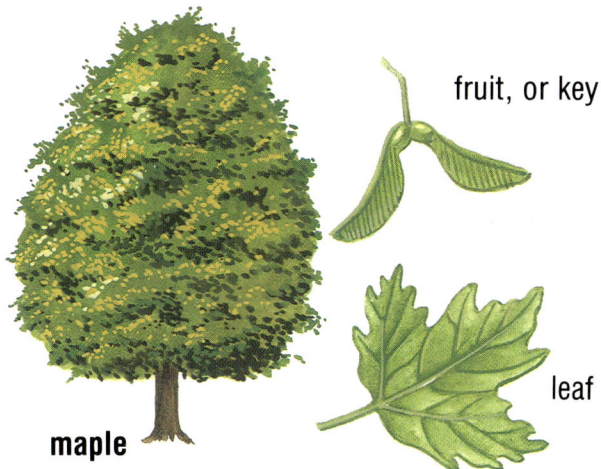

Broadleaf trees, such as the maple, lose their leaves in winter. They produce flowers and fruits.

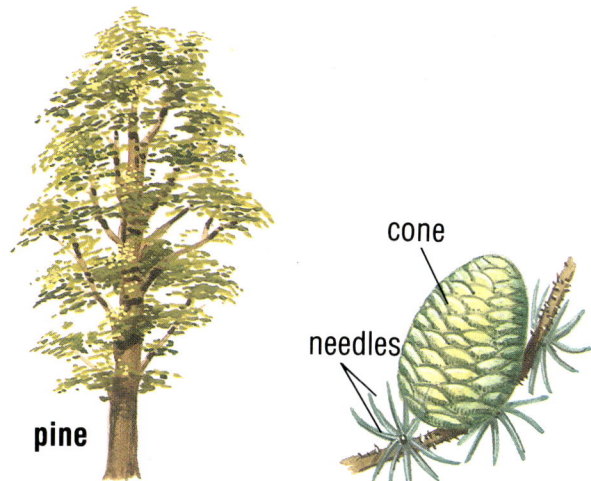

cone

needles

pine

Needleleaf trees, such as the pine, have thin, pointed leaves called needles. They bear seeds in hard cones.

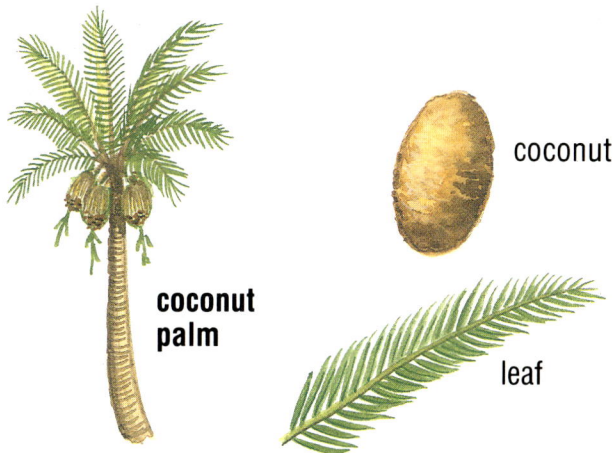

coconut

coconut palm

leaf

Palm trees, such as the coconut palm, have huge leaves with no branches. Their fruits grow in clusters beneath the leaves.

cone

cycad

leaf

Cycad trees, such as the South African cycad, produce large, heavy cones. They grow only in tropical regions.

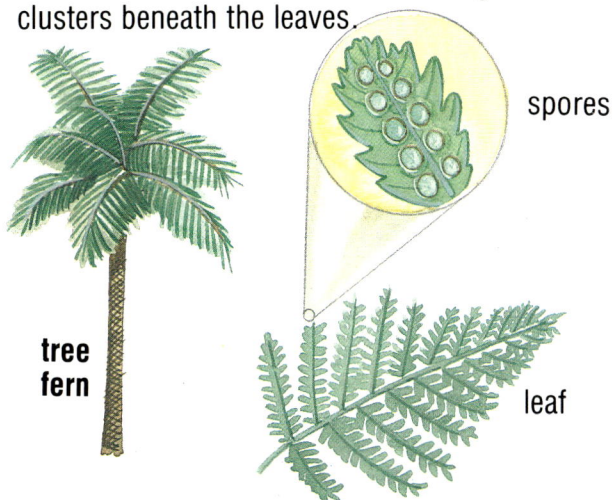

spores

tree fern

leaf

Tree ferns reproduce by means of spores. They are the only trees with no flowers, fruit or seeds.

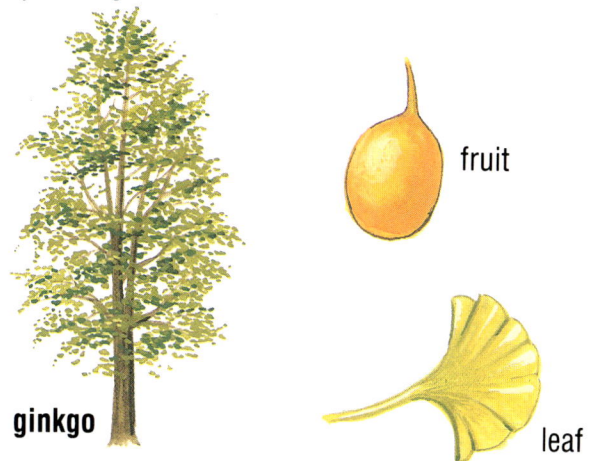

fruit

ginkgo

leaf

Ginkgo trees are a species on their own. They produce seeds without fruit or cones.

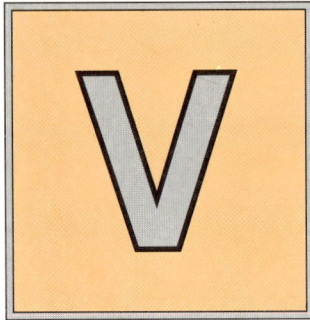

V

vanilla   *noun*
Vanilla is a **climbing plant** that is part of the orchid family. It is grown in tropical areas such as Mexico and Madagascar, where the air is hot and damp.
The extract from the vanilla pod is sometimes used to flavour chocolate and ice-cream.

variegated   *adjective*
Variegated describes the **foliage** of a plant. In a variegated plant, the leaves or stems are striped or spotted in different colours. Variegated plants are often green and white. Gardeners have bred variegated varieties of many different species.
The variegated shrub looked splendid in the herbaceous border.

vascular plant   *noun*
A vascular plant is one of a large group of plants. The vascular plants include the **club mosses**, **horsetails**, **ferns**, **gymnosperms** and **angiosperms**. Their stems contain special cells for carrying food and water.
As we travelled into the cold Arctic, we found fewer and fewer vascular plants.

club moss

cross-section of club moss stem showing vascular system

vegetable ▶ page 152

vegetation   *noun*
Vegetation is the overall plant cover of an area or region. It includes the tiny **mosses**, the **grasses** and **herbs**, right through to the tallest **trees**. As vegetation **decays**, it returns minerals and other chemicals to the soil, forming **humus** and **peat**.
Tundra and tropical rain forest are both types of vegetation.

vegetative reproduction   *noun*
Vegetative reproduction is a major method of reproduction in the plant kingdom. It happens when plants produce offspring without involving **sexual reproduction**. Sometimes, the parent plant sends out **runners** from which new plants grow. Many garden plants are **propagated** by taking **cuttings**. This is also a type of vegetative reproduction.
In vegetative reproduction, the young plants are all exactly the same as the parent.

vein   *noun*
A vein is a tube-like structure in a leaf. The veins carry the **xylem** and **phloem** vessels along the leaf. Veins make special patterns in the leaf surface. Some plants have parallel veins, and in others the veins spread out, or branch.
He held the leaf up to the light to see the pattern of veins.

veld   *noun*
Veld is an open, dry **grassland**. It is found on the high plateaux of southern Africa. The main plants of the veld are **grasses**, and there are very few trees.
The farmer rode out across the veld to round up his cattle.

vessel   *noun*
A vessel is a long tube of special **cells** in a plant. Most **angiosperms** and some **ferns** have vessels. The vessels carry food and water around the plant, in the **phloem** and **xylem**.
The biologist looked at the long vessels under the microscope.

vine *noun*
A vine is a **climbing plant**. Vines use other plants, such as trees, as a support. They cling on to their branches using **tendrils**. Vine is also the name for the **grape** vine. Grape vines are grown in areas with Mediterranean climates, to make wine.
The forest trees were festooned with vines.

grape vine

violet *noun*
Violet is a group of low-growing, flowering plants. There are more than 500 species of violet. They grow throughout the world, usually in shady woods and meadows. Each flower grows on a separate stalk. The flower has five petals, and has a very sweet smell. Violets are used to make perfumes, wine, tea, and the flowers are also eaten.
Violets sometimes have yellow or white flowers, but are usually blue or purple.

virus *noun*
A virus is a kind of tiny living thing, called a micro-organism. Viruses cause many **diseases** in plants and animals. The virus enters a healthy cell and then forces that cell to make more viruses. This causes the infected cells to burst and die. More and more cells are then attacked.
Tobacco mosaic disease is caused by a virus.

W

walnut *noun*
Walnuts are large, deciduous **trees**. They are found in east Asia, Europe and America. Walnuts have large, edible **seeds**. The wood of the walnut tree makes excellent furniture and veneer.
Walnut seeds give oil, used in cooking and to make salads.

wasteland *noun*
A wasteland is an area of open land which has not been **cultivated**. It is also open country which was farmed once, but which has been left to go back to **nature**.
In urban areas, wasteland is land which has been cleared of buildings, but left open.

water *noun*
Water is a clear liquid, with no smell or taste. It is made from the **gases**, hydrogen and oxygen, and is mainly found in the seas, rivers and lakes, and as rain. Many other **chemicals** dissolve in water. When water is solid, it is called ice, and as a gas it is called water vapour.
All life depends on water.

water cycle *noun*
The water cycle is the process by which water leaves the sea and returns to it. In the Sun and wind, water **evaporates** from the surface of the Earth as water vapour. This vapour forms clouds in the sky, which drop rain onto the Earth. The water cycle is completed when the water flows through the ground in rivers and back to the sea.
Without the water cycle, plants and animals could not live on dry land.

vegetable *noun*

A vegetable is food that comes from leaves, roots, stems, buds or seeds of a plant. Bulbs and buds can be eaten, too. Plants which are eaten are also called vegetables. Vegetables include food crops such as beans, peas, carrots and potatoes.

His diet included a lot of vegetables.

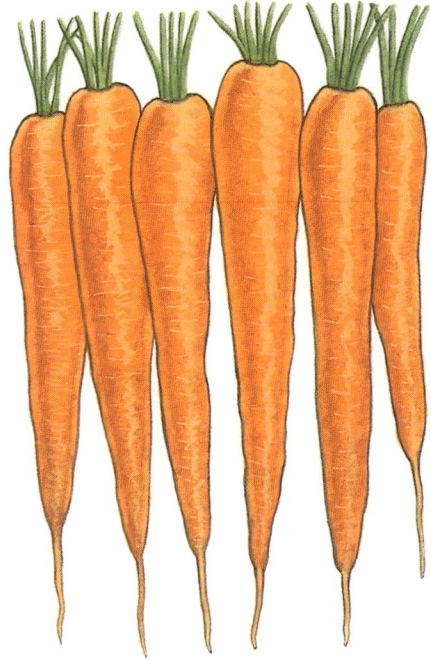

In vegetables such as carrots, the roots are eaten.

In vegetables such as asparagus, the stems are eaten.

In vegetables such as peas, the seeds are eaten.

The tuber is the part of the potato plant that can be eaten. It is the edible part.

The leaves are the edible parts of spinach.

The flower is the edible part of cauliflower.

The bulb is the edible part of an onion.

The fruit is the edible part of an aubergine, or egg plant.

water plant *noun*

A water plant is any plant which grows in the water. Some water plants, such as duckweeds, float on the water. Others grow submerged but root in the mud at the bottom. Other kinds grow in the shallow water at the edges of lakes, rivers and ponds. They emerge to flower above the surface. Many water plants have air spaces in their stems to help them float.
The river was choked by a thick growth of water plants.

water lilies

fanwort

water pollution *noun*

Water pollution is the collection of impurities or unwanted substances in the water. Sewage sometimes causes water pollution of streams and rivers. Other sources of water pollution are waste chemicals from factories, and fertilizers from farmland.
The water pollution was so bad that the fish all died.

water storage *noun*

Water storage describes the way in which plants store water in their cells. Pores called **stomata** in the leaves of many plants open to allow water to **evaporate**. This controls the level of water in the plant. **Cacti** and other **succulents** store water in their fleshy stems. Plants that grow in cold climates have thick, waxy leaves from which water does not easily evaporate.
Because their water storage is so efficient, cacti can provide something to drink for thirsty animals.

wattle *noun*

Wattles are large **trees** found in Australia. There are over 600 kinds of wattle tree. The wood of the wattle is used for timber, and the bark for tanning leather. Wattles are often planted near farms as windbreaks, or grown in plantations. Sunshine, silver, cedar, boree gidgee and mulga are all examples of wattles.
The wattle trees protected the farm buildings from the storms.

wax *noun*

Wax is a waterproof coating produced by plants. Many plants have a coating of wax over their leaves and stems. This prevents the plants from losing too much moisture. Some plant waxes, such as those from the leaves of the carnauba palm, are harvested commercially. Other vegetable waxes include candelilla wax, sugar cane wax, and bayberry wax.
The thick, shiny leaves had a covering of wax on their surface.

weed *noun*

A weed is a plant that is growing where it is not wanted. Many weeds produce lots of seeds and quickly colonize new ground. Weeds are often considered a pest because they weaken the main crop by competing with it for food and water. They can also harbour pests and diseases.
The farmer sprayed the weeds to kill them.

purple loosestrife

greater plantain

black bindweed

lesser burdock

welwitschia *noun*
The welwitschia is the only member of a **family** of plants. It lives in the dry, stony desert of south-western Africa. Its long **tap root** grows far down into the ground. A single pair of long, leathery, green leaves grows down a cone-like trunk and spreads on the ground. The desert winds split the leaves into ribbons. These leaves continue to grow throughout the plant's life, which can be several hundred years.
Some welwitschia plants are known to have lived for up to 2,000 years.

wetland *noun*
A wetland is any area of land in which the surface is normally waterlogged. Wetlands include open water and boggy **habitats**. A wetland may be fresh water, brackish or salt water, depending upon its location. Wetlands contain animals and plants which are **adapted** to the wet conditions.
The marshy wetland covered the floor of the valley.

wheat *noun*
Wheat is a plant that belongs to the **grass** family. It is the world's most important **crop**. Wheat has a single stalk that grows up to 1.5 metres high. At the top of each stalk is the head, which carries from 30 to 50 **kernels**. The ripe kernels are used to make flour for bread, pasta and breakfast cereals.
Over the years, scientists have developed many new varieties of wheat.

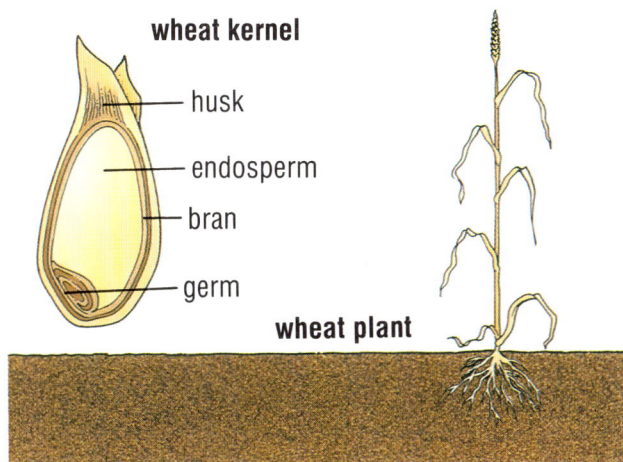

wheat kernel
- husk
- endosperm
- bran
- germ

wheat plant

whorl *noun*
A whorl is a ring of leaves or flowers on a plant stem. Many plants, such as horsetails, have their leaves arranged in whorls up the stems. The flowers of many kinds of orchid, such as the spotted orchid, are arranged in whorls.
The leaves grew in whorls around the stem of the bell heather.

bell heather

wild *adjective*
Wild describes something which is not cultivated or domesticated by people. Wild plants and animals live their lives free in their natural **environment**. Wild **habitats** are those most untouched by people or human influences.
Garden plants have been bred from their wild ancestors.

wilderness *noun*
A wilderness is any uninhabited and uncultivated region. A wilderness may be a dry, sandy desert or an area of snow and ice such as Antarctica. Even a tropical forest could be called a wilderness, if it is unchanged by people.
Antarctica is one of the last areas of true wilderness left on Earth.

wildflower ► page 156

wildlife *noun*
Wildlife is the natural **flora** and **fauna** of a region or **habitat**. It includes all the organisms, including fungi, plants and animals. All around the world, wildlife is under threat from increasing pollution, industry and building.
The nature reserve protected the wildlife of the area.

wildflower *noun*

A wildflower is any species of flower that is naturally found in the wild. True wildflowers are those which are native to a particular region or habitat. Some wildflowers have been introduced from elsewhere and then become part of the wild **flora** of a region. *The woodland contained many pretty wildflowers.*

1. Dog's-tooth violet is a woodland plant found in eastern Europe.

9. Iris cristata grows in the hills and beside the streams of the Great Smoky Mountains, USA.

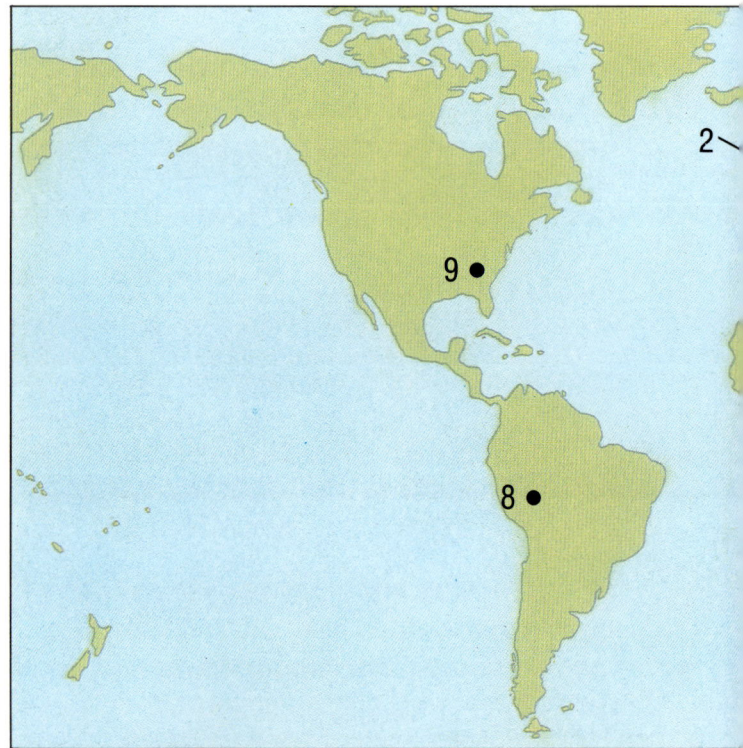

8. The fragrant flowers of the four o'clock plant open late in the afternoon. It grows wild in Peru.

7. Central Africa's glory lily has bright red flowers with long stamens.

2. The bluebell grows wild in the woods of the British Isles.

3. A beautiful, white member of the leontopodium genus is a herb native to China.

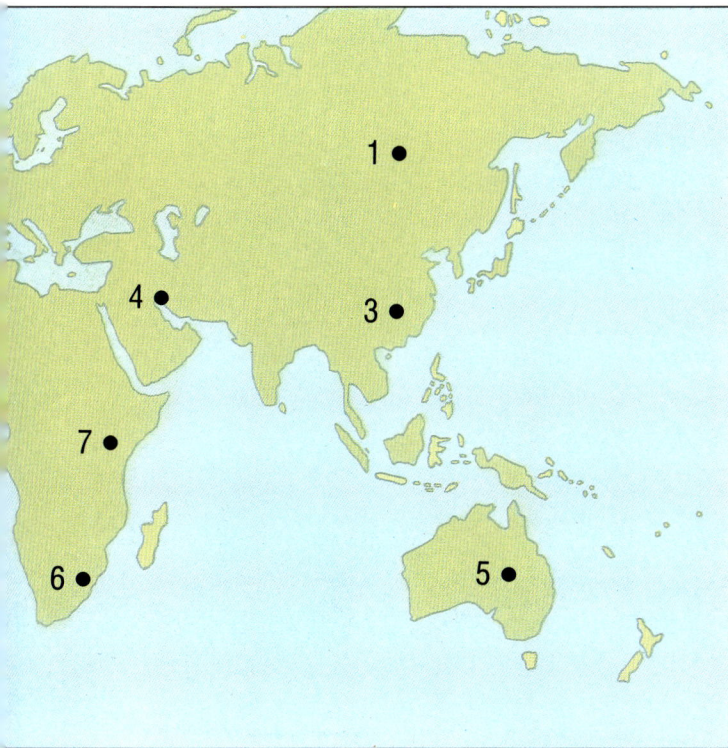

4. The tall safflower thrives in the hot, dry climate of the Middle East.

6. The blue aster carpets the ground after rain in the South African bush country.

5. Sturt's desert pea opens spectacular scarlet flowers in the scorching heat of the Australian desert.

willow *noun*
Willows are deciduous **trees.** There are about 300 kinds of willow, that are found mostly in northern temperate countries. Willows have soft wood, and flexible branches. They are usually found growing near water. The twigs of some willows are used to make baskets. Cricket bats and clogs are also made from willow wood. Black willow, pussy willow and crack willow are all examples of willow trees.
The willows trailed their branches in the river.

windbreak *noun*
A windbreak is a structure that provides shelter from the wind. Many farms and buildings in open places are sheltered by windbreaks. A line of trees is often planted as a windbreak, with quick-growing species such as cypress or poplars often being used in temperate areas.
The farmer planted a line of trees as a windbreak.

wood *noun*
1. A wood is a collection of **trees** growing in one place. Woods often contain many different species of tree. Woods are long-lasting and **regenerate** if left undisturbed. Some woods are managed for the production of **timber**. Many plants and animals live in woods.
The hill slopes were covered by an ancient wood.
2. Wood is the tough, outer covering that develops under the **bark** on the stems of some plants. **Trees, shrubs** and other **perennial** plants develop wood in their older stems. Wood contains large amounts of the chemical lignin which makes the wood hard and solid. Wood supports the above-ground parts of the plant and protects the stem from insects, and sometimes from fire. Wood is a valuable **natural resource**.
We cut down the trees and used the wood for building.

woodland *noun*
Woodland is land which is covered by a **wood**, or woods. In many inhabited areas, woodland grows in a patchwork pattern with farmland and grassland. In earlier times, woodland covered much larger areas of the lowland in the temperate regions of the world.
The area of woodland was reduced to make way for farms.

woody stem *noun*
A woody stem is a stem with a large amount of wood in tissues. Trees and shrubs have strong, woody stems.
The bush was supported by its woody stem.

World Conservation Strategy *noun*
The World Conservation Strategy is a special document about the world's **environment**. It was drawn up in 1980 by organizations including the **World Wide Fund for Nature**. It recommends how global **conservation** problems can be tackled, so that plants and animals can be preserved and people can live in harmony with nature.
The countries tried to follow the guidelines of the World Conservation Strategy.

World Heritage Site *noun*
A World Heritage Site is a kind of nature **reserve**. It is a natural area of special importance. Some World Heritage Sites conserve areas where the geology is interesting, others are set up to conserve **rare** plants or animals.
The reserve was declared a World Heritage Site.

World Wide Fund for Nature ▶
page 159

World Wide Fund for Nature *noun*
The World Wide Fund for Nature is the world's largest private, international **conservation** body. It has more than four million supporters and 27 associated organizations on five continents. In North America, it is still known by its earlier name, the World Wildlife Fund.
The aims of the World Wide Fund for Nature are to conserve the natural environment and ecology essential to life on Earth.

The WWF has the panda as its symbol. The organization has done much to protect this rare animal.

The WWF works constantly to protect rain forests, one of Earth's most important natural resources.

The WWF has shown the need to protect the decreasing numbers of gorillas in Africa.

Some countries have changed their fishing methods to protect the bottle-nosed dolphin. The WWF is working towards a complete ban on killing dolphins.

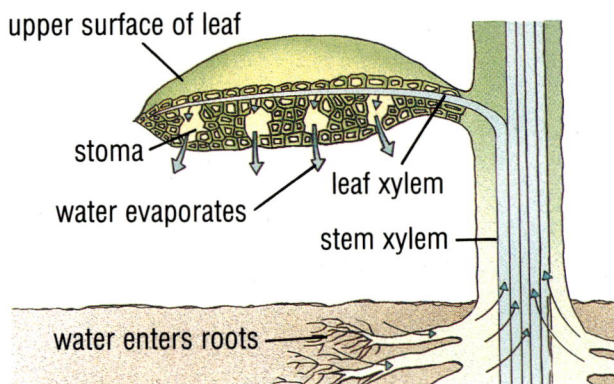

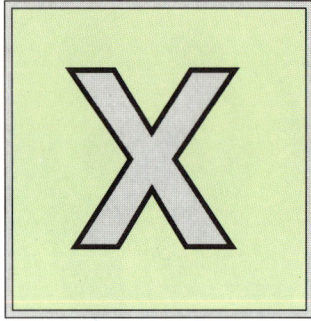

xerophyte *noun*
A xerophyte is a plant that is specially
adapted to grow in very dry areas, such as
deserts. Xerophytes have thick, waxy leaves,
or narrow, pointed **spines**. Many of them
also have **succulent** stems, which store
water. Cacti are examples of xerophytes.
*The desert plants were nearly all
xerophytes.*

xylem *noun*
Xylem is tissue found in most plant **stems**.
The xylem cells are arranged in bundles of
long tubes. The xylem carries water and
dissolved minerals from the roots around the
other parts of the plant.
*He could see the xylem in the cross-section
of the plant stem.*

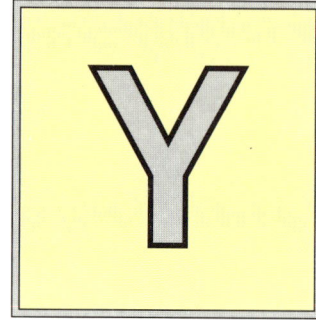

upper surface of leaf
stoma
water evaporates
leaf xylem
stem xylem
water enters roots

yam *noun*
Yams are a kind of tropical **vegetable**. They
grow in **tropical** regions, such as West
Africa, the Caribbean and South Pacific.
There are hundreds of different kinds of yam.
The yam itself is the swollen stem of the
plant, a little like a large potato. It is a source
of starch and can be eaten when cooked.
Yams are also used to provide valuable
medicines.
*The farmer loaded the yams onto his cart
and took them back to the village.*

yeast *noun*
Yeasts are microscopic **fungi** which live on
plants and animals, or in the soil. Yeast cells
grow and multiply very quickly in substances
containing sugar. They break down sugars
into alcohol and **carbon dioxide**. This
process is called fermentation, and is an
important part of bread-making and making
wine and beer.
*The yeast formed bubbles of carbon dioxide
in the bread dough.*

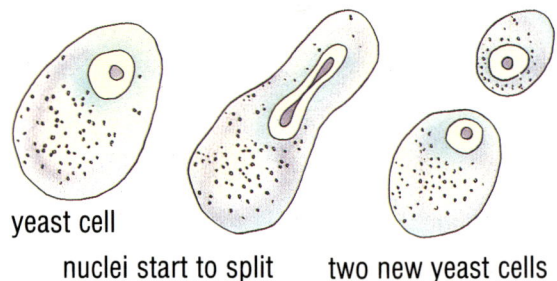

yeast cell
nuclei start to split   two new yeast cells

160